Tax Law and Racial Economic Justice

Tax Law and Racial Economic Justice

Black Tax

Andre L. Smith

LEXINGTON BOOKS
Lanham • Boulder • New York • London

Published by Lexington Books
An imprint of The Rowman & Littlefield Publishing Group, Inc.
4501 Forbes Boulevard, Suite 200, Lanham, Maryland 20706
www.rowman.com

Unit A, Whitacre Mews, 26-34 Stannary Street, London SE11 4AB

British Library Cataloguing in Publication Information Available

Library of Congress Cataloging-in-Publication Data

Smith, Andre L., author.
Tax law and racial economic justice : black tax / Andre L. Smith.
pages cm.
Includes bibliographical references and index.
ISBN 978-1-4985-0365-5 (cloth : alk. paper) — ISBN 978-1-4985-0366-2 (electronic)
1. Taxation—Law and legislation—United States—History. 2. African Americans—Taxation—Law and legislation—United States. 3. United States—Race relations—History. 4. African Americans--Economic conditions. 5. Racism—Economic aspects—United States. 6. Fiscal policy—Social aspects—United States. I. Title.
KF6289.85.S65 2015
343.7304089'96073—dc23

2015004332

™ The paper used in this publication meets the minimum requirements of American National Standard for Information Sciences Permanence of Paper for Printed Library Materials, ANSI/NISO Z39.48-1992.

Printed in the United States of America

To Lauren, Jasmyne, and Marley

Contents

Preface

Before we discuss how taxation and tax law contributes to the study of race and racism, before we reveal that the first instances of affirmative action, or intentional governmental assistance to assist one race, were tax laws in South Carolina designed to encourage the presence and increase the economic fortunes of white men, and before we discuss black people and taxation from Ancient Egypt to twenty-first-century America, let's first deal head-on with the concept of race.

Since race is not real, it should be disavowed entirely, say the post-racialists. Race cannot be boiled down to a phenotypical, biological, or cultural essence. Race is constricting and stands in the way of one's personal autonomy. It is divisive. It is merely an ideological construct. Naomi Zack asks, if race has no consistent basis in biology, genetics, phenology, why acknowledge it at all?[1]

While race is a "mere" ideological construct, so is the line between the United States and Mexico, and pretending that it does not exist invites certain consequences. There are privileges in society assigned to those perceived as white and demerits for those perceived as black. Even though whiteness does not have the value it once had, it would be foolhardy for black people to disavow racial solidarity when others have not. According to philosopher Charles Mills, "That race should be irrelevant is certainly an attractive ideal, but when it has not been irrelevant, it is absurd to proceed as if it had been."[2] Embracing "blackness" is then an act of self-defense, for the political and economic fates of blacks have improved in times before only to be retarded by those who would enjoy the benefits of greater white cohesion.

Post-racialism in the hands of equity obstructionists represents an intentionally false claim of victory over racism designed to dampen society's enthusiasm for addressing white socio-economic-political supremacy.[3] It fails to recognize or address the historical redistribution of wealth from blacks to whites, along with the foreclosure of many lucrative markets to blacks. It ignores the fact that racial discrimination can be imposed without expressing the goal of racial subordination, that racial inequality can and has been maintained through subterfuge, that overt discrimination is but one way to maintain racial hierarchy.

Post-racialism also refuses to recognize that race relations and civil rights for blacks improved in the past only to be viciously and violently taken away. Consider how the gains of Reconstruction were taken away and slavery reinstituted under the Jim Crow convict leasing-sharecropping system. It refuses to recognize that the absence of black solidarity contributed to the African slave trade in the first place. At its worsts, it is designed to ignore imperfections in the market relating to race, including and especially those least susceptible to public, legal interference. For these reasons, pretending not to "see" race maintains, rather than eliminates, a racial caste socio-political-economic system in the United States.

One of the principal techniques of the post-racialist is to reduce the concept of racism to mere discrimination; that way, any attempts to address the material subordination of black people somehow becomes discrimination.[4] Under this perverse conception, post-racialism makes racists out of those of us who seek justice for black people, and celebrities of those who encourage society to ignore racial subordination and thereby help maintain the status quo of inequality. In the Rules of Racial Standing, Derrick Bell predicted that black people who publicly assist the post-racial movement would be given superior racial standing.[5]

Another problem with post-racialism is that it pretends that our racist history has little to no relationship to the degraded economic position of black people in the United States today. It places all of the blame for rampant black poverty on black people for supposedly adopting a prurient, violent, slothful social culture. Now, to the extent there are segments of black people who attach themselves more than those in other racial groups to violence, prurience and slothfulness, it is clearly the responsibility of black people to address and counter such trends whenever and wherever and however they originate and flourish. It is unreasonable to expect others to address vestiges of the "slave" mentality. But post-racialism ignores the fact that counter-productive elements of black culture, like, say, gangster hiphop, are fully aware of their counter culture status and defend themselves, not unreasonably, by pointing to the millions of blacks who play by the rules, who have pretty much assimilated into "American" culture, who go to work, school, and church regularly, and who are still left at the end of the day with nothing more than they started with, and sometimes less.

To the extent post-racialism is based on the idea that racism and racial inequality ended with de jure discrimination, it is simply wrong: consider a game of Monopoly where one of the players is not allowed to go around the board for a significant number of dice rolls, meanwhile all of the other players are not so restricted and are able to earn money and invest in property. The game is not fair once the restricted player is allowed to participate on equal terms, because the other players have accumulated more wealth and property to use to their advantage. Not only will the disadvantaged player find it hard to stay afloat, he or she will likely be put out of the game.

A truly absurd consequence, known to all who have played Monopoly, is that when a player is unlikely to earn enough money to pay the expenses they are likely to incur going around the game board, they roll the dice often hoping to land in jail! Moreover, the game cannot be considered fair by pointing to the fact that once every so often a once-disadvantaged player who, with cunning, with skill, and a few lucky rolls of the dice will overcome the initial circumstance and win the game. It is to that person's credit that she succeeded against enormous obstacles. It does not discredit others who were unable to fight through the disadvantage. In shorter words, neutral rules and principles alone do not necessarily produce equal opportunity.[6]

In some respects, individual blacks have more opportunity to advance economically than ever before. I would even concede (enthusiastically!) that racism as a global system of white economic and political supremacy has been in slow decline for about one hundred years. But I disagree that its complete disintegration is inevitable. Its decline has been due to the strident efforts and sacrifice of justice-minded people, and no less is required to finish the job. In the context of legal architecture, critical race legal theorists (and critical race tax theorists!) embrace this responsibility.

Daria Roithmayr, for one example, has written extensively on how private market exclusions in the past, like the National Realtors Association's restrictions on black home purchases, have led to today's racial economic inequality.[7] She calls it "locked-in" inequality. Juan Perea similarly demonstrated how twentieth-century economic assistance programs, like the G.I. bill, were designed and implemented in ways that disproportionately benefited whites. In a broader context, Douglas Blackmon's *Slavery By Another Name* won the Pulitzer prize by demonstrating how blacks were almost entirely excluded from taking advantage of the most lucrative markets in America during both slavery and twentieth-century Jim Crow.[8] I hope that by identifying tax laws designed to exclude blacks from lucrative markets and redistribute wealth from blacks to whites, this work comes close to shedding as much light on the topic these and other authors have done.

This work is dedicated to the many who have helped me think over these issues over the years, including, but certainly not limited to, Derrick Bell, the Howard University School of Law, Beverly Moran, Dorothy Brown, Alice Gresham Bullock, Luther Clark, Mildred Robinson, J. Clay Smith, Lisa Crooms-Robinson, Spencer Boyer, Carlton Waterhouse, Deborah Post, Calvin Johnson, Daria Roithmayr, Anthony Infanti, David Brennan, Darryl Jones, Karen Brown, Kimberle Crenshaw, James Hackney, Anthony Farley, Emma Coleman Jordan, Angela Harris, Cheryl Harris, Todd Clark, Taunya Banks, Reginald Mombrun, Kenneth Nunn, Lenese Herbert, Okianer Christian Dark, Francine Lipman, Keeva Terry, Darryll K. Jones, Stacey Holmes-Hawkins, Carla Pratt, Ediberto Roman, Linda Ammons, Stanley Fish, Leonard Strickman, Rhonda Williams, Samuel Myers, Keisha Stokes-Edwards, Tima McGuthry-Banks, Erica Chaplin, Derrick White, and countless others.

Support for some of the research contained herein was provided by the Widener University School of Law, Wilmington, Delaware, as well as the Florida International University College of Law, in Miami, Florida.

NOTES

1. Naomi Zack, Philosophy of Science and Race (2002); Naomi Zack, Race and Mixed Race, (1993).
2. Charles Mills, Blackness Visible: Essays on Philosophy and Race (1998); The Racial Contract (1997).
3. Eduardo Bonilla-Silva, Racism Without Racists (2008).
4. Stanley Fish, *Reverse Racism, Or How the Pot Got to Call the Kettle Black*, The Atlantic Monthly (November 1993) ("Reverse Racism is a cogent description of affirmative action only if one considers the cancer of racism to be morally and medically indistinguishable from the therapy we apply to it. A cancer is an invasion of the body's equilibrium, and so is chemotherapy; but we do not decline to fight the disease because the medicine we employ is also disruptive of normal functioning. Strong illness, strong remedy: the formula is as appropriate to the health of the body politic as it is to that of the body proper.")
5. Derrick Bell, Faces at the Bottom of the Well (1992).
6. Andre L. Smith, *Boycotts, Interest Convergence, and Asymmetrical Market Failures Relating to Race*, 56 Howard Law Journal 891 (2013) (Wiley A. Branton Symposium Issue); *Race, Law, and the Free Market: A Critical Law and Economics Conception of Racism as Asymmetrical Market Failures*, 4 Georgetown Journal of Law & Modern Critical Race Perspectives 39 (2012).
7. Daria Roithmayr, "*Locked In Segregation*," 12 Virginia Journal of Social Policy and the Law 197 (2004); "*Locked In Inequality: The Persistence of Discrimination*," 9 Michigan Journal of Race and Law 31 (2003).
8. Douglas Blackmon, Slavery By Another Name (2009).

Introduction

This project presents six chapters on tax and race: 1) Does it Matter What Slaves Thought "Direct Tax" Meant?, 2) PreColonial African Tax Experiences, 3) Taxes and the Rise of White Supremacy (1600–1900), 4) Interlude: "No Reparation Without Taxation," 5) Taxes and the Demise of White Supremacy (1900–2015) 6) and Critical Race Tax Theory in Twenty-first-Century American Legal Architecture.

Together, they demonstrate that there is practically no area of human activity where race is irrelevant. They are intended to promote a greater understanding of how the history of race relations in the United States produced the economic inequality and injustice black people experience today. The findings and conclusions herein support scholars who advocate for reparations,[1] Equal Protection Clause and thirteenth amendment scholars who advocate for affirmative action,[2] as well as tax scholars whose critique of the standard conceptions of tax fairness relies on the concept of an unjust "baseline."[3] In fact, the first examples of "affirmative action," American legal institutions acting affirmatively to advance the economic interests of one race, were tax laws designed to encourage the presence of whites and discourage the presence of blacks in antebellum South Carolina.

While later chapters will deal more specifically with how American taxation redistributed wealth from blacks to whites and excluded blacks from lucrative markets, chapter 1 is both an exercise in legal theory and an example of how race is relevant in even the most esoteric and abstract circumstances. *Does it Matter What Slaves Thought Direct Tax Meant*, uses race and taxation as tools to criticize neo-textualism in legal interpretation, specifically the plain meaning rule to be exact.[4]

Chapter 1 makes the point that a thorough consideration of plain meaning must include the meanings attributed to a word by different "interpretive communities," to the extent such meanings differ from the dominant one.[5] Judges trying to gather the plain meaning of "Direct Tax" in the U.S. Constitution must research and incorporate the views of women, blacks, native americans, or any group whose interpretation differs from the dominant construct, especially since it is widely accepted that white males at the time of the Constitution had no idea what direct tax was supposed to mean.[6] Two years after publishing this as an article in the *Widener Journal of Race, Economics and Law*, Supreme Court Justice Antonin Scalia and Judge Richard Posner of the 7th Circuit Court of

Appeals engaged in a spirited public debate precisely over the issue whether legal, deliberative processes should require judges to become historians.[7]

Chapter 2 answers skeptics who read chapter 1 and doubt whether slaves could have had *any* thoughts about what "direct tax" meant in the U.S. Constitution. The myth of black inferiority begins with the false notion that European conquest, slavery, and colonization brought civilization to Africa specifically, and dark-skinned people generally. Many Americans, both black and white, are still unaware that centralized government in Africa predates the trans-atlantic slave trade by centuries if not millenia. Recognition for the pre-colonial African states of Nubia, Ethiopia, Ghana, Mali, Songhay, Kanem, Hausa, Kongo, Kuba, etc., is long overdue. Thus, in this chapter, we present examples of African taxation (tribute, excise taxes, poll taxes, income taxes) going back over five thousand years.[8]

Considering the high rate of illiteracy amongst whites in eighteenth-century America, a slave captured from an aristocratic African family, like Equianoh the African, or Prince Abdur Rahman, would have as good and valuable an understanding of what "direct tax" meant as anyone else.

Chapters 3 and 5 represent a tax history of race and racism in the United States. Chapter 3 demonstrates how the tax laws of the United States have historically been conscripted toward the installation and maintenance of socio-political-economic white supremacy. This chapter focuses on tax laws that redistributed wealth from blacks to whites, those that excluded blacks from lucrative markets and the voting franchise, as well as those that helped establish a racial hierarchy. Slavery itself was nearly a 100 percent tax on Black labor, and so was Jim Crow era convict-leasing/sharecropping system. Excise taxes on the slave trade redistributed wealth which should have vested in Black laborers from the slave-owners to poor white southerners, and perhaps to the North in even greater amounts due to the Federal Tariff. In addition, discriminatory occupational taxes excluded inchos from lucrative markets, and poll taxes disenfranchised blacks so that whites could conscript state governments toward social and economic supremacy. On the expenditure side, millions of dollars which should have vested in black laborers were redistributed in the form of government services and anti-poverty programs designed exclusively for whites.

Chapter 4 is something of an interlude. Chapter 3's discussion of how tax law redistributed black wealth to whites as well as excluded blacks from lucrative markets supports scholars who believe that black people are owed reparations for slavery, as well as Jim Crow apartheid. It is indeed curious that tax laws have been ignored in the context of reparations—especially since one of the early substantial works on reparations was written by one of the more famous tax professors in American legal history, Boris Bittker.[9]

In chapter 4, I engage with reparations scholar Carlton P. Waterhouse about whether and how a reparations program would be taxed by the federal government.[10] Professor Waterhouse and I agree that the optimal reparations program would eschew payments to individuals in favor of funding organizations designed to "repair" the black community. Such organizations, however, may face challenges to their non-profit tax status to the extent employment and other internal operations are limited to blacks, or to the extent the benefits of the organization are distributed strictly to black people.[11]

Chapter five, *Taxes and the Demise of White Supremacy in the United States*, identifies the role taxation had in the civil rights movement. At first, the Civil Rights Movement succeeded in attacking neutrally written tax laws that were designed to maintain racial subordination. For example, the twenty-fourth Amendment's prohibition against poll taxes in 1964 reflects a direct assault on American apartheid. Since then, a national taboo against express advocacy for white supremacy emerged. But, two tax cases in the early 1980s, *Bob Jones v. US* (1983), and *Allen v. Wright* (1984), presage the Supreme Court's twenty-first century, "post-racial" attitude, where the government pays lip service to racial equality while ignoring inequality in actual practice. Bob Jones stands for the proposition that federal statutes should not be interpreted in ways that exacerbate racial inequality. But Allen v. Wright holds that black people generally don't have standing to force the government to eradicate racism even when it is illegal.

The Bob Jones court's intrusion on white privilege in the private sphere was perhaps the last straw before a long, sustained conservative assault on so-called "judicial activism." The very next year after Bob Jones, the court chastised itself in *Chevron v. NRDC* (1984), holding that the judiciary was no longer the branch of government entitled to interpret federal statutes. Neo-forpsm, neo-textualism, and neo-positivism has been on the rise ever since. Nevertheless, chapter 6 demonstrates how none of these jurisprudential "stopping rules" actually prevent legal decision makers from considering racial phenomena.

Chapter 6 identifies critical race theory and critical race tax theory as counter-movements to post-racialism and neo-formalism. Despite the current absence of facially discriminatory tax laws in the United States, critical race tax theorists remain vigilant in exposing when and where neutrally worded tax laws create, maintain or exacerbate disparate economic impacts relating to race.[12] But the challenge faced by critical tax theorists is exemplified by *Banks v. US* (2006), where the Court literally marginalized the issue of race by reducing it to a footnote.

Therefore, toward a wider acceptance of critical race tax theory as a creditable part of the legal academy, I offer in this chapter the concept of "asymmetrical market imperfections relating to race" as a rhetorical construct by which critical tax scholars can describe racially disparate impacts.[13] The benefit of adopting "asymmetrical market imperfections" is its consistency with several of the most current theories, aesthetics, and attitudes about law. Considering racism as AMI is consistent with neoclassical economic conceptions of efficiency, with the modern conception of tax fairness, the Rawlsian concept of justice as a fairness, and with each major technique of statutory interpretation or construction.

NOTES

1. Carlton Waterhouse (2009); Roy L. Brooks, Atonement and Forgiveness: A New Model for Black Reparations (2004); Alfred Brophy (2008)
2. Charles Lawrence, "*Unconscious Racism Revisited: Reflections on the Impact and Origins of The Id, the Ego, and Equal Protection*" 40 Conn. L. Rev. 931, (2008).
3. Neil Buchanan, "*The Role of Economics in Tax Scholarship,*" in Beyond Economic Efficiency in United States Tax Law. Ed. by David A. Brennen, Karen B. Brown and Darryll K. Jones) (2013); Nagel & Murphy, The Myth of Ownership (2002)
4. Andre L. Smith, *Boycotts, Interest Convergence, and Asymmetrical Market Failures Relating to Race,* 56 Howard Law Journal 891 (2013) (Wiley A. Branton Symposium Issue); *Race, Law, and the Free Market: A Critical Law and Economics Conception of Racism as Asymmetrical Market Failures,* 4 Georgetown Journal of Law & Modern Critical Race Perspectives 39 (2012).
5. Stanley Fish, "There is No Textualist Position" San Diego Law Review (2005)
6. Calvin H. Johnson, Righteous Anger at the Wicked States: The Meaning of the Founders' Constitution (2005).
7. "Judges are not competent historians," Hon. Richard Posner, ABA Journal, August 2012.
8. Michal Tymowski, The Origins and Structures of Political Institutions in Pre-Colonial Black Africa (2009); Claessen & Skalnik, The Early State (1978); Claessen & Skalnik, The Study of the State (1981).
9. Borris Bittker, The Case for Black Reparations (1972).
10. Smith & Waterhouse, *No Reparations Without Taxation,* Pittsburgh Tax Review (2010)
11. David Brennan, *Race and Equality Across the Law School Curriculum: The Law of Tax Exemption,* 54 J. Leg. Educ. 336 (2004)
12. Race and Economics, Ed. Jordan & Harris (2006)
13. Andre L. Smith, *Boycotts, Interest Convergence, and Asymmetrical Market Failures Relating to Race,* 56 Howard Law Journal 891 (2013) (Wiley A. Branton Symposium Issue); *Race, Law, and the Free Market: A Critical Law and Economics Conception of Racism as Asymmetrical Market Failures,* 4 Georgetown Journal of Law & Modern Critical Race Perspectives 39 (2012).

ONE

Does it Matter What Slaves Thought "Direct Tax" Meant?

When I was first on the market to become a law professor, I had a dinner interview during which one of the tenured folks looked at me quizzically and asked, "Why tax?" The question was clearly relevant, since I was applying to become a tax law professor. But it was also tinged with an accusation. I paused, and she clarified her question, making the charge explicit, "I mean people are dying on death row, and you're worried about taxes?"

Obviously, she had read my resume, which included short stints with Al Gore's (failed) presidential campaign, the Democratic National Committee, and the NAACP National Voter Fund, and concluded that I would make a good liberal soldier on the faculty. Except that, here I am at dinner speaking reverently about the Internal Revenue Code (IRC, or the Code) and enthusiastically about the myriad ways it can be interpreted. "I mean, liberty is more important than property, right?" she added.

I was certainly prepared to answer the generic "why teach tax" question. It's a job interview, after all. But I was a bit put off by the tone of her question, feeling as if I had just been accused of being a sellout. The table of five diners became slightly tense in the nanoseconds I took to respond. One of the others, hearing her question the same way I heard it, looked away from the table, as if to say "aw shit, this is not going to go well." On the other hand, an older gentleman, a retired judge who later tried to recruit me to the Republican Party as he drove me back to my hotel, looked up from his plate of food, giddily anticipating a confrontation between two people he had assumed up to that point would be aligned against him.

"Without property, I don't know how much you are at liberty to do," I replied. This would be far from the only time in my career that I failed to meet progressive expectations in the legal academy.

Sometime later, a mentor of mine for whom I still have quite a bit of scholarly affection questioned why I often use neo-classical economics as an analytical construct in my writings on race. He was referring to Audre Lord when he asked, "aren't those the master's tools?"[1] My left eyebrow rose, betraying my attempts to remain honorific and expressing my disagreement without permission. I chose *not* to say, "ain't nothing master got, we didn't give him."

You see, I am not a Democrat or a Republican, I am neither liberal nor conservative. I consider myself a pragmatic, Black Nationalist—one who believes that black folks (however constructed) must realistically assess the costs and benefits of each and every invention, tool, construct, theory and strategy available toward redemption.[2] I also have a Pan-African or Afrocentric attitude toward blackness, which means I believe that black people (however constructed) have a special connection to Africa and that Africans wherever situated on the globe have participated in the forward march of "civilization" as much as any other group of people on the planet.[3] Therefore, I believe that there is hardly any invention, tool, construct, theory or strategy—including neo-classic economics—that belongs to white people.

For our present example, this chapter takes an esoteric legal question like "what is the precise meaning of Direct Tax in the U.S. Constitution" and shows how "textualism," the jurisprudential technique most favored by today's political conservatives, actually requires judges to consider race in many legal controversies, while purposivism and modern dynamics, the jurisprudential techniques most favored by today's political progressives, actually ignores what eighteenth-century black people had to say in respect of the U.S. Constitution.

TECHNIQUES FOR DELIBERATING OVER THE U.S. CONSTITUTION

The original purpose of this chapter was to show that textualism has little to no efficiency advantage over other statutory construction techniques, contrary to some scholarly suggestions.[4] Textualism, done right, can consume as much time and resources as dynamism, purposivism or intentionalism. This is because textualism requires, first, a two-step analysis of both plain meaning and statutory context and, second but more importantly, an investigation into various interpretive communities and a determination as to the meaning each would ascribe to a text. For example, the word "income" varies in breadth and scope depending on whether the interpretive community consists of lawyers, tax lawyers, accountants, laypersons, etc.

For another example, there is little agreement on what is meant by "Direct Tax" as used in the U.S. Constitution. Thus, textualism requires a judge to undertake the arduous activity of determining what each community thought Direct Tax meant in 1787, including women, slaves, free blacks, Native Americans, etc. This is of particular importance when, as with the debate over Direct Tax, the major or predominant interpretative group (white males) equivocates on the matter.[5] Consequently, it cannot be said that the plain meaning rule is a less costly endeavor than divining intent or considering foreseeable consequences.

Adrian Vermeule and Cass Sunstein presented the argument that textualism is a less costly activity than the consideration of legislative purposes.[6] Behind each statute might lay a multitude of purposes to consider, each perhaps requiring the exercise of some discrete expertise. Purposivism would thus require a judge and her clerks to acquaint themselves with different fields of study in order to decide each case. Dynamism, being a broader inquiry into foreseeable consequences than purposivism, would be even more costly. However, Vermeule and Sunstein's charge of relative inefficiency can stand only when purposivism and dynamism are compared against an overly simplistic and unrealistic conception of textualism.

Proponents of textualism typically offer little more to the would-be textualist other than "focus on the text," as if the correct answer will simply wash over you after mere concentration. Some refer the would-be textualist to the "canons of construction" for guidance. In fact, Justice Scalia has authored a how-to book on textualism.[7] But, as will be discussed, real textualism, particularly the part that relates to plain meaning, requires a number of calculations and admits more judicial discretion than is typically acknowledged. By asking whether the thoughts of slaves matter with respect to the legal question what is a "Direct Tax," I intend to prove simply that a text-based analysis is not necessarily more efficient than a purposive one.

In the end, no, I do not know what an individual slave would think Direct Tax meant—although in chapter 2, I intend to prove that some would have sophisticated thoughts on the matter if asked. Those not interested in the particulars of jurisprudence and legal theory may want to skip ahead to chapter 2's discussion of African taxation. Those who are interested exclusively by the issues of tax and race in the United states may be forgiven for jumping ahead to chapter 3.

Now what will represent a huge political irony to some is that Justice Scalia's brand of originalist textualism accords the most respect to the views of slaves on constitutional issues.[8] Similarly, it accords the most respect for women's views. His theory requires judges to consider what the text of the Constitution meant to the people of the United States. He considers the Federalist Papers not as evidence of the Framers' intent but as evidence of what the People thought specific words meant.[9] But, even if the Federalist Papers represent the best evidence of original constitutional meaning, they do not constitute the sole evidence of what the people of the United states understood. Thus, Scalia's originalist textualism requires judges deciding constitutional questions to consider to some degree and to the extent possible the meaning most likely supplied by blacks, women, and perhaps Native Americans, especially if there is evidence that their understanding differs to some extent from the dominant public sphere of the time.

Other theories of constitutional interpretation, like originalist intentionalism and dynamism, ignore slaves' views on constitutional matters. Dynamists who believe in a "Living Constitution," encourage judges to consider which decisional choice in a constitutional case is most consistent with most of our most important modern day social principles, as well as legal ones.[10] Dynamism is very inclusive and could be said to permit judges to consider among myriad factors what people at the time of enactment generally thought the Constitution meant.[11] But dynamic interpretation is most often offered as a distinct alternative to constitutional originalism. In contrast with originalism, the most popular conceptions of dynamism care hardly at all for the views of those alive at the time of the Constitution's drafting (dead hand control).[12]

Ultimately, the meaning of Direct Tax depends on the deliberative technique employed. Those who try to interpret the meaning of words as they were understood at the time of enactment may settle on a meaning different from those who reconstruct the meanings of words to represent modern understandings and concepts.[13] Still, between those who privilege original meanings and between those who promote a living constitution there is little convention as to how those meanings are determined under either scheme.[14] An originalist might emphasize most the meanings intended by the authors, the meanings as understood by the ratifiers, or the meanings as understood by the people of the United States. A realist on the other hand might accept original purposes rather than meanings, attempt to translate original meanings into the language of modern times, or reject original understandings entirely.[15] This is why legal interpretation or deliberation is more art than science, and claims of efficiency are tenuous at best.

Considering slaves' views, by itself, neither legitimates nor discredits a deliberative/interpretive technique. Ironically, the technique that embraces slaves' views, textualism, is considered by some progressives to be simply a means of ignoring the pleas of the disempowered, while some of the techniques that ignore slaves' views, like dynamism and purposivism, are credited amongst progressive interest groups.[16] It does, however, suggest that textualism requires empirical inquiry and is incomplete without evidence as to the meanings slaves and women would assign to words used in the Constitution. Considering slaves' views demonstrates that textualism does not necessarily provide efficiency advantages.

If the views of slaves are indeed relevant under textualism, the questions that immediately follow under the textualist regime are "how important" and "can it be discovered" and if so "at what cost"?[17] It is the poverty of American history that the answer to the first question is, according to a similar textualist application, that consideration of slaves' views are discounted by forty per cent; and that the unlikelihood of discovering their views is due not to an inability of African immigrants to think on the matter but to the fact that their views were neither sought nor preserved.[18]

SLAVERY AND "NO DIRECT TAX WITHOUT APPORTIONMENT"

By 1787, the Articles of Confederation had proven a failure, specifically because it did not provide a viable means for the federal government to pay the revolutionary war debts, the nonpayment of which would leave the fledgling country vulnerable to renewed attacks.[19] When the federal government demanded sums from the states in order to pay the debt (i.e., requisitions) the states failed to comply.[20] The Articles of Confederation neither provided a means for levying upon the States' property nor a means of revenue-raising other than requisitions.[21] Even while in rebellion against the British, the states poorly funded the Revolutionary War, several times turning its back financially on George Washington and his armies.[22] In 1781, Rhode Island vetoed a federal impost tax on exports, and the impotence of the Articles became too apparent to ignore and apparently too deep-seeded to simply amend.[23] In 1783, New York also vetoed a federal impost.[24] For the country to survive, the federal government had to become more powerful. It needed to raise revenue directly, without the states as a conduit.[25] It needed at least the power to tax exports and imports, and perhaps collect sin taxes on the sale of "undesirable" goods. Thus, the committee responsible for amending the Articles of Confederation scrapped it entirely and constructed a new document, the U.S. Constitution, which gave the federal government considerably more power, most especially the power to lay excise taxes.[26]

According to Calvin Johnson, the Constitution could not give the federal government the power to tax without dealing with the controversy over slavery.[27] By 1787, slavery was considered an evil by many, but it persisted due to the peoples' drunkenness with economic advancement.[28] Slavery violated moral and religious principles of the day as well as the principles of "liberte" which had enthralled colonialists and inspired them to revolt against the English.[29] But slave labor, being cheap by definition, competed well against more expensive nonpropertied white labor, not just in terms of the cost of running a tobacco or rice farm but also in terms of blacksmithing and other urban occupations.[30]

South Carolina and other states would not tolerate a prohibition on slavery in the Constitution itself, and they feared that a Congress controlled by the northern states would tax slavery out of business.[31] Many northerners may have wanted to end slavery for various reasons, but they believed apparently that the colonies needed to unite for economic and military reasons and could not if slavery were challenged.[32] Slaves far outnumbered white South Carolinians and constituted 40 percent of Virginians, which made the poor whites who lived there fearful and led them to develop numerous techniques toward squelching the enslaved Africans' want of freedom (maiming, whipping, lynching, killing, threatening to sell children to distant slave owners).[33] Still, representatives from South Carolina had long threatened that there be no union if the institution of slavery was at all threatened.[34]

Framers of the U.S. Constitution sought to design a federal government with more power to tax than it previously had under the Articles of Confederation, yet without the power to end slavery.[35] Ultimately, they achieved their goal, but not before serious discussion and negotiation over the federal government's powers generally and the power to tax specifically. The Constitution does not outlaw slavery, and it offers a grace period for ending the importation of slaves (which was agreeable even to slave states since the number of enslaved Africans relative to free whites in the South had become dangerously high, and because the importation of more slaves would cheapen the commercial value of those already held).[36]

It gave the federal government the power to lay excise taxes, except that it prohibited confiscatory taxes on slave importation and restricted Congress ability to tax exports made from slave labor.[37] It also retained the federal government's power to tax the states directly (requisitions), but added an apportionment requirement this time. Whether to count slaves as people or property if the government were to tax the states directly under a rule of apportionment became what is infamously known as the Three-fifths Clause.[38]

Most important to this discussion, however, is that they neglected to define precisely what "Direct Tax" meant. Here, I ask how much the thoughts of slaves count toward what the people of the United states as an interpretive community understands a word in the Constitution to mean? Perhaps their views are relevant but discounted to three-fifths that of a white man? Despite the fact that reconstructing the views and history of marginalized groups is difficult and costly, we ought not to make the mistake of ignoring the full humanity of a specific group of people in exchange for convenience.

THE POLITICAL IMPORTANCE OF "DIRECT TAX"

The debate over "Direct Tax" corresponds to the modern day question whether the federal government should/can impose a wealth tax. The income tax is a tax on income earned from a specific period, but only if that income has been "realized." Thus, a person whose wealth has dramatically increased may not owe any income taxes at all, even if their property has increased in value, so long as the taxpayer has not sold it or disposed of it voluntarily for cash, services or other property. Even if this wealthy person realizes income in a given year, the Internal Revenue Code contains numerous provisions which reduce one's tax liability. Recently, the mega-billionaire, Warren Buffet, admitted that his "effective tax rate" is less than his secretary's.

Tomas Piketty's *Capitalism in the Twenty-First Century* has garnered a lot of attention for its wealth tax prescription.[39] Some years ago, Beverly Moran also proposed a wealth tax, contending that it is more consistent with the capitalism Adam Smith envisioned when he wrote *The Wealth of Nations* over two hundred years ago.[40] If a government's primary purpose is to protect wealth, then the wealthy should be the primary funders of government (via taxation). Such proposals are supported by Bruce Ackerman's theory that the Direct Tax Clause, if not all provisions of the Constitution even remotely relating to slavery, is invalid on moral grounds.[41]

Opponents of a wealth tax, however, believe the Direct Tax Clause imposes a serious limitation on the Federal government's power to tax individuals, and prohibits a wealth tax specifically, or even income tax without apportionment.[42] A third position, Calvin Johnson's, is that the Direct Tax Clause is a valid constitutional restriction but only concerns the Federal government's relationship with State governments, and poses no serious restriction on its relationship with the people of the United states directly. Professor Johnson has not expressed any desire for a wealth tax, but his scholarship and theory of the Constitution supports it.[43]

The earliest case, Hylton, held that a tax on the ownership of carriages, what we would call a property tax, was not a Direct Tax. However, the Supreme Court held years later, in Pollock, a 5-4 opinion, that an income tax is so close to a tax on property that it is unconstitutional as a Direct Tax. Eventually, the Sixteenth Amendment was enacted to reverse the Supreme Court's decision in Pollock and allow the government to tax incomes without apportionment.[44]

Now because scholars have recently been discussing the propriety of a tax on held wealth and whether such a tax would be scuttled as a Direct Tax in need of apportionment,[45] and because Hylton and Pollock are inconsistent, some scholars have tried to wrangle its meaning by focusing on the history of the provision.

According to Ackerman, the Direct Tax limitation was a political expedient used to facilitate a compromise between the northern and southern states, but one which was illusory in that the authority to levy Direct Taxes on the states had already proved useless under the Articles of Confederation because the states refused to pay it and the federal government had no means or will to forcibly collect it.[46] He argues that the Sixteenth Amendment along with the New Deal Amendments to the Constitution declare in principle that the federal government's economic regulatory powers are not limited in any meaningful way.[47] Thus, he would not, as Calvin Johnson might, limit the Direct Tax clause to requisitions, capitation, and property taxes on real estate. Ackerman would disavow the whole Direct Tax deal as anachronistic on two counts, that its strictures have been extended past its intended scope and that it is irreparably tainted by its entwinement with slavery.[48]

According to Calvin Johnson, the Pollock Court was completely incorrect as well as overtly political when it held that the income tax was a Direct Tax.[49] Hylton was close enough in time to the constitutional convention that the justices are assumed to be aware of the debates and compromises. There, the Supreme Court held that the Direct Tax clause could only be extended past requisitions to those taxes which could reasonably be apportioned.[50] An income tax cannot be apportioned because, in addition to political ridiculousness, it would fail the constitutional requirement of uniformity: if Congress sought to raise $1 trillion under a rule of apportionment, it would have to require each state to produce an amount based on its percentage of national population, which would require a low tax on states with high per capita income and a higher tax rate on individuals from states with a low per capita income.[51]

During the Civil War, Congress enacted an income tax that withstood a challenge to it as a Direct Tax.[52] But the Pollock Court, operating under a renewed vigor for the protection against governmental deprivations of property and economic liberty, (i.e., Lochnerism), put the burden on Congress to either push through a tax that would disproportionately burden poorer people generally and poorer states specifically, or scrap the idea altogether.[53] Calvin Johnson hopes the Supreme Court will find an appropriate opportunity to reverse Pollock, expressly, and reestablish the rule in Hylton that a Direct Tax only refers to requisitions from the states and taxes on the ownership of land.[54]

Eric Jensen disagrees.[55] He does not seek to defend the Pollock Court against charges of Lochnerism, but he does defend the Direct Tax clause as an important and vital restraint on federal power, one that would require Congress to apportion any so-called wealth tax and navigate the furor such an apportionment regime would inspire. He contends that, even if the Framers had less than a concrete conception of what constituted a Direct Tax, and even if the Direct Tax clause was a straw provision to facilitate a political compromise, it is the job of legal practice to read the Constitution's provisions coherently and supply meaning to them.[56]

The Constitution prohibits capitation taxes as well as Direct Taxes without apportionment.[57] Also, at least one of the Federalist Papers describes Direct Taxes as including requisitions, poll taxes and real estate taxes.[58] Taken as a whole, Jensen suggests that Direct Taxes are those levied on accumulated wealth and which cannot be avoided by engaging or not engaging in a particular transaction.[59] Jensen argues that the Constitution establishes a form which can reasonably be extended by analogy to newer concepts. He asks, would the Constitution have been approved by the people of the United states in 1787 if they knew that the new federal government could tax their wealth directly?

HOW THE LAW THINKS ABOUT DIRECT TAX

The debate over the Direct Tax limitation of the U.S. Constitution illustrates the relative indeterminacy of words and the usefulness of more precisely delineated jurisprudential decision procedures.[60] Words are naturally vague and ambiguous, even if not perfectly so. Adjectives are especially problematic.[61] It is usually the "open-ended" clauses of the Constitution which give the judiciary such pause.[62] Invariably, those open-ended clauses include an adjective that necessarily means something different from one person to the next.[63] What process is due? Was the search or seizure reasonable? In the case of the income tax, the Pollock dealt with whether a tax on all transactions garnering income was the functional equivalent of a direct assault on wealth? How *direct* must the tax be for the Constitution to require Congress to apportion it amongst the states by population? Nouns are problematic as well, particularly with respect to phenomena which was previously inconceivable. Later legal arbitrators are often stymied by whether the text of law extends its provisions over modern inventions which a previous legislature could not conceive. Consider modern technology and freedom of speech. Recently, we had a case dealing with whether Obamacare levied a "tax."[64] If Congress passed a wealth tax, there would then be a case dealing with "direct."

Also, to the extent "Direct Tax" is a term to be taken as a whole, as a proper noun, it is naturally unclear whether the term applies to taxes not yet conceived of in 1787. Jensen asks whether the people of the United states would approve a Constitution expressly authorizing the unlimited taxing power Ackerman's construction would give it.[65] The reason this counter-factual question has little force however is because it is doubtful whether any American government of the time, whether state or federal, had the bureaucracy necessary to levy an income tax on a national citizenry.[66] One might argue that we still don't. If the income tax had been a known concept and a viable possibility for the federal government in 1787, pondering such a question might be seen as determinative.

Originalist Intentionalism

Whatever slaves may have thought Direct Tax meant, it does not matter under originalist intentionalism, the practice of interpreting text by discerning the intentions of its author(s).[67] To intentionalists, words have no meaning outside the intent of their author.[68] They are only concerned with what the authors intended, consult the Federalist Papers and other sources like Federal statutes of the time for evidence of what meaning the Framers intended for words in the Constitution to have. Thus, an intentionalist judge would not care what slaves thought because none were drafters of the Constitution. As such, their views are wholly irrelevant. Intentionalists would consider the views of slaves if the People are the authors of the Constitution or that the Framers intended to use words as they were most plainly understood by the People.

Originalist Textualism

Some originalist textualists might consider the meaning a slave may supply to the words Direct Tax, others would not. Textualism emphasizes the meaning people assign to text they encounter.[69] In our legal system, the Supreme Court, Justice Scalia in particular, encourages the legal deliberator to select the meaning that is plain.[70] In the case of a meaning that is less than plain, the deliberator usually considers other sources, like textual context, indicia of intent and purpose, modern dynamics, etc.[71] Of course, a chauvinistic textualist would not consider other sources, instead choosing the meaning of the word that is plainest even if not plain in the abstract.[72] In other words, if plain meaning in the abstract requires, say, 75 percent of people to agree upon a word's construction, a chauvinistic textualist may still reject all forms of context and choose the meaning as understood by only 51 percent.

Understandings of the Ratifiers

Textualism presents a core question that must be answered before one determines whether it matters what slaves thought Direct Tax meant: To whom must the text be plain? Different communities will often supply different meanings to the same word.[73] For example, the definition of income differs depending on whether one is talking to an economist adherent to Haig-Simons or a tax lawyer relying on *Glenshaw Glass v. Commissioner*.[74] Income requires realization to one, but not the other. Stanley Fish calls these "interpretive communities," and the exact number breadth of such communities depends on the context. Thus, whether a textualist will consider what slaves thought Direct Tax meant depends on the interpretive community our deliberator chooses to privilege. It is a matter of discretion.

Whether the thoughts of slaves matter to a textualist, then, depends on whether the deliberating textualist focuses on the understanding of those "Ratifiers" of the Constitution, or rather the understanding of the People alive and residing in the United states at the time of ratification.[75] Consequently, a textualist who privileges the Ratifiers as an interpretive community would ignore the views of slave, since no slaves were ratifiers.

Understandings of the People

Justice Scalia's brand of textualism, on the other hand, indeed concerns itself with what slaves thought Direct Tax meant.[76] His originalist textualism emphasizes the meaning the people of the United states supply to text. According to Scalia, he does not rely on the Federalist Papers to determine what the authors of the Constitution intended, but to discover what the people of the United states took the words in the Constitution to mean. The Federalist Papers, presumably being the best source of meaning, are obviously not the only items of evidence.

None of the Federalist Papers were written by slaves, so we cannot be sure that the Federalist Papers represent the meaning of Direct Tax, or Liberty, or Property, or Cruel and Unusual, as understood by those African immigrants. African slaves came from civilizations some of which had contact with and understandings of terms and concepts familiar to newly-immigrated Europeans.[77] We know that many captured slaves were part of their homeland's aristocracy and were indeed familiar with if not expert in governance and law.[78] Thus, the reason we do not know what African slaves thought Direct Tax meant is more likely to be that they were not asked.

For that matter, it is not free from doubt whether the Federalist Papers represented the meanings as would be understood by eighteenth-century women.

This article does not require that the meanings of words and phrases in the Constitution as understood by African slaves should trump the understanding of newly-immigrated Europeans. For one thing, it is not certain whether there is a difference at all. We are coming to understand that all of the world's legal systems, if not their cultures as a whole, have been quite syncretic for some time.[79] Instead, it is an attempt to highlight the fact that plain meaning is inherently empirical and, as such, the discovery process should include all relevant sources. That plain meaning textualism's empirical nature encourages historical research into the lives of Africans and Africa is as interesting sociologically as it is ironic politically, but it does not by itself privilege textualism over other deliberative techniques—like intentionalism, purposivism, or dynamism—in a juristic sense.

Justice Taney, in *Sanford v. Scott* (the Dred Scott case), claimed that slaves were not included in the people of the United States.[80] If he is correct, then Scalian textualism would ignore their views. However, others on the same court disputed this claim. We also acknowledge through modern social and legal understanding that Taney was simply wrong. African immigrants were people of the United States, even if immoral laws of the time excluded them from the polity.

Realism

Realism in constitutional understanding is represented most cogently by the notion of a Living Constitution.[81] Under this style of interpretation, if it can be called that, judges deliberating over the Constitution choose the meaning that best serves modern society. Living Constitution scholars are comfortable with the reality that meanings of words and phrases change over time. In its most radical form, living constitutionalism ignores the understandings and intentions of eighteenth-century persons, regardless of their status as authors, ratifiers or mere citizens.[82] In a milder form, however, living constitutionalism or constitutional realism might attempt to maintain some tether between modern meanings and original text.[83]

The Living Constitution

Adherents to living constitutionalism do not care what slaves thought at all about Direct Tax, or what any other phrase in the Constitution meant. Generally speaking, they contend that we ought not govern ourselves based on the ideals of an eighteenth-century, euro-male dominated, slave holding society.[84] Even if the thoughts of slaves were to be counted, judges will likely continue to emphasize the meaning understood by slaveowners more. Instead, the Constitution may legitimately be reconstructed through judicial opinions, so that the supreme law of the land is more symmetrical with the ideals of the people.[85] While living constitutionalism is credited with (or discredited for) expanding the notions of privacy and equality, it cares not at all for what slaves thought terms in the Constitution meant, as it does not care what anyone in the eighteenth century thought.

Translation

According to Lawrence Lessig, judges who rely on modern understandings can still be faithful to text.[86] For some, judges must rely on original understanding in order to be faithful to a written Constitution; otherwise they defeat the purpose of memorializing that huge social contract in the first place.[87] Lessig, on the other hand, believes that translating the original text into modern terms does not cast constitutional deliberation adrift into the sea of judicial legislation.[88] Words are inherently imprecise representations of concepts people share. So the trick of fidelity, according to Lessig, is to stay faithful to the concept the text identified, rather than adhere to the static meaning of a word or phrase.[89]

A legal decision maker stays faithful to a concept in the same way a translator of literary texts identifies the concepts a word in one language identifies then reiterates those concepts using the terms of another language. In constitutional translation, first a judge imagines the concepts that words and phrases of the Constitution are intended to represent, then he reiterates the concept in terms of modern understanding. For example, a translationist does not rely on the meaning of liberty as understood by the people or intended by the Framers, but instead identifies the word liberty as imperfectly representative of the concept of responsible personal autonomy and translates that into what personal autonomy means today. In order to translate old words into modern parlance a judge must have evidence and an understanding of what concepts an eighteenth-century writing is trying to represent. Thus, such a translationist may care to consider African conceptions of liberty or property or Direct Tax. However, a translationist might, in a way similar to an originalist textualist or intentionalist, restrict his focus to the concepts as understood by Framers or Ratifiers, which have nothing to do with what slaves thought.

Purposivism

John Hart Ely and Stephen Breyer's kind of constitutional purposivism is attractive to most critical race legal scholars today, but it ignores the views of slaves.[90] Purposivism is the privileging of consequences a legislature (or author) intended for a judge to consider.[91] It is distinct from intentionalism in that it focuses on consequences whereas intentionalism is concerned strictly with meaning.[92] According to Ely and Breyer, the structure of the Constitution commits us to the preservation and widening of a participatory democracy.[93] According to this deliberative technique, the most important consequence to consider in constitutional cases is which choice better preserves or widens participation in our governmental processes. With respect to this determination, the views of slaves as to Direct Tax or anything else is irrelevant.

Natural Law

Natural law stands for the proposition that law is not man-made, it precedes humankind.[94] The most difficult aspect of instituting natural law as a legal system is determining what natural law is in order to determine whether there has been a departure from it? That question is not answered here. Here, we note that under the natural law paradigm, whatever the source of it law is universal and binds us all. Thus, African methods of discovering the divine are just as relevant as any other.[95]

CONCLUSION

In *United States v. Murphy*, a panel of the DC Circuit used Scalian textualism to hold that damages relating to mental anguish were not income within the meaning of the Sixteenth Amendment and, thus, not subject to the income tax.[96] Scalian textualism stands for the proposition that when deliberating over words in the Constitution a judge should emphasize the meaning held by the people of the United States. According to Judge Ginsburg, the author of the DC Circuit's initial decision (which was reversed en banc), the people of the United states who enacted the Sixteenth Amendment did not understand income to include damages received on account of mental anguish. Although that panel reversed itself, Judge Ginsburg's opinion exemplifies the rising currency of Justice Scalia's jurisprudential teachings generally and his constitutional deliberative technique specifically.

But Scalian textualism is easier to describe than it is to apply, because determining what the people of the United states understood a word to mean at the time of enactment requires research and assessment, both involving rigor, procedure as well as discretion.[97] The same word has different meanings to different people.[98] Even if there is substantial symmetry between what two people believe a word to mean it is unlikely that their conceptions can ever be perfectly symmetrical. Of course, the law (and human cooperation generally) relies on tendencies, symmetries, and other "close-enoughs." Thus, Scalia, the Supreme Court, and others in the practice examine many different types of evidence to determine what the people understood a word to mean, including dictionaries, the Federalist Papers, English legal texts, etc.

Adherents to Scalian textualism, however, have not spent much if any effort exploring the meaning of words as understood by those who had no influence on dictionaries, the Federalist Papers, or English legal texts. Of course they would be wasting their time if it is true that propertied, white males who controlled these discourses accurately reflected the meanings understood by slaves, women, nonpropertied white males, Indians, etc. Such is a reasonable assumption for them to make even if based on the uncomfortable notion that as controllers of power-constellations, propertied white males determined ultimately what others thought words meant. However, I suspect that that assumption while somewhat reasonable is largely inaccurate, that marginalized groups tend not to succumb simply to the whims of power-brokers, that they tend to inculcate within their own cultures differing meanings and understandings regarding lots of stuff.

Moreover, to the extent a word or phrase like "Direct Tax" had no identifiably determinate meaning between propertied white males of the time, it is gainful under Scalian textualism, perhaps even required, to explore the meanings held by others. To that end, this article claims that an aristocratic slave captured from a well-to-do African family would have had ideas and understandings regarding terms in the U. S. Constitution, including what "Direct Tax" might mean.

African concepts of taxation, government, economic liberty, etc., are irrelevant to deliberations over the meaning of "Direct Tax," only because a deliberative procedure of the Supreme Court may deem such views practically or jurisprudentially out of bounds, not that they do not exist. For instance, Bruce Ackerman's approach to the Constitution would ignore the views of slaves since his constitutional interpretive style privileges understandings of the New Deal era. By contrast, Justice Scalia's version of text based originalism seems to require consideration of the views of slaves, as well as women, Indians, etc. Adrian Vermeule and Cass Sunstein might permit judges to ignore considerations they do not have time or expertise to analyze and evaluate. Ignoring the views of all the People might be forgivable as expedient, but it is certainly not excused, especially as an academic rather than jurisprudential matter.

Again, what slaves thought Direct Tax meant might not matter to Professor Jensen for several reasons. Under non-originalist constitutional jurisprudence, income tax can be considered a Direct Tax because there are good reasons to do so. Even some originalists would not care, particularly those advocating an intentionalist approach to the Constitution. And even those who, like Scalia, attempt to divine the meanings of words as they were understood by the people of the United states might refuse to consider the views of slaves, either because they were not at that time included as people of the United States, because their views are adequately represented by slave masters or subsumed by the legal ethos of the day, or because there is not enough evidence to determine what slaves thought about such matters or because it would cost too much time and money to investigate what slaves thought.

Consider that if the views of slaves are to be considered, then such views might be controlling with respect to a state like South Carolina, where slaves outnumbered whites. But even in that situation a judge might discount the views of slaves by two-fifths, in accordance with the U.S. Constitution.

What slaves thought Direct Tax meant matters most under Scalia's version of originalist textualism, because it is concerned with the understandings of the people of the United States, of which slaves were a minority. Lawrence Lessig's translationist deliberator considers the views of slaves to a lesser extent, as that judge seeks to identify the concepts old texts are trying to identify then translates them into modern language. Similarly, natural law theorists should be interested in any way, style or method of identifying what Nature requires of us, including the means by which Africans recognize those duties. Originalist intentionalism and living constitutionalism does not at all consider what slaves thought Direct Tax meant. Neither assigns any deliberative emphasis to the understandings of the people of the United states at the time of enactment, and thusly does not care what slaves thought the words and phrases in it meant.

A poverty of American history is that we do not know what slaves thought Direct Tax or any other term of the Constitution meant. This is due to our collective ignorance, not theirs. Many slaves were members of aristocratic families in the many African societies from which they were plucked. The famous story of Equiano the African illustrates this point.[99] Consider that African societies had for thousands of years been familiar with complex taxation, ancient Egypt having the oldest recorded tax system. Consider also that for several centuries the West African empires of Mali, Songhai, and Ghana organized government in a quasi-federal manner. Thus, it is entirely conceivable, perhaps even likely, that slaves captured from aristocratic environments would have an understanding of taxation implementation, and Direct Tax specifically. If it does anything at all, hopefully this chapter inspires more investigation and exposure of African civilizations incorrectly thought to be bereft of high culture.

NOTES

1. Audre Lord, The Master's Tools Will Never Dismantle the Master's House, speech The Second Sex Conference, New York, New York (1979).
2. Tommie Shelby, We Who Are Dark: The Philosophical Foundations for Black Nationalism (2008).
3. Molefi K. Asante, Afrocentricity (1988).
4. Adrian Vermeule, Judging Under Uncertainty (2006).
5. Calvin H. Johnson, *Fixing the constitutional Absurdity of the Apportionment of Direct Tax*, 21 Const. Comment. 295 (2004); Erik M. Jensen, *Interpreting the Sixteenth Amendment (By Way of the Direct-Tax Clauses)*, 21 Const. Comment. 355 (2004); see also Bruce Ackerman, *Taxation and the Constitution*, 99 Columbia Law Review 1 (1999).
6. Cass R. Sunstein & Adrian Vermeule, *Interpretation and Institutions*, 101 MICH. L. REV. 885 (2003); Vermeule, Judging Under Uncertainty (2009).
7. Antonin Scalia & Bryan Garner, Reading Law: The Interpretation of Legal Texts (2012). But see, William N. Eskridge, Jr., The New Textualism and Normative Canons , 113 Colum. L. Rev. 531 (2013)
8. Antonin Scalia, A Matter of Interpretation: Federal Courts and the Law (1997).
9. Id.
10. See, e.g., William N. Eskridge, Dynamic Statutory Interpretation (1994); Bruce Ackerman, *The Living Constitution*, 120 Harv. L. Rev. 1727 (2007).
11. William N. Eskridge, Dynamic Statutory Interpretation 34 (1994) ("The arguments for textualism as the foundational method in statutory interpretation are strong ones"); see also, Ronald Dworkin, *The Arduous Virtue of Fidelity: Originalism, Scalia, Tribe, and Nerve*, 65 Fordham. L. Rev. 1249 (1997).

12. For a middle ground position, see Lawrence Lessig, *Fidelity in Translation*, 71 Texas L. Rev. 1165 (1993).

13. This is, after all, the fuss over constitutional and statutory construction. See Ronald Dworkin, *The Arduous Virtue of Fidelity: Originalism, Scalia, Tribe, and Nerve*, 65 Fordham. L. Rev. 1249 (1997); Andrew Oldenquist, *Is the Death Penalty on Life Support? Retribution and the Death Penalty*, 29 U. Dayton L. Rev. 335 (2004) ("Scalia and Oxford professor Ronald Dworkin offer contrary views about the application of the Eighth Amendment").

14. Andre L. Smith, The Deliberative Stylings of Leading Tax Law Scholars, 61 Tax Law 1 (2008).

15. William N. Eskridge, Dynamic Statutory Interpretation 205-308 (1994). These scholars can be described as realist, though each of their methods of deliberating over the Constitution differs markedly from each other. John Hart Ely, Democracy and Distrust (1980), Stephen F. Breyer, Active Liberty (2005); Bruce Ackerman, *The Living Constitution*, 120 Harv. L. Rev. 1727 (2007); Lawrence Lessig, *Fidelity in Translation*, 71 Texas L. Rev. 1165 (1993).

16. The beef over methods of statutory and constitutional construction is after all political. See Phillip P. Frickey, *From the Big Sleep to the Big Heat: The Revival of Theory in Statutory Interpretation*, 77 Minn. L. Rev. 241 (1999). But see, "the death of theory," James Hackney, "Legal Intellectuals in Conversation." 2012

17. Adrian Vermeule, Judging Under Uncertainty (2006).

18. This notion follows and relies upon Professor Diop's tracing of African cultural unity through five thousand years of recorded history, back to Ancient Egypt and Nubia. Cheikh Anta Diop, PreColonial Black Africa (1987).

19. Calvin H. Johnson, Righteous Anger at the Wicked States: The Meaning of the Founders' Constitution 19 (2005) ("What is there to prevent an Algerine Pirate from landing on your coast and carrying your citizens into slavery? . . . You have not a single sloop of war" quoting a Hugh Williamson of North Carolina).

20. Calvin H. Johnson, Righteous Anger at the Wicked States: The Meaning of the Founders' Constitution 15–26 (2005).

21. Robin L. Einhorn, American Taxation, American Slavery 119 (2006) ("When the champions of the Constitution attacked the 'imbecility' of the Articles of Confederation, they were talking about these rounds of state legislative action and the power of a single state to frustrate the rest. Mostly, they were talking about the defeat of the impost."); Calvin H. Johnson, Righteous Anger at the Wicked States: The Meaning of the Founders' Constitution 15–26 (2005).

22. Calvin H. Johnson, Righteous Anger at the Wicked States: The Meaning of the Founders' Constitution 15–26, 32–39, 37 (2005) ("With the end of the Continental dollar, the Army in the field survived primarily on impressments . . . involuntary seizures from civilians with the misfortune of living within reach of the army as it moved or camped.")

23. Calvin H. Johnson, Righteous Anger at the Wicked States: The Meaning of the Founders' Constitution 26–29 (2005).

24. Id.

25. Calvin H. Johnson, Righteous Anger at the Wicked States: The Meaning of the Founders' Constitution 40–99 (2005).

26. Id.

27. Robin L. Einhorn, American Taxation, American Slavery 118 (2006) ("Regardless of whether the apportionments rested on population or wealth, they had to include decision about how to treat slaves: how to count them as persons or hot to count them as property.")

28. Calvin H. Johnson, Righteous Anger at the Wicked States: The Meaning of the Founders' Constitution 182–86 (2005).

29. Id.

30. Robin L. Einhorn, American Taxation, American Slavery 122 (2006) ("Slavery crowded out free labor"). By the mid nineteenth century, slave-owners assigned con-

siderable numbers of slaves to urban occupations. See George Ruble Woolfolk, *Slavery and Taxation in the AnteBellum South,* Journal of Southern History (1960); John Hope Franklin and Loren Schweninger, Runaway Slaves: Rebels on the Plantation 33–37 (1999).

31. Calvin H. Johnson, Righteous Anger at the Wicked States: The Meaning of the Founders' Constitution 182–84 (2005) ("In South Carolina, Anti-Federalist Rawlins Lowndes would oppose the Constitution because 'Negroes were our wealth, our only natural resource; yet behold how our kind friends in the North were determined soon to tie up our hands, and drain us of what we had!'")

32. Robin L. Einhorn, American Taxation, American Slavery 138–45 (2006).

33. Id. at 33, 94 (2006). John Hope Franklin and Loren Schweninger, Runaway Slaves: Rebels on the Plantation 33–37 (1999).

34. Robin L. Einhorn, American Taxation, American Slavery 120 (2006) ("If it is debated, whether their Salves are their property ... there is an end of the Confederation" quoting Thomas Lynch, delegate from South Carolina). According to Calvin Johnson, Madison tried at the Virginia Ratifying Convention to convince George Mason and Patrick Henry that the apportionment requirement in the Constitution prevented Congress from taxing slavery out of business. Mason and Henry didn't buy it, arguing (correctly) that Congress could set forth a formula that requires states to pay their full quota by way of a slave tax, which would lead to mass manumission. Calvin H. Johnson, Righteous Anger at the Wicked States: The Meaning of the Founders' Constitution (2005).

35. Calvin H. Johnson, Righteous Anger at the Wicked States: The Meaning of the Founders' Constitution 183–85 (2005).

36. Robin L. Einhorn, American Taxation, American Slavery 138–45 (2006); Calvin H. Johnson, Righteous Anger at the Wicked States: The Meaning of the Founders' Constitution 183–86 (2005).

37. Paul Finkelman Slavery and the Founders: Race and Liberty in the Age of Jefferson (2001).

38. Id.

39. Tomas Piketty, Capitalism in the Twenty-First Century (2014).

40. Beverly Moran, *Capitalism and the Tax System: A Search for Social Justice,* 61 SMU L. Rev. 337 (2008).

41. Bruce Ackerman & Anne Alstott, The Stakeholder Society (1999); Bruce Ackerman, *Taxation and the Constitution,* 99 Columbia Law Review 1 (1999).

42. E.g. Erik Jensen, The Taxing Power (2005).

43. Calvin H. Johnson, *Fixing the constitutional Absurdity of the Apportionment of Direct Tax,* 21 Const. Comment. 295 (2004); Francis R. Jones, Pollock v. Farmers' Loan and Trust Company, 9 Harv. L. Rev. 198, 198 (1895).

44. Pollock v. Farmers' Loan & Trust Co. ("Pollock I"), 157 U.S. 429 (1895); Pollock v. Farmers' Loan & Trust Co. ("Pollock II"), 158 U.S. 601 (1895). Pollock II, 158 U.S. at 618 ("[W]e are unable to conclude that the enforced subtraction from the yield of all the owner's real or personal property . . . is so different from a tax upon the property itself, that it is not a direct, but an inDirect Tax, in the meaning of the Constitution."). Francis R. Jones, Pollock v. Farmers' Loan and Trust Company, 9 Harv L. Rev. 198, 198 (1895) (the Court "deliver[ed] an opinion in which is laid down a doctrine that is contrary to what has been accepted as law for nearly one hundred years"). Knowlton v. Moore, 178 U.S. 41, 106–7 (1900).

45. U.S. Const. amend. XVI.; Bruce Ackerman & Anne Alstott, The Stakeholder Society (1999);Eric Rakowski, *Can Wealth Taxes be Justified*? 53 Tax L. Rev. 263; Beverly Moran, *Capitalism and the Tax System: A Search for Social Justice,* 61 SMU L. Rev. 337 (2008).

46. Bruce Ackerman, *Taxation and the Constitution,* 99 Columbia Law Review 1 (1999).

47. Id.

48. Id.

49. Calvin H. Johnson, *Fixing the constitutional Absurdity of the Apportionment of Direct Tax*, 21 Const. Comment. 295 (2004).

50. Hylton v. United States, 3 U.S. (3 Dall.) 171, 172, 181 (1796).

51. Calvin H. Johnson, *Fixing the constitutional Absurdity of the Apportionment of Direct Tax*, 21 Const. Comment. 295 (2004).

52. Pacific Insurance Co. v. Soule, 74 U.S. (7 Wall.) 433 (1869).

53. Pollock v. Farmers' Loan & Trust Co. ("Pollock I"), 157 U.S. 429 (1895); Pollock v. Farmers' Loan & Trust Co. ("Pollock II"), 158 U.S. 601 (1895). Pollock II, 158 U.S. at 618 ("[W]e are unable to conclude that the enforced subtraction from the yield of all the owner's real or personal property . . . is so different from a tax upon the property itself, that it is not a direct, but an inDirect Tax, in the meaning of the Constitution.").

54. Calvin H. Johnson, *Fixing the constitutional Absurdity of the Apportionment of Direct Tax*, 21 Const. Comment. 295 (2004).

55. Erik M. Jensen, *Interpreting the Sixteenth Amendment (By Way of the Direct-Tax Clauses)*, 21 Const. Comment. 355 (2004).

56. Erik M. Jensen, *Interpreting the Sixteenth Amendment (By Way of the Direct-Tax Clauses)*, 21 Const. Comment. 355, 370 (2004) ("Professor Johnson is correct, of course, that the founders didn't understand all of the consequences of the provisions they created... But the appropriate response to criticisms of that sort is 'So what?'. . . We do the best we can.").

57. U.S. Const. Art. I, sec. 9.

58. See The Federalist No. 21 (Alexander Hamilton).

59. Erik M. Jensen, *Interpreting the Sixteenth Amendment (By Way of the Direct-Tax Clauses)*, 21 Const. Comment. 355 (2004).

60. Scholars debate the degree with which this is true, with some arguing that legal terminology is fairly determinate and others believing that it is almost perfectly indeterminate. For a balanced exposition, see Lawrence M. Solan, *Vagueness and Ambiguity in Legal Interpretation*, in Vagueness in Normative Texts (2005).

61. Ruth Vatvedt Fjeld, *The Lexical Semantics of Vague Adjectives*, in Vagueness in Normative Texts (2005).

62. John Hart Ely, Democracy and Distrust (1980).

63. Of course some adjectives like "thirty-five years of age" are more determinate than others like reasonable, due, equal, necessary, substantial, etc. Ruth Vatvedt Fjeld, *The Lexical Semantics of Vague Adjectives*, in Vagueness in Normative Texts (2005).

64. National Federation of Independent Business v. Sebilus, 567 US ___ (2012)

65. Erik M. Jensen, *Taxation and the Constitution: How to Read the Direct Tax Clauses*, 15 Journal of Law and Politics 687 (Fall 1999).

66. Robin L. Einhorn, American Taxation, American Slavery (2006).

67. Stanley Fish, *There is No Textualist Position*, 42 San Diego L. Rev. 629, 649 (2005).

68. Id.

69. Antonin Scalia, A Matter of Interpretation: Federal Courts and the Law 16–18 (1997).

70. Antonin Scalia, A Matter of Interpretation: Federal Courts and the Law 16 (1997) ("When the text of a statute is clear, that is the end of the matter.").

71. Andre L. Smith, *The Deliberative Stylings of Leading Tax Law Scholars*, 62 Tax Lawyer 1 (2008).

72. Allan Madison, *The Tension Between Textualism and Substance-Over-Form Doctrine in Tax Law*, Santa Clara Law Review (2003); cf. Manning, John F. "*Textualism and the Equity of the Statute*," 101 Columbia Law Review 1 (2001). Vermeule and Molot.

73. Stanley Fish, Is there a Text in This Class?: The Authoritativeness of Interpretive Communities (1980).

74. Commissioner v. Glenshaw Glass Co., 348 U.S. 426 (1955).

75. Although not discussing constitutional deliberation specifically, Jellum & Hricik acknowledge that the plain meaning rule admits some discretion as to which interpretive community a judge should emphasize. Jellum & Hricik, Modern Statutory Interpretation 46 (2009) ("Should the ordinary meaning apply unless the legislature

has expressly adopted a technical meaning in the statute? Or, should courts use the technical meaning if the statue is direct5ed to a technical audience?").

76. Antonin Scalia, A Matter of Interpretation: Federal Courts and the Law 38 (1997).

77. Implicit in Diop's claim that the African has a distinct culture is the understanding that it differs from others, including Europe. Cheikh Anta Diop, PreColonial Black Africa (1987).

78. See, e.g., Terry Alford, Prince Among Slaves: The True Story of an African Prince Sold into Slavery in the American South xv (2007) ("from time to time African princes and kings had wound up as slaves").

79. P.G. Monateri, *Black Gaius: A Quest for the Multicultural Origins of the "Western Legal Tradition"*, 51 Hastings Law Journal(2000).

80. Scott v. Sanford, 60 U.S. 393 (1857).

81. Bruce Ackerman, *The Living Constitution,* 120 Harv. L. Rev. 1727 (2007).

82. Id.

83. Lawrence Lessig, *Fidelity in Translation,* 71 Texas L. Rev. 1165 (1993). See also John Hart Ely, Democracy and Distrust (1980) (contending that the structure of the U.S. Constitution exemplifies a commitment to greater participatory democracy, and that that non-text based commitment should be determinative in hard cases); Stephen F. Breyer, Active Liberty (2005).

84. See, e.g., Sanford Levinson, *How the United states Constitution Contributes to the Deficit of Democracy in America,* 55 Drake L. Rev. 859, 875–76 (2009). But see Charles R. Kesler, Thinking About Originalism, 31 Harv. J.L. & Pub. Pol'y 1121, 1127–128 (2008).

85. Bruce Ackerman, *The Living Constitution,* 120 Harv. L. Rev. 1727 (2007).

86. Lawrence Lessig, *Fidelity in Translation,* 71 Texas L. Rev. 1165 (1993). See also Todd E. Pettys, *The Myth of the Written Constitution,* 84 Notre Dame L. Rev. 991 (2009) (contending that Living Constitutionalism is text based).

87. Antonin Scalia, A Matter of Interpretation: Federal Courts and the Law (1997).

88. Lawrence Lessig, *Fidelity in Translation,* 71 Texas L. Rev. 1165 (1993).

89. Id.

90. John Hart Ely, Democracy and Distrust (1980); Stephen F. Breyer, Active Liberty (2005).

91. Aharon Barak, Purposive Interpretation in Law (2005).

92. Andre L. Smith, *Deliberative Stylings of Leading Tax Law Scholars* (2008); Jellum & Hricik, Modern Statutory Interpretation 245 (2009).

93. John Hart Ely, Democracy and Distrust (1980); Stephen F. Breyer, Active Liberty (2005).

94. An example of a natural law approach to constitutional construction is Adamson v. California, 332 U.S. 46, 70 (1947) (Black, J., dissenting), overruled in part by Malloy v. Hogan, 378 U.S. 1 (1964).

95. Asa G. Hilliard III, *African Origins of Justice* (1992) (paper representing speech given to Georgetown University Law Center's Black Law Student Association) (on file with author).

96. *United states v. Murphy,* 460 F.3d 79, 92 (D.C. Cir. 2006). Gregory L. Germain, *Taxing Emotional Injury Recoveries: A Critical Analysis of Murphy v. Internal Revenue Service,* 60 Ark. L. Rev. 185 (2007).

97. Hon. Richard Posner, *Judges are not Competent Historians,* ABA Journal, August 2012.

98. Stanley Fish, *There is No Textualist Position,* 42 San Diego L. Rev. 629, 649 (2005).

99. Vincent Carretta, Equiano, the African: Biography of A Self-Made Man (2005).

TWO

Pre-colonial African Tax Experiences

To speak of taxes, law and government in pre-colonial Africa is "to lay oneself open to a number of criticisms."[1] According to eighteenth-century Scottish philosopher, David Hume, upon home James Madison relied for his views of government and nationhood:

> I am apt to suspect the Negroes, and in general all other species of men, to be naturally inferior to the whites. There never was any civilized nation of any other complection than white, nor even any individual eminent in action or speculation. No ingenious manufactures among them, no arts, no sciences. . . . Such a uniform and constant difference could not happen, in so many countries and ages, if nature had not made an original distinction between these breeds of men.[2]

Fortunately, in the twenty-first century, it is widely accepted that African statesmanship extends back to antiquity.[3] In fact, some leading economists suggest that the degree of ease with which post-colonial African states are adapting to global economics relates to the degree to which those states were previously committed to pre-colonial centralization and governance.[4]

Still, Western academics—at least legal ones—have been warned not to identify with Afrocentricity or other kinds of negrophilia.[5] When Patricia Williams tried to infuse the legal discussion of race with her well-informed personal narratives, then Chief Judge of the 7th Circuit, Richard Posner, accused her of "suppressing" all other viewpoints, and then attempted to discredit her by associating her with those "irresponsible" Afrocentrists: "I should have thought that Williams, as a lawyer and an academic, would have wanted to place as much distance as possible between herself and [Afrocentricity] rather than to embrace uncritically one of its representative wild claims."[6]

Shall we discredit the wildly celebrated accomplishments of America's "founding fathers" to the extent they relied on scholars whose views are racially problematic, like Hume?[7] False notions of white racial superiority clearly required an eventual Afrocentric response, especially since many irresponsible and racist claims by Eurocentric scholars have remained "sticky," to say the least.[8] Borrowing Posner's words, "To pretend otherwise is an evasion."[9]

More than twenty years has passed since the Posner-Williams spat, so we will not dwell too much on past beef and illogical taboos, except to acknowledge that many of the claims of the Afrocentric movement have proven true, even if others have not.[10] Thanks to venerated scholars such as Cheikh Ante Diop and S.O.Y. Keita, etc., it is now commonly accepted worldwide that Egypt is in Africa, that its origins were in the South, and that its science, governance and culture influenced cultures outside of Africa.[11] It is also commonly accepted that statehood, a system of governance more complex than a simple chieftancy or kingdom, was established in all parts of Africa before European contact.[12] A century ago, each of these claims were considered "wild" and "irresponsible."

That some Afrocentric claims have not proven true, and sometimes plainly untrue, cannot seriously provide the basis for discouraging the examination of a simple question, a question that is entirely devoid of racial hubris, the question that links all "legitimate" Afrocentric ideals and scholarship: "How does history look from the perspective of Africa or Africans?"

TAXATION AND AFRICAN CULTURAL UNITY?

African states prior to the Christian era include Khem (Egypt), Kush and Meroe and Napata (Nubia), Punt (Ethiopia), and Carthage (Libya or Tunisia). During the first century of the Christian era, African statehood was reduced to Aksum (Ethiopia), Meroe (Nubia), and the Berber States (Libya).

By the eighth century, statehood expanded both westward and southward: Egypt, Morocco, Nubia, Ethiopia, Ifriqiya, Ghana, Tekrur, and the Swahili states of East Africa. Still centuries prior to European colonization, African states of the thirteenth century included, Egypt, Ifriqiya, Morocco, Nubia, Ethiopia, Kanem, Mali, Songhay, Ife, Yoruba, Great Zimbabwe, Mogadishu, Malindi, Mombassa, Zanzibar, Kilwa, Sofala, and Wolof.

And immediately prior to the African Diaspora and European colonization, sixteenth-century African states included Egypt, Turkish Ifriqiya, Morocco, Funj, Adal, Ethiopia, Swahili states, Bornu, Hausa, Kebbi, Nupe, Kuarafarfa, Songhay, Mali, Wolof, Mossi, Bono-Mansu, Yoruba,

Benin, Congo, Luoango, Tio, Bunyoro, Buganda, Monomotapa and Malawi.[13]

> In the pre-colonial epoch, beginning in the first half of the 1st millennium AD and continuing until the end of the 19th century, Sub-Saharan Africa was characterized by the emergence and existence of early forms of statehood. . . . [T]hey never covered the whole territory of Sub-Saharan Africa; until the end of the 19th century, they coexisted with tribal organizations, segmentary systems and chiefdoms. . . . European colonial expansion put an end to the independent evolution of the sovereign early states of Sub-Saharan Africa, of all types and stages of development.[14]

But does it make sense to speak of Africa in such monolithic tones? Can Africa be considered one gigantic political entity? Or is "Africa" a modern conception that was unknown to the ancient peoples of the continent, and moreover a conception that is useless in terms of accurately describing the diverse people and geography?

Africa's size makes it somewhat difficult to construct a unified African culture. Africa's land mass is many times larger than Europe. It is several times larger than North America. In fact, several ancient West African civilizations, like Songhay, were larger than all of what is now Western Europe. Further convoluting Africa's cultural unity are myriad, smaller, stateless societies that have always existed within and between the borders of Africa's more elephantine nations and empires.

In addition to the difficulties posed by Africa's size, West Asian and European colonization and subjugation confound the exploration of African cultural unity. Hostile to indigenous leadership and organization, colonizers and subjugators destroyed (and are still destroying) many artifacts and documents describing African cultural and political institutions. They often forbade the operation of native cultural and political institutions which retarded and sometimes destroyed them, and imposed upon the populace foreign languages, borders and legal systems. Undoubtedly, all parts of Africa have been impacted by contact with Europeans, Asians, and Americans.

But, despite fairly recent colonial subordination, features of African philosophy and notions of justice extending back to antiquity permeate the legal processes and institutions of African states as they existed before the terror of both the transatlantic oceanic and transindian oceanic slave trades, and then European colonization. This holds true also for African taxation. In fact, a particular style of taxation can be counted among things that seem distinctively African, like divine kingship, queen mothers, matrilineal succession, education through agegroup sets (i.e., fraternities and sororities), the drum, etc.

Almost all African states governed over several provinces, which sometimes presided over regions, and always over villages. This corresponds to the federal, state, county, and local authorities that comprise the United States. Heads of state appointed provincial governors who were required to provide military support and taxes to the state. In return, heads of state were required to distribute wealth gathered by the central authority back to the provinces. "Such systems, in which rulers required fidelity and assistance in return for granting power over a certain territory, have often been termed African feudalism in the literature."[15]

While it is true that all parts of Africa have been influenced by outsiders, it is also true that such influence was usually limited and often times indirect. The great Roman civilizations had extensive contact with North and West Africa, perhaps as deep as the Senegal River. And East Africans traded with nations as far as China during the first millennium, AD. As gold became internationally recognized as currency, interest in trade with Africans increased gradually yet dramatically.

Still, areas containing the most lucrative gold mines in the African interior were rarely conquered by non-Africans. Roman legions could drive only so far into Africa because African terrain was inhospitable to chariots. The wheel was simply not an efficient tool in Africa's forest zones. Moreover, the prevalence of the tse-tse fly hampered the domestication of horses and camels. Thus, Arab (and Roman) invaders were limited by the environment. Not until the late nineteenth century was the entire continent colonized by outsiders, and even then only for a few decades.

It is also wrong to assume that high civilization in pre-colonial Africa was due solely to Islamic influences. Even though many medieval African rulers converted to Islam, it was next to impossible in most cases for them to force a majority of their subjects to convert to a foreign religion. In fact, Islamic historians, merchants and travelers routinely questioned the piety of African rulers.[16] Arab sources also tell us that African Muslims, particularly those in West Africa, practiced Islam in a distinctly African way. These sources repeatedly mention Kharadjitism as a troublesome degradation or alteration of Islam practiced amongst the blacks of West Africa. In fact, it was not uncommon for stricter Islamic groups in West Africa to war upon or enslave other Africans who were not thought to be true or devout. The treatment of women was a particularly contentious matter, as traditional African societies and religions permitted far more of a public life for women than sharia law allows. We can still see this dynamic in action in West Africa today with respect to the militant group, Boko Haram.

Of course, the heavy influence of Islam on the East African Swahili states cannot be denied. Similarly, the beautiful hodgepodge of Mediterranean culture heavily impacts polities on the coastline of North Africa. We can further concede that the people and rulers of the West African empire of Songhay were considerably more devout Muslims than their predecessors, in Ghana and Mali. Still, there are vast regions in sub-Saharan Africa, several vast regions in fact—the Guinea Bay, the Congo River Basin, the savannahs of southeastern Africa—that developed statehood with little to no Mediterranean or West Asian contact.[17]

Ultimately, Mychal Tymowski is convinced that most of the state institutions over the course of African history were largely of indigenous development. He acknowledges that scholars describe the bulk of African states as "secondary" ones; ones that have borrowed the idea of statehood and many of its accoutrements from others. But he also acknowledges that, "it should be strongly stressed, once again, that the great majority of all states that have ever been created in the world, not only in Africa, are secondary ones."[18]

According to Tymowski, we should not attribute African statehood and civilization to others. But then the question remains, if all African states are secondary, from where do they originate? Mali was modeled after Ghana, but the origins of Ghana are unknown. Borno was modeled after Kanem, but the origins of Kanem are unknown at this time.[19]

This brings us to the controversial question of whether sub-Saharan culture emanates from the ancient Nile Valley civilizations of Egypt, Nubia and Ethiopia? Which, in addition, raises another controversial question of which of these has priority? Afrocentric scholars are convinced that Nile Valley civilization spread to all parts of Africa.[20] Others disparage Afrocentric scholars as peddlers of fantasies and invented homelands. But if African states cannot claim the Nile Valley as their progenitor, then they are all the more astounding for the early development and originality.[21]

According to Cheikh Ante Diop, a historically contiguous African culture can be identified, despite the vastness of size and the influence of non-African cultures. Throughout Northeast, Southern, Central, and Western Africa, similarities abound in terms of governance, language, cosmogony, etc. African societies have been more likely than any others to employ a matriarchal system of inheritance and power succession. Versions of the Bantu language are spoken by well over half the people on this immense continent. Traditional African societies have always been more apt than any other place in the world to educate and indoctrinate youth through fraternal rites. Similarities in cosmogony and arts have been noted (perhaps overemphasized).

ANKOLE: A TRADITIONAL AFRICAN STATE?

It should be helpful here to contrast Ankole, in southwestern Uganda, a state which appeared to have developed over millennia without much Islamic or European contact, with, Jimma Abba Jifar, a nineteenth-century state in the region of southwestern Ethiopia, which operated under an

Islamic superstructure imposed upon a "traditionalist" African population.

In Ankole, the melding of several agricultural villages along with groups of herders produced a state where the pastoral group, the Hima, a minority group, seemed to dominate the Iru, an agricultural group. The royal family was Hima and they alone were allowed to own cattle. Farming communities of the Iru, were taxed for agricultural products, crafts, beer and corvee labor. The Hima also exclusively controlled trade outside the villages. They also developed a system where the Hima might lend nonproductive cattle to the agriculturalists in exchange for a portion of the surplus. The Hima were also taxed a portion of their cattle by the central authority. The ruler was known as Mugabe, and his princes, rather than appointed officials, were responsible for tax collection.

The Ankole experience is fairly typical of pre-colonial African states south of the Sahara who had little contact with Islam, the Mediterranean or European traders. It is known to some as "African Feudalism," and taxation is central to it.

Others, however, reject the term "feudalism" when discussing African taxation because, as a rule, African states incorporated a reciprocity principle in their taxation that was not present in typical, European feudal relationships. Whereas European feudal taxation does not require the state to redistribute tax revenue to the subjects in that and other provinces, African taxation was not designed to enrich rulers, but to redistribute the goods produced in one region of the nation to other regions who produce something different. Rather than describe African taxation as feudalistic, it is probably more precise to call it "reciprocal." Whereas a feudal lord "owned" the land and the people on it, to do with as he pleased, the African monarch was responsible for the land and the people on it, and taxation and distribution were the means for fulfilling their divine charge.

> [T]he ruler was supposed to guarantee his community's well-being. The ruler's strength and prestige depended on fulfilling this function and on effectively caring for the whole community subjected to him. This was the manifestation of the reciprocity principle, so important for wielding power, according to which the subject population, in return for respecting the ruler and providing him with gifts and taxes, expected to receive care, gifts in return, and, above all, to be assured of security, order, and well-being. This latter was understood not only materially, in terms of wealth, good crops, and lack of natural disasters, but also in terms of the fertility of women and general felicity.[22]

In the typical African reciprocal tax arrangement, central governments required each province to pay their taxes in the form of a mandated agricultural, pastoral or craft product, which the central government then redistributed to other provinces that did not produce those goods. So one province might be required to pay taxes in cotton, another in iron works, etc. The ruler gained admiration by redistributing these items back to the provinces. In some cases, the ruler and his family were forbidden from taking or consuming any of the produce—a far cry from the absolute monarchy some claim for pre-colonial African rulers. The central government typically collected excise taxes from merchants (foreign and domestic) in the same way and for the same purposes.

When the ruler failed to honor the reciprocity principle of taxation, or when times were bad and blame placed on the ruler, the council of elders had the right to kill the king.[23] By ritual, the king was killed and then reborn, and continued to rule. In rare instances, the king was actually killed. Such was the power of certain councils to check the authority of the monarch. Succession to the throne by the next ruler was not ordinarily by primogeniture, where the eldest son had a right to the throne. Instead, most pre-colonial African states provided for "dynastic selection" where the council of elders chose the most able of the king's surviving sons who had been certified by the Queen Mother—an official state title with ceremonial and political responsibilities. Usurpers were rare and typically left out of the oral histories recited by griots.

JIMMA ABBA JIFAR: TAXATION IN AN AFRICAN STATE WITH ISLAMIC SUPERSTRUCTURE

In contrast with Ankole, the short-lived state of Jimma Abba Jifar exemplifies an African state with an Islamic superstructure governing a population that persisted in following traditional religions and customs.[24] The Jimma state was located in what is now southwestern Ethiopia. Its capital was Himrata and represented an area peopled by the ancient Himyarites, a kingdom subordinate to the rulers of the great state of Axum. Jimma is considered one of the five Galla states that arose at a time when the central authority of Ethiopia was being pinched by Europeans (i.e., Italy). By the time of its demise, around 1932, Jimma (or the Himyarites) was again paying tribute to the emperor of Ethiopia.

By examining Jimma, we might better understand the dynamics of earlier African states whose rulers had converted to Islam while the bulk of the people had not (e.g., Ghana, Mali, Songhay, Kanem and Bornu). The ruler and perhaps most of the ruling class of Jimma Abba Jifar were Muslims and "protectors of the faith." Still, however much the ruling class aligned with Islam and Arabia, the people of Jimma, while facing a famine, forced the ruler at least once to adopt a divine character and perform traditional rituals heretical toward Islam. Yet, unlike traditional African governance, there was no official position for Queen Mother or the ruler's elder sister. Unlike traditional African taxation, there was no reciprocity requirement.

Because of its Islamic superstructure, Jimma also contrasted with traditional African states where land could not be bought and sold by individuals. Farming was the occupation of the vast majority. And in Jimma, a family could own their own land or sharecrop on someone else's. Provincial governors were almost always derived from the wealthy.

Not surprisingly due to its Islamic superstructure, Jimma maintained a vibrant slave market. Yet there were opportunities for upward mobility. A conquered person with talent who had adopted Islam could rise from a slave to a high official, to whom the central monarch could appropriate lands, thus becoming a person of nobility. The markets of Himrata were the most lucrative of the five Galla states of southwestern Ethiopia. Caravans seeking to trade in these markets paid tolls and taxes at the border and at several tollgates. Among the goods traded were ivory, hides, cotton, grain, coffee, musk, gold, etc. Armed state officials maintained law and order and collected taxes. Provincial officials were subordinate to those of the state.

Nineteenth-century Jimma had a code of laws, a penal system, and a judiciary with courts of appeal. Officials were appointed by the central authority, rather than elected or selected through local laws or customs. Hardly any government office was gained through kinship or heredity. Central government officials had very specific duties, including "tax-collector, market judge, courier, border guard, jailer, military officer, and so on."[25] These central government officials had priority over provincial governors who were prohibited from collecting taxes. These features of "modern governance" reflect the imposition of an Islamic superstructure over autochthonous customs. In other words, the modernity of law and governance in Jimma was linked to subjugation.

In its declining years, however, provincial governors had obtained from the central government the right to 10 percent of the tax collected. This dynamic might be seen as a resurgence of the typically African "reciprocity" rule of taxation. However, those governors could not collect it themselves, nor were they permitted to maintain a standing armed force. "According to informants, a governor could not even send a large group of armed men in pursuit of bandits preying on caravans in his districts. He had to send word to the palace and request that troops be sent to deal with the problem."[26] These governors could, however, demand corvee labor, adjudicate minor offenses, and collect "irregular" taxes or bribes.

Central government tax officials toured the country annually, taking census and collecting taxes. They had the authority to exempt from regular taxation those performing military service or those who served as border guards or who had some other obligation to the central authority. Artisans either gave their services directly to the monarch or paid their tax in craft products. Tax was levied on the holding of cattle, but after that by the poll. Taxes were often paid in currency; salt at first, then

Maria-Theresa thalers. By the late nineteenth century, a considerable portion was diverted to Ethiopia's emperor Menelik II.

The king of Jimma Abba Jifar protected foreign merchants and also received taxes, tributes and gifts from them, but the king had no duty to redistribute what was collected, as was the case in "traditional" African societies. The king's protection freed merchants from the customary laws of the villages and counties. This may have been the way both Islam and slavery were protected and promoted against the interests of the commoners who were traditionalists. Similarly, the monarchs of medieval Mali and Songhay seemed at times to be more courteous to wealthy and powerful Arab merchants than to the commoners of the state.

TAXATION AS AN INTEGRAL FEATURE OF EARLY AFRICAN STATEHOOD

Taxation has played a role in African governance since the beginnings of Nile Valley civilizations.[27] Regardless of whether a central authority arose from within an ethnic group or if one ethnic group overtakes another, there arose a chief and central administration that required taxes from those within and outside of the group. Poll taxes simply for the privilege of living on controlled lands were the simplest form of taxation/authority. But the obligation to pay corresponded to an obligation to protect. After that fundamental dynamic was established, more sophisticated taxation followed.

Thousands of years before the christian era, Egypt, Nubia and Ethiopia were not only involved in international trade but sometimes intercontinental trade as well (between Africa and West Asia). Discovered tablets show that by the beginning of the Christian era, Egypt had income, excise, estate and other special taxes, complete with exemptions, collection due process, and perhaps even tax shelters. Systems of governance in Nubia and Ethiopia often resembled that in Egypt, and it is possible that their tax systems had similarities.

Then, from the first to the eighteenth century AD, from the Muslim north, the Swahili Coast in the east, to the Bantu south and west, African civilizations instituted excise and poll taxes and collected requisitions or tribute from states within their federations and from conquered and colonized states surrounding their empires. Some of these tributary payments, particularly those from states within a greater African empire, resemble the requisitions and direct taxes required of colonies and states under the Articles of Confederation and the U.S. Constitution.

Failure to pay taxes or tribute has always been tantamount to rebellion, in Africa and elsewhere.

Taxation is integral to the anthropological study of "the state," generally, and in Africa, specifically: "[O]ne characteristic of most, if not all, early states deserve special attention because it may well turn out to be one of their distinctive features. I am referring here to the significant role played by the early state itself in the direct exploitation of the producers through taxation, compulsory labor and other obligations . . ."[28]

Moreover, the modernity of a state relates to the complexity of its tax system. An "inchoate" state taxes its citizens through the exaction of agricultural or pastoral produce, as well as occasional corvee labor projects, like maintaining roads or establishing an irrigation system. In a "tribal" or "clan" setting, there is typically one class of people and very little economic differentiation between members. Several tribes, clans, ethnic groups, etc., coming together in one territory often produces a kingdom, which is also typically supported by a tax in-kind on each village, usually to support whatever military aims there may be (advance or defense). Scholars still debate how and why several kingdoms might come together and form an inchoate state with a centralized authority.

Some have argued that a "state" is a strictly European concept, describing the emergence of centralized political communities in Western Europe between the fourteenth and sixteenth centuries AD, Mychal Tymowski rejects this conception, as it denies statehood, for no good reason, to Asian, African and pre-Columbian American polities. Instead, the state—or centralized governance over distinct peoples in a given territory—is common to every continent, and emerged over five thousand years ago in Egypt. Tymowski also seeks to avoid the state as a normative quality, as in something "better" or "more civilized" than a tribe or kingdom or clan. Instead, it is merely a description of complexity, for there are many scholars, often of a Marxist persuasion, who believe the state is the primary mechanism for privileged minorities to exploit unfortunate majorities.

The ruling class of an "inchoate" state begins to differentiate itself from the ruled by the establishment of governmental officials who take little to no part in economic production. Governance, at higher levels first, and then later at lower levels, becomes a full-time occupation. Sometimes, a group finds itself with an agricultural surplus which supports trade and requires regulation. Here, taxation of produce and trade supports the endogenous growth of a central government that can establish internal order as well as protect citizens from outsiders. For an overly-simple example, if members of the community decide to grow corn, the community itself will likely decide and enforce rules regarding who can touch the corn and when.

Other times, one group conquers another and establishes itself as the ruling class, supporting itself by taxation on subordinate groups. At other times, a state is organized for defensive purposes. It is historically typical in Africa, whatever the circumstances of origin, that the ruling class is supported by, yet also subject to, taxation.

In an inchoate state, the position of tax collector or head of the treasury usually starts out as a relative of the ruler and remains hereditary, but becomes appointed by the ruler from outside the family after some time, and outside the ethnic group some further time after that—to someone totally dependent on and loyal to the ruler, solely. This transition to a merit based system from a hereditary one roughly describes the transition from an inchoate state to a so-called typical or transitional state.

In a "typical" state, taxation in the form of tribute is paid regularly by subordinated groups to the central government, whereas such taxes in an inchoate state are thought to be intermittent or ad hoc. At the next level, a "transitional" state, "taxation had developed into a well-defined system, with a complex apparatus to ensure its regular flow."[29] Features of taxation that suggest a "transitional" or complex state include codified taxes, payment in currency rather than in-kind, cabinet or court level tax officers, "ad valorem" taxation, and appointed tax collectors having no kinship ties to the ruler or ethnic affiliation to the ruled.[30] The central, sub-Saharan state of Kuba was a transitional, early state. The short-lived East African state of Jimma Abba Jifar was also considered "transitional." Rulers of Songhay, Bunyoro, Buganda and sixteenth-century Congo appointed and removed officials without regard to their ethnicity or affiliation with the ruler's clan, which represents either a typical or transitional state.

In typical and transitional pre-colonial African states, court dignitaries administered government, including the collection of taxes. In Ethiopia, Mali, Sonhay, Hausa, Bornu, Benin, Ashanti, Mossi, Fulbe and Congo, the highest officers included deputy rulers and regents, often performing military functions. In Africa, kings did not lead or even participate in warfare. Lesser dignitaries managed the economic affairs of the state, including the supervision of markets, roads, waterways, harbors, and of course taxes in the form of customs, road levies, and poll taxes.[31] The Mandinke Empire, for example, enlisted over twenty court dignitaries, including the *korei-farma*, the minister dealing with the white (Arab) population. The cabinet level official responsible for taxes was the *fari-mundio*.

TYPES OF TAXES IN PRE-COLONIAL AFRICAN STATES

Slavery in pre-colonial Africa usually resulted from conquest, and taxation in the form of corvee labor was the typical means of subordinating the captured. Prisoners of war were often settled on land dedicated to the king or the central government. "[Y]ield from these estates was supplemented with the revenue obtained from taxes, tributes and the other sources . . ."[32] These types of villages could be established by provincial governors, regional administrators or village chiefs. Either the slave/prisoners were taxed a particular portion of what they grew, or they were required to maintain a separate field the entire yield of which belonged to the king and central authority.

Because monarchs had more control over the slave/prisoner villages than they had over kin and fellow ethnic relatives who had traditional and customary rights, African rulers sometimes entrusted talented former slaves with important government positions. It is in this context that in Africa, a person from a newly conquered group might become a slave to the king, and yet become a high official (possibly even ruler himself). For example, the Mamluks were once slaves in Egypt who took full control of the nation-state for over two and a half centuries, creating a separate ruling group. The biblical story of Joseph is also instructive.

Taxation in the form of tribute and corvee labor was not only a ubiquitous aspect of early statehood in Africa, but also around the globe. Obviously, several African states submitted to Arabic and European slave demands and profited significantly from the capture and sale of other Africans. Still, revenue from slavery, either from their sale or agricultural exploitation, was, as a rule, not the predominate source of revenue for African states. "[E]ven in states where the ruling groups were inclined to capture and sell people and derived great profits from this, slavery did not become a numerically dominant phenomenon in the system of internal social forces. Most of the population of these states consisted of subjects living in their village communities and providing taxes to the ruler."[33]

Tribute is a tax paid to the central government by subordinate groups within or outside of a state. Tribute was obtained by conquering tribes, kingdoms and other states and requiring annual payments from the conquered in-kind, in labor, or in currency. A treaty called the Bakt between Nubia and Egypt, in 641 AD, probably represents the most famous of these. A more subtle means of subordination involved the conquering state securing safe passage through another state's territory for commercial or military purposes. Smaller states sometimes paid tribute to more than one "protector" state. Although tribute and tax are virtually synonymous, it seems that the term tribute is used in the literature to designate the subordination of distinct peoples over another, whereas tax is used to describe intragroup exactions.

When one African state conquered another polity, the next question was usually whether to incorporate the conquered people into the conquering state by claiming the land and placing a central government official over the region who would collect the taxes and remit them to the ruler's court. Or, the conquering state could allow the conquered to govern themselves so long as they collected and paid taxes to the conquerors. The reciprocity principle of African taxation seems to govern in the former cases but not the latter. A major factor in this decision was the distance between the conquered people and the capitol of the conquerors. Of course, the conquered can one day become the conquerors, a feat the Fulani accomplished as one time subjects of the Hausa before becoming conquerors in their own right.[34]

While provincial and regional governors were likely to be appointed by the ruler, village chiefs were typically elected or selected according to pre-state laws and customs. They might rule undisturbed so long as taxes were paid and people were supplied to the state for military or public works projects.[35]

Early statehood in Africa stems from many factors including population density, war, and technological advancements. More sophisticated taxation followed these innovations. After the advent of iron hoes, stock breeding, iron smelting, and metal smithing, Sub-Saharan African states produced surpluses that supported large states through taxation.[36] Cattle and ivory, along with the mining of salt, copper and gold added to the tax base. Reports of intensive gold mining in Ghana go back to the eighth century AD.[37] The international trade of goods to and from required a level of efficient organization that, unfortunately, is not widely appreciated and seldom acknowledged.

More complex African states had markets where numbers of people and merchants participated for themselves, not on behalf of the sovereign. In these states, revenue was garnered in the form of road and border tolls, market excise taxes, and numerous other fees. The rulers and merchants of West African empires of Ghana, Mali and Songhay were notorious middlemen who oversaw the trade of salt from their North for gold from their South. Citizens were allowed to trade gold dust, but nuggets of a certain size all belonged to the king. Mansa Musa, considered by some, including *Forbes Magazine*, the wealthiest ruler in the history of the world, bragged that he taxed every gold trade and received a mithkal of salt for two-thirds its weight in gold. Other rulers regulated the trade of metals (like copper and iron) in a similar manner. Controlling and protecting trade routes, including checkpoints, marketplaces, ports, and towns, was essential to the might of African states, like Ghana, Mali, Songhay, the Hausa city-states, Kanem-Bornu, the Lunda and Kazembe states, and the Swahili Coast of East Africa.[38]

In a small state, the ruler was likely to make an annual tour of the state, displaying royal grandeur, taking census, dispensing justice, and collecting taxes. In a medium sized state, the ruler was less likely to tour, and provincial governors were more likely required to travel and attend court, bringing with them the tax collected (after keeping some for himself). In larger, more complex states, central government tax collectors assessed and collected taxes outside of the presence and purview of the central ruler or the provincial governors. In fact, in Jimma, the central government prohibited provincial governors at all times from collecting taxes or from levying their own internal taxes. There, central authority was so complete that provincial governors could not have armies, nor could they pursue criminals outside of the state, as that was the exclusive responsibility of the state.

Not all pre-colonial African states had cities, but the ones that did often taxed urban denizens based on their craft specialization. Cities were also the manufacturing hubs of the state, where the raw goods collected as taxes were then processed into that which was necessary for the maintenance of the state. For example, the tax on city blacksmiths might consist of an obligation to process metal ore collected as tax from the provinces into military armaments. Urban potters and weavers were probably taxed similarly.

Anthropologists consider the use of currency in tax collection a sign of modernity. Salt and salt bars were currency in a variety of African states and polities, both in the East and the West. Cowrie shells were another popular form of currency. Other forms of currency included raffia cloth, copper ingots, gold, cola nuts, salt bars, and beads. Obviously, gold was a fairly ineffective form of currency because of its plenty. [39]

Again, a central tenet of African taxation, however, was the concept of reciprocity. While the "divine ruler" technically owned all the land and could do as he please, it was recognized everywhere that the ruler was responsible for the general welfare of his subjects. Thus, the giving of taxes to the ruler triggered a reciprocal responsibility of the ruler to lavish the people with gifts. These gifts would be in the form of produce from the other provinces which the receiving province could not produce for themselves.

Great land mass and environmental diversity produced a diverse economy, and the ruler was ultimately responsible for redistributing the goods from one sector to the others, usually by requiring each province to pay its taxes in a kind designated by the ruler. A ruler might require one province to pay their taxes in cotton, while another in sorghum or millet or some other grain, while another pastoral province may be required to pay in cattle. Similarly, the ruler sometimes held a monopoly on international trade, using the taxes collected to trade for foreign luxury goods which he would then distribute to the provinces, thus increasing his prestige, authority and power. It is said that African rulers were not concerned much with hoarding wealth as they were with controlling the distribution of it.

The central government's inability to collect and redistribute taxes could lead to the fall of not just the ruling dynasty, but to the state itself. Refusal to pay taxes or tribute was, and is, tantamount to rebellion. But the question was whether the central authority could do anything about it. If a subordinated tribe or ethnic group refused to pay taxes, the central government may not have the revenue or authority to deal with the recalcitrant. Or, provinces and villages may come under pressure to pay tribute to another regional power or state.

Ultimately, there are not only certain commonalities with respect to pre-colonial African states, but also commonalities with respect to the characteristics, composition, and functions of their tax systems:

> Vansina proposed defining an African state in the pre-colonial epoch as a politically sovereign organization headed by a ruler having sacral features, and delegating power to his representatives in the field. . . . Taxes, in addition to their economic importance, have a political and symbolic role, because their payment is a form or recognizing the ruler's authority, while refusal to pay constitutes rebellion. There are various forms of taxes, from payments in kind in the products being local specialties, through the provision of labour and military contingents, to market charges, road tolls or court fees. Part of the ruler's revenue comes from trade and cultivation of the ruler's own estates. The burden of taxes and services to be provided is counter-balanced by the ruler's duty to distribute gifts. Wealth is the right to control the flow of goods rather than the right to possess them.[40]

Perhaps the most important understanding emanating from an examination of taxation in Africa is the falsehood of absolute, despotic monarchs ruling simple tribes and governing over unsophisticated economies. Pre-colonial African rulers were normally constrained by a ruling council and were almost always required to respect the reciprocity principle in taxation, where the ruler was not permitted to enrich himself but was required to redistribute that which was collected. The reciprocity principle was not designed to eliminate all subordination, however, as there was no extended requirement that the ruler distribute goods equally or in proportion to what was given. "The reciprocity system is in force, but is imbalanced."[41]

TAXATION DURING AFRICAN ANTIQUITY

According to S.O.Y. Keita, the Badarians (4000 BC–3200 BC) are possibly the first African civilization, if the development and commitment to agriculture identifies the existence of civilization or at least law and society.[42] Their remains are found in Northeast Africa, between a fertile but drying Sahara and the Nile River valley. At this time, Nubia is referred to as Ta Seti ("Land of the Bow"), and what will be Egypt is divided into two lands, Upper Egypt in the south and Lower Egypt to the north. Little is known, however, about taxation or governmental organization generally in these lands, except that John A. Wilson believes that Old Kingdom Egypt's legal procedures derive from these early societies.[43]

Old Kingdom Egypt

Over 5000 years ago, before any successful invasion of Egypt from outside of Africa, everyday Egyptians operated within an intense legal structure governing most aspects of their lives. Egyptian dynasties were committed to the development of the administrative government and were quite familiar with numerous forms of taxation, including tributes, tariffs, poll taxes, and, eventually, the world's first estate tax.

Old Kingdom Egyptians developed a legal system with procedures of law designed to settle disputes and administer government based on principled and reasoned deliberation and to afford protection of the system on equal grounds to all citizens. According to Aristide Theodorides, Old Kingdom Egypt "attained from the outset, during the Old Kingdom, a high level of institutional and juridical development, which was subsequently distorted by the intrusion of religious practices. Not only did Egypt not surpass this level in the later phases of her development, she may even perhaps have failed to reach it again, despite the efforts of her rulers and thinkers."[44]

For thousands of years, later dynasties tried to restore Egypt to its Old Kingdom greatness, including attempts to restore its principles of due process and equal protection. Eventually, Egypt became more cosmopolitan and Mediterranean during the Middle and New Kingdoms, until it became increasingly "non-African" in character: Hellenic in the first millennium BC, Roman around the turn of the millennium, and Islamic in the seventh century AD.

The original name for Egypt is Khem, or "Land of the Blacks." Some argue that "black" in this context is a reference to the color of the soil. However, consider that "Ethiopia" is a reference to the phenotype of its people, "land of the sun burnt faces." Note also that "Sudan" is Arabic for "land of the blacks" and refers not only to the geographical location where Nubia was once located, but also to sub-Saharan West Africa. "Maur" (which eventually evolved to Moor) was a term used by Romans to denote a land with people of dark skin. Thus, for "Khem" to be a reference to the soil rather than phenotype would make it an anomaly.[45]

That Old Kingdom legal experience developed endogenously and should be considered African in character is supported by Diodorus' belief that Egyptian culture originated from the South. The Great Court instituted by the earliest Egyptian dynasties were to be staffed by the "Great Men of the South." According to Wilson, "legal procedure was followed in Egypt, but the specified practice must have stemmed from the customary law of the land before there was a unified state."[46] When Egypt was unified by Menes (the Scorpion King), around 3200 BC, the conquerors came from the South.

This first Egyptian dynasty began what is known as the Old Kingdom era. From 3200–2000 BC, Egypt developed its statehood, originated systems of writings, applied the sciences, and built all of the pyramids. Old Kingdom Egyptians traveled and traded broadly—conquering, controlling and taxing areas outside of Africa.

However, much Old Kingdom pharaohs are portrayed today as having almost unbounded authority and were to be revered as gods, the principles of Ma'at were greater than the pharoah's whim and were the standards against which his decisions were judged. Whatever its origin, the principles of Ma'at and the governments of the Egyptian dynasties at all times respected the concept of privately held property. By its fourth Dynasty, Egypt had a national archive where they stored deeds, contracts, wills and royal decrees. Wilson describes Old Kingdom government as an "elaborate bureaucracy," including several cabinet-level ministers. Agents of the Egyptian state operated under the direction but somewhat removed from personal control of the pharoah. In fact, by around 1350 BC, the pharaoh could no longer make law by decree.

Even more remarkable was that Egyptians of deep Antiquity accepted women as full legal persons. Egypt was known to have on occasion female Pharaohs.[47] During the Middle Kingdom era, a common woman could exercise whatever legal rights every other citizen of her day was supposed to have. Aristide Theodorides recounts a story about an Egyptian woman who sued her father for goods he owed to her and her husband.[48] Unlike Western societies up until close to our own time, women were neither the property of their fathers nor their husbands.

During the earliest days, the vizier was required to "walk forth every day, so that poor or timid people might also have a chance to appeal to him for justice."[49] The First Dynasty relied on a member of the royal family to serve as vizier, which at that time appears to be a combination of attorney general and chief justice. By the Fifth Dynasty, however, the vizier is no longer related to the king, and resembles what we might call today a cabinet member.

The vizier administered the Egyptian court system, which includes the Great Court and the Six Great Courts on which local judges served. As a member of cabinet subservient to the king, who in turn was adjudged against the principles of Ma'at, the vizier did not enjoy much personal discretion. According to Wilson, "the king's charge to the vizier is very detailed, insists upon the strictest impartiality and also directs that all of the vizier's judicial activity be carried out in conformance with the regulations and that everything be done in conformance with the precedent therefor."[50]

Stare decisis was apparently an important concept in the Old Kingdom, a practice which relates both to equal protection as well as due process. A judge's "individual authority was thoroughly limited by known precedents and procedures from the past."[51] On one hand, Diodorus claimed that at least five Old Kingdom pharaohs instituted codified laws. On the other, these laws have not been discovered; meanwhile contemporaneous codes have been found throughout West Asia. Egyptian courts are believed to have forty rolls of past precedent available to each judge in the courtroom and were to decide accordingly. Only during the first intermediate period was there ever a doubt as to whether any individual had recourse to the courts as a matter of right. Notably, Egyptian legal procedure recognized the importance of lawyers yet restricted their duties, as they believed excessive lawyering favored the rich.

According to Russ VerSteeg, "it was customary, though not required, for a judge to apprentice as a clerk in the court prior to the time that the king promoted him to a judgeship," a process for selecting "federal" judges similar to our own.[52] Pharaohs sometimes appointed special commissions to preside over particular cases, such as when Ramses, concerned with the appearance of impartiality, convened a special commission to try conspirators against his regime. Egypt may have had other "nonfederal," local courts to hear minor petitions and accusations of petty crime. From time to time, the vizier's commissioners visited and consulted with the local judges.

The Old Kingdom developed numerous tax systems. The most informal form of taxation was tribute either paid by or paid to Egypt by other nations. When conquering lands on the Arabian peninsula and northwards toward Palestine, the Egyptians required payment in exchange for autonomy. During periods of decline, Egypt was required to pay the likes of Nubia or the Macedonians to keep them from attacking.

Taxes on individuals were a normal part of Egyptian life from the very beginning. Pharaoh's of the very first dynasty (3000–2800 BC) levied an annual poll tax. Local "nomarchs" collected these poll taxes. Instead of money, tax collectors sometimes received payment in kind. Tax payments were stored in a national treasury, to be redistributed to the population. Thus, it is possible that Old Kingdom Egypt like the rest of Africa thereafter taxed under a reciprocity principle where the obligation to pay taxes was followed by an obligation of the ruler to redistribute.

Through taxation and redistribution, the economy of a state could be more effectively planned and diversified. In Egypt, cotton was probably collected as tax, processed in cities, and redistributed as garments by the central authority to a larger portion of the population. One of the earliest known Egyptian officials was responsible for the storerooms and workshops, while another was in charge of distribution. Egyptian taxes also included ad hoc levies dedicated to specific activities like military campaigns. Taxes on exports and imports, along with the establishment of tariff-free zones, were also part of Old Kingdom Egyptian tax administration.

As early as the fourth Dynasty, Egyptian governments issued tax exemption charters. Corvee labor was a tax paid by the Egyptian citizenry. However, the idea that the pyramids and other impressive Egyptian buildings were built by subjugating the whole of the population and committing them to slavery is probably fantastic. "It is likely that corvee for the maintenance of what irrigation works existed at that time, together with the custom of conscripting men for expeditions to quarries and mines, constituted the legal basis for the right to summon laborers for public works, among which the construction of pyramids figured prominently; but this does not mean that the peasants and workmen were legally or social slaves or serfs."[53] Requiring citizens to labor on public works projects for the benefit of the state like the establishment and maintenance of roads and harbors or even compulsory military service was ubiquitous in Africa and around the globe.

The Egyptian tax system during the Old Kingdom is phenomenally comprehensive for its time. It was not modern in the sense Robin L. Einhorn uses the term.[54] In her discussion of taxation in the United States, pre- and post-Revolutionary War, she suggests modernity is to be judged by both a commitment to the progressivity of tax incidence philosophically and to appraising the commercial value of property administratively. However, considering the over-mystification of Egyptian government and society and the still prevalent attitude that Egyptian civilization was prelogical,[55] it is very important to detail Egypt's commitment to taxation as a means for maintaining responsible government and a harmonious society.

Most of these developments relating to taxation and governance occur in Egypt before any of the Greek city-states even existed. And while it is dangerous to assume that Egyptian experiences in taxation spread to Nubia and Ethiopia, it seems equally reckless to assume they did not. Quibbling about whether Cleopatra was black or whether Napoleon shot off the nose of the Sphinx is really a distraction and misses the point that, two thousand years before Greek, Roman, Persian or Arab subjugation of North East Africa, Egypt had already developed a complex state styled government; and its influence spread in every direction.

Middle and New Kingdom Egypt

After 2000 BC, Egypt faced threats from the Assyrians and the Persians to their northeast, and after around 500 BC from the Greeks and Romans to their north. After the first intermediate period (2280–2060), the Middle Kingdom (2060–1785) returned Egypt to a dynastic order. The pharaoh Horenheb was noted for restoring order and integrity to Egyptian tax administration after a period of societal decline. pharaoh Sensuret I extended Egypt's power during this time to include the Nubian Empire of Kerma and demanded annual tribute from them. Similar demands were made of the Libyans.

Still, more West Asian invasions occurred, bringing upon Egypt a second intermediate period of political upheaval. Recently discovered texts show that New Kingdom Egyptians (1580–1085) were heavily burdened by income taxes, and openly chafed under their weight.[56] This is probably the result of foreign subjugation. Eventually, the Nubians led by Piankhi retook Egypt and, through Taharqa and the Twenty-fifth Dynasty, briefly restored its prominence.

Hellenistic Egypt relates to the period in Egypt after the fall of the New Kingdom Dynasties to Alexander the Great through eventual Roman conquest around 350 AD. According to Stephanie Willbanks, the first estate tax was instituted in Egypt around this time.[57] Furthermore, the Egyptian estate transfer system contemplated a trust system where a trustee holds property and distributes income therefrom to a class of intended beneficiaries. P. G. Monateri maintains that Egyptian law remained firmly Egyptian even after Greek then Roman conquest, "Egyptian national law remained in force even after the Antonian Constitution."[58] In fact, Monateri relays Revilliout's claim that the Greek "'Law of Persons and General Jurisprudence' were of Egyptian origin."[59]

During periods of Egyptian decline, the Nubian empires of Kush, Meroe, and Napata were developing. Also, the Ethiopian city states of Punt and Aksum were growing in international importance near the Red Sea. Carthage, formerly Libya to the Egyptians, became a major power, challenging Roman hegemony in the Mediterranean.

Ethiopia (Punt, Axum)

After Egypt's 3000 year run as one of the most advanced civilizations in the world, the Axumite Kingdom represented the preeminent African state. Goods from the African interior were distributed internationally through the Ethiopian port of Adulis.

As Europeans eventually subdued almost the whole African continent, Ethiopia successfully fended off the Italian army and is known as one of the only states in Africa to remain independent almost throughout its entire five thousand year history. Its leader at that time, King Haile Selassie I, is revered to this day as a divine king by the Rastafarian religious order.

Ethiopians are represented in ancient literature by Punt, the Himrayites, and Axum. The term "ethiopia" is Greek, meaning the sun-burnt people. When Herodotus relays that "the Ethiopians believe themselves the oldest of all peoples," it is unclear whether he is speaking specifically of the Axumites or of Nile Valley Africans generally.[60] This discussion of Ethiopian taxation, then, will concentrate on that which is known about Axum, which became a world power after the fall of Egypt to the Romans, Greeks, Assyrians and Persians.

The Axumite Kingdom bordered Nubia (Meroe) and had long-established contacts with Egypt. It also bordered southern Arabia, which had its own flourishing civilization at the beginning of the Christian Era. Axum's position on the Horn of Africa and at the south of the Red Sea provided protection from Roman hegemony in the north as well as vast opportunities for trade with India and ports east. In fact, Rome in the fifth century AD attempted to deploy an economic embargo to thwart the growing power of Axum.

Axumite wealth stemmed from the role of middlemen between foreign traders and goods that could only be secured from Africa's interior, like ivory, obsidian, antimony, mercury, hippopotamuses, giraffes, leopards, etc. Large caravans regularly traveled to the interior. Taxation of this trade was a major source of revenue for the Axumite kings. "The heyday of this trade was from the first century BC to the early third century AD. It is commented upon in the works of Strabo, Pliny, Claudius Ptolemaeus and Heliodorus, as well as in Pseudo Arrianus' Periplus of the Rythrean Sea."[61]

Axum was located on a high plateau, which gave it protection from invaders and where great wealth could be stored. Besides the capitol, there were other cities and towns, including Adulis and Matara, which specialized in trade and craft production, rather than herding and agriculture. The city of Axum was expansive and contained large, multi-story buildings, due to their use of clay mortar in construction. Farmers and cattle breeders on the periphery were taxed to support the economy of the city. Between the third and eighth century AD, Axum produced gold, silver, and copper coinage. Foreign merchants were required to pay tribute to the king as early as the third century. Whether taxes were paid in coin is unclear. "[T]he first reports of trade duties in the Axumite kingdom, although not entirely reliable, date from the sixth century."[62]

The Axumite rulers governed over numerous peoples and territories, each of which owed regular tribute to the king. The king toured these territories annually or biennially, taking census and collecting taxes along the way. Some territories, such as the Himyarites, governed themselves and paid a tax in exchange for their independence. The kings of Ethiopia were and are still known as the "king of kings." At one time, it is believed that Axum held over ninety-nine separate kingdoms under their sway, presumably under a tributary relationship.

Nubia (Kush, Napata, Meroe, Kerma)

Nubia was referred to in different times as Ta-Seti, Kush, Kerma, Meroe, Napata, Makuria, Alodia, and Nuba. It is now known as the Sudan and the South Sudan. It lay directly south of Ancient Egypt and had a complex relationship with its northern neighbor, Egypt. It is West of Ethiopia. The Nile runs through its length from south to north.

It was once recognized as one of the most powerful kingdoms on Earth. Despite being one of the primary sources of gold for the ancient world, Nubia was never conquered during antiquity by the Romans, Greeks, Assyrians, or Persians, although it has been subject to Egypt on several occasions. It eventually developed its own system of writing. And the indigenous or African character in high times is suggested strongly by, among other things, its prominent matriarchy—the fact that it was often governed by women, (e.g., the Candaces).

The relationship between Egypt and Nubia, particularly before the Christian Era, is rich with cooperation and conflict. Yet the precise nature of the relationship at different times during the ancient period remains unclear. Part of the controversy stems from the fact that Greek and Roman writers describe Africans using terms like "Ethiopian" to sometimes identify a specific political entity while at other times they may be referring to Africans generally in racial terms.

At least twice in antiquity, however, Egyptians dominated Nubia and required her to pay annual tribute. At times, Egyptian administration of Nubia included Egyptian personnel as tax collectors. However, Diodorus, for one, wrote that Egypt was a colony of Nubia. During the Old and New Kingdoms, Nubian pharaohs reigned over Egypt.

Social developments before this time in terms of law, religion and other forms of social organizations are decidedly African. "It was only toward -3000 that a distinct difference developed between the civilization of the lower, Egyptian part of the Nile Valley and that of the upper, Nubian part."[63] More pyramids were eventually built in Nubia than in Egypt.

Nubians were famous for iron smelting, dubbed the "Birmingham of Antiquity." Its archers were world-renowned. When strong, Nubians maintained exclusive access to gold and ivory from the African interior. Egyptians as far back as the Old Kingdom imported gold, steel and other items from Nubia and then traded them to other parts of the ancient world. The ability to protect that position of exclusive intermediary to Africa's entire would determine their global importance once gold became accepted currency throughout the globe, and the ability to tax those trades helped establish the wealth of the nation.

On the other hand, Egypt and Ethiopia had the power to control trade coming from outside of Northeast Africa. When Europeans and Western Asians took control of these trade routes, the powers of interior African states diminished. By the dawn of the Christian era, Nubia was subjugated by Mediterranean Egypt. In 641, the Bakt required Nubia to pay Egypt an annual tribute.

Still, medieval Nubia enjoyed a glorious almost thousand year epoch, as it became a great Christian empire during the latter half of the first millennium and beginning of the second, only to fall to Islam in the thirteenth century AD, like Egypt. Afrocentrists tend to assume that each societal decline in Nubia likely produced great migrations throughout Africa, leading to the spread of Nile Valley culture south- and westwards. "Traditional" scholars tend to discount this likelihood.

MEDIEVAL NUBIA, EGYPT, AND ISLAMIC NORTH AFRICA

Egypt and Nubia's presence as great ancient African civilizations declined at the hands of a rising West Asian civilization, the Arabs. Until approximately the fifth century AD, the Nubian-Kushite Empire governed over much of Southern Arabia, while the Roman Empire controlled Northern Arabia and the Middle East. But in the sixth century AD, Arabia turned the tides.

With the aid of Ethiopians, Mohammed united Arabia under the banner of Islam. Under this new religious fervor Arabians rejected Nubian, Roman, and Persian authority and then began to conquer lands outside of Arabia. Egypt fell under their power, and become the first African state to be converted to Islam. According to Al-Jahiz, a "black" muslim living in ninth-century Iraq known as one of Islam's great polymaths, "white" muslims eventually became hostile toward Africa and Africans and sought to subjugate them for their resources, particularly gold.[64] After several campaigns, spanning several centuries, Arabs converted almost all of Northeast Africa to Islam. Islamic taxes have been imposed in these countries for centuries.

Around 641, Islamic Egypt signed the Bakt. Part of the tribute was to be paid in slaves, who were likely obtained from lands Nubia may have conquered to its south, from their jails and prisons, or both. Little is written about this relationship between the seventh century and twelfth century which suggests either an equilibrium had been reached or a re-emergence of the Nubians, for Arab sources generally ignore the unflattering, while Nubian sources on the other hand have disappeared.

In the twelfth century AD, Egypt became the seat of power in the Islamic world. Included in their administration were import and export duties, poll taxes, and tributes from subjugated states within the empire. The Mameluk Empire under Saladin distributed tax revenues as a means of securing the loyalty of the army, the leaders of which were apparently seen by Egyptians as more Turkish or Kurdish than Egyptian. By the thirteenth century AD, the Abbuyyid Empire also caused major upheaval in Nubia and regions to the south by demanding again the annual tribute in slaves. Several reprisals from Nubia are reported, both militarily and by way of refusing its obligations under the Bakt.

Eventually, Egypt turned Nubia "into raiding country." A poll tax was levied on non-Arabs and thousands of slaves were taken. The demand for slaves increased such that they were soon taken from Nubia itself—which likely caused substantial migration and cultural diffusion. Conversion to Islam typically offered a way to avoid enslavement and the tax, but Arab-Egyptians sometimes even enslaved the Nubians who had converted. This chain of events—conversion, external slave raiding, internal slave taking—repeated itself with respect to West Africans and their relationship with Islam, and then again with respect to European slavers and Christianity.

Islamic civilization spread through North Africa, up the strait of Gibraltar into Spain. By 1180, almost all of the North African coastline was annexed, with the Almohads levying a lucrative land tax on non-Muslims. Excise taxes on the trade of goods were levied alongside property taxes.

Besides military conquest, taxes, or rather exemptions therefrom, were partly responsible for the conversion of peoples from traditional African religions to Islam. For example, in the thirteenth century AD, the Banu Marin and Banu Wattas levied taxes over the peoples of Morocco. As in Nubia, the Banu Marin restricted its poll tax (and perhaps its slaving) to non-Muslims, which likely encouraged religious conversions in large numbers. By this time, many factions rivaled for control over North Africa, including Almohad civilian governors, Almohad religious leaders, the Banu Ghaniya, the Banu Marin, and Renaissance Christians, some of whom offered their rule as protection from taxation.

By the fourteenth century, power and governance in North Africa was centralized in Islamic hands. Their Mediterranean empire stretched from Northwest Africa to Arabia and included parts of Southern Europe. Islamic hegemony in this part of Africa remains today. Taxes, such as the Zakat, are supposed to be collected in accordance with the Koran.

This tax history of North Africa, particularly North-West Africa is incomplete to the extent it does not deal seriously with taxation in the Moorish Empires--a project for another day.

WEST AFRICA

With control over a major source of the medieval world's gold, the nations of medeivel West Africa could afford and indeed consumed the best of the world's goods and supported the most advanced scholarly academies of their day.

> The principal source of revenue for the sovereigns of Black Africa, from antiquity to modern times, from the Indian Ocean to the Atlantic, i.e., from the Nubia of Herodotus and Diodorus Siculus to the Ghana of Bakri and the Mali of Ibn Battuta and Khaldun and the Songhay of Sadi and Kati, was gold extracted from mines. . . . It contributed powerfully to the economic prosperity of the country; it quite certainly meant the sovereigns did not have to overwhelm their respective peoples with taxes and tariffs.[65]

Ghana, and its successors, Mali and Songhay operated for the most part as confederations, with a central state subduing adjacent kingdoms from time to time and either governing them directly or requiring from them large tax payments in exchange for some degree of autonomy.

While these West African civilizations were definitely influenced by Islamic-African civilizations to the north, their customs and culture remained intact to a degree sufficient to identify distinctions between indigenous cultures and imposed Islamic customs, particularly with respect to law. Diop contends that distinct and identifiable facets of these indigenous cultures point toward African cultural unity from times of ancient Egypt and Nubia.[66]

Taxes were paid in kind, coin, and by other mediums of exchange. Cowry shells, being relatively scarce and easy to carry but hard to conceal and impossible to counterfeit, served as a medium of exchange throughout many parts of the continent. Salt was another. Gold pieces and other metal ingots were also used. West Africans instituted taxes as a form of economic regulation and diversification. For instance, gold being plentiful in West Africa but scarce in Europe and West Asia, West African kings taxed its trade heavily in order to extract rents from foreigners. At times, taxes on the import of unworked copper garnered the most revenue for the Mali Empire, as their merchants traded it to nations in the interior for their gold at the rate of "one mithkal of [copper] for two-thirds its weight in gold."[67]

Like elsewhere in Africa, West African states used taxation to institute a caste or reciprocal system of economic production. Central governments demanded tax payments exclusively in quantities of produce the empire expected of them. In certain societies, poll taxes on farmers were paid in kind, but on a graduated scale with a cap, (i.e., ad valorem). Goods collected by the central authority were then redistributed back to the provinces, thereby supplying each province with a variety of goods from the whole of the state.

Orderly administration probably signified to citizens and foreigners alike the sophistication and might of the empire, or the lack thereof when tax administration is arbitrary. Of Ghana, Mali, and Songhay, the three most notable pre-colonial West African empires, each took great pains to institute a regulated tax system, and several rulers were credited with severely punishing those governors who exacted unlawful taxes from the people. "[R]evenues from imperial estates; the zakat or tithe, for the poor; taxes in kind levied on harvests, herds and fishing; taxes and customs duties on commercial transactions; special levies on the merchants in the towns; the spoils of almost annual war, etc. This income paid for the upkeep of the court, the administration and the army, and for giving presents and alms."[68]

A West African empire would typically collect internal requisitions from its member states, as well as collect tribute from vassal states outside the empire's direct administration. The relationship between West African empires and North African empires was also marked by tributary arrangements, with revenue flowing either way depending on the balance of power at the time and was paid in produce, metals, and slaves toward the colonial era. As well, African nations closer to the interior, like those located in today's Nigeria, exacted tribute from each other as a typical form of conquest and subordination. For example, in the area known today as Nigeria, the kingdoms of Katsina and Kano instituted a poll tax by collecting requisitions from conquered chiefdoms in the form of iron bars.

Ghana

Ghana exists as a political entity perhaps as far back as 400 BC. It lasts as a political entity for over 1.500 years, eventually overtaken by Mali, then Songhay. Around 700 AD, the Soninke Clan advanced the use of iron smelting toward weaponry and united Ghana under its might. A tenth-century Moor, Ibn Hawkal, believed the king of Ghana to be the "richest sovereign on earth." In the eleventh century, the Spanish Moor, Al Bakri describes the Ghanaian city of Aoudaghast as "a very large city with several markets . . . filled with fine houses and solid buildings."[69]

Dispute resolution by a state court system was an essential feature of government in not only Ghana, but also later in Mali and Songhay. West African courts, like ancient Egyptian ones, sought to mediate the dispute and reconcile the parties. Al-Bakri refers to Ghana's court of justice. Ghana's twelfth-century king, Takruri, was also widely known for his commitment to the just cause.

Cheikh Anta Diop contends that the Ghanaian Empire was involved in international commerce, complete with an excise tax system, as early as the Roman destruction of Carthage in the second century BCE. This system survived the fall of Ghana, and lasted through Mali and Songhay into colonialism. One Arab historian records a tax of one gold dinar per load of salt imported and two dinars for each load exported. Five gold mithkals was the rate for copper, and ten for all else. Excise taxes were collected in Timbuktu by local officials who would then distribute the proper share to whichever federal rulers there might be, whether Ghana, Mali, Berbers, or Songhay. By the eighteenth century AD, all parts of West Africa instituted systems of merchant taxes, including market days and taxes on caravans as they crossed borders.

Diop notes a religious veil over West African systems of taxation. He contends that "one's goods and crops that ritual decreed must be turned over to the sacrosanct authority who linked the two worlds, so that order might be maintained in the universe and nature continue to be fruitful."[70] Perhaps he is referring to zakat, or tithe dedicated to alleviation of poverty, which was instituted by West African societies ruled by Muslim governors. However, he attributes this tax to Ghana at a time before Islamic prevalence in West Africa. Apparently, a Ghanaian dynasty ruling between the sixth and eighth centuries AD collapsed due to the peoples' perception that taxes were being administered in a manner against their spiritual principles.

Ghana's decline in the thirteenth century is reported by the Arab historian Ibn Khaldum who described how the North African Almoravids subdued Ghana, taxed it and rendered it vulnerable to further conquest by its neighbors, the Sosso. By 1238, the great Mali king, Sundiata, captured what remained of Ghana from the Sosso, placing it within the new Mandinke Empire.

Mali

Mali was founded by Mansa Allakoi Keita in 1213 and became a world power within twenty-five years by conquering its neighbor Ghana, before Mali itself was eventually conquered around 1475 by another West African neighbor, Songhay. At its height around the early 1300s, Mali was as large as Western Europe. So committed to the use of government toward the absence of chaos and strife, Ibn Battuta said of the Mandinke, "the Negroes are of all peoples those who most abhor injustice . . . complete and general safety one enjoys throughout the land."[71] Even after its golden era, according to Howard Zinn, "European travelers in the sixteenth century were impressed with the African kingdoms of Timbuktu and Mali, already stable and organized at a time when European states were just beginning to develop into the modern nation."[72]

In 1324, special taxes were levied to fund Mansa Musa's famous thirteenth-century hajj to Mecca, which ultimately brought unparalleled cosmopolitanism to Mali. During his famous pilgrimage to Mecca, Mansa Musa carried with him such extreme gold and luxury and exciting so many merchants from Portugal, Italy, Egypt and North Africa that traders from those areas descended upon Mali in great number, enriching it with tax revenues. He lavished the Middle East with so much gold its price dropped internationally by one-seventh.

Mali's wealth allowed it to focus on specialization, learning and the development of professional classes. It was renowned worldwide for its universities and schools of higher learning. Regarding Malian legal and scholarly sophistication, Leo Africanus reported that "In Timbuktu, there are numerous judges, doctors, and clerics, all receiving good salaries from the Mansa. . . . More profit is made from the book trade than from any other line of business."[73] Mahmud Kati, from Syria, records 150 to 180 schools in Timbuktu alone, with Muslim scholars attending from faraway places such as Europe, West Asia, North Africa and other parts of sub-Saharan Africa. Ancient historian Abderranman es Sadi tells of an Arab who sought to practice law but wanted to avoid Timbuktu initially because it was full of "legal experts." Remarkably, the city of Jenne was thought by many to be even more advanced than Timbuktu, because its universities taught medicine, including surgery.

Mali embraced the administrative nature of government. It had as many as twelve provinces. To govern them, Sundiata, its greatest king, appointed cabinet level officers, including ministers of foreign affairs, treasury, commerce, sanitation, fishery, forest, and agriculture, a head inspector, and lieutenant governor. Each department employed lower ranking officials. The government played a significant role in regulating the economy, including encouraging interstate and foreign trade, controlling exports, taxing imports, and setting production quotas. Typically, a member of state council was responsible for collecting the empire's share of taxes from the local government, while in local government the administrator in charge of the official marketplace collected taxes assessed on the citizens.

Ibn Battuta attributes to the Mandinke legal system an appeals process where the Mansa (or king) serves as the court of last resort. Lower court proceedings were attended by governmental ministers. Battuta admires, "They do not confiscate the property of any white man who dies in their country, even if it be uncounted wealth. On the contrary, they give it into the charge of some trustworthy person among the whites, until the rightful heir takes possession of it."[74]

Songhay's rise stemmed from Mali's decline. Beginning in the mid-fifteenth-century Mali was under pressure from the Islamic Tuareg people to their north, from small coastal kingdoms armed by the Portuguese, and from the rising of Songhay, a former Malian province. In 1433, the Tauregs captured several Mali cities, including the venerated Timbuktu and other large capital cities such as Gao. Meanwhile, coastal kingdoms were breaking ranks and trading with the Portuguese without paying taxes to the central government.

The breakdown of order depressed the gold trade. Finally, Sonni Ali successfully led neighboring Songhay's forces against the Taureg and reasserted authority over several areas that had aligned themselves with the Portuguese.

Songhay

Songhay first emerged as a powerful kingdom in the eleventh century. Despite the fact that since 1019 Songhay's Askia was Muslim, Songhay leaders such as Sonny Ali, who came to the throne in 1464, identified with indigenous religions and were hated by devout Muslims. Askia Muhammad (or Askia the Great), on the other hand a devout Muslim whose reign lasted from 1493–1528, pushed the empire's borders to the Atlantic, east toward the Sudan, and northwest into the Sahara—a region larger than Western Europe. Songhay universities at Timbuktu, Djenne and Gao taught theology, grammar, rhetoric, logic, astrology, astronomy, history, geography, medicine, science and math. These universities granted different levels of academic degrees.

The universities at Timbuktu were not attended solely by citizens of Songhay or Mali. They were internationally renowned. Songhay's immense wealth allowed them to support schools that were the envy of the world and regularly attended by North African muslims, Europeans, West Asians, and sub-Saharan Africans. In fact, so committed to education were the West Africans that Askia Muhammad is famous for instituting public kindergarten. Aristocrats from West African societies were well-schooled in the liberal arts, and those that found themselves captives on American shores, like Equiano and Prince Abdur Rahman, could have contributed to the understandings of justice held by eighteenth-century Americans, if only they were asked.

Askia the Great is also renowned for increasing the sophistication of Songhay government. He is credited with "codifiying the legal system, centralizing his bureaucracy, establishing a more effective banking and credit system, and providing education from kindergarten through the University of Sankore in Timbuktu."[75] Askia Muhammad established a court of appeals separate from and greater in power than the Askia, the Islamic-styled Kadi.

Reports regarding twelfth-century Borno and thirteenth-century Kanem also identify judges, magistrates and jurists.

By the time Songhay ruled over most of West Africa in the sixteenth century, it employed a panoply of taxes, including taxes on estates, the zakat or Muslim tithe dedicated to the poor, in kind poll taxes on agriculture, herding and fishing, general and specific excise taxes, and import and export tariffs. Sometimes, the tax system of a particularly successful merchant area would survive the transition from one empire or conqueror to the next, as it did in the infamous city of Timbuktu, which resided at different times under the regime of the Mandinke, the Tuaregs and Songhay. The local governors continued to collect taxes and regulate market activity under an apparently locally devised scheme and distributed a share of revenues to whichever central administration ruled over the larger area.

Songhay's government took great pains to regulate international and intranational trade, their efforts including a tax system designed to maintain stable pricing for its most lucrative export, gold. They also instituted poll taxes and tariffs as a means of controlling the economy. Songhay allowed some of its conquered protectorates to govern themselves in exchange for requisitions or tribute.

While the religious aspect of taxation was probably designed to promote obedience to the tax collector and the empire more generally, rulers clearly had more earthly and practical ideas about tax administration. Askia Muhammad, for example, encouraged agricultural production at times by lowering taxes on certain farmers. Like other West African societies, poll taxes were collected in kind so as to collect revenue and to institute a caste system of economic regulation. But Askia Muhammad's fifteenth-century Songhay introduced government tax appraisers and a progressive scheme, a graduated scale depending on wealth.

The Songhay Empire flourished until the late sixteenth century, when Morocco, long a rival of Songhay, finally gained a military advantage through the use of muskets. War with Morocco lasted until 1618, until Morocco was eventually repelled. But the victory was hollow and the glory days were over. The empire had become weak through prolonged external warfare and with the help of the Portuguese who pinched its coastal trade and supported internal warfare with ammunition and weaponry. "From that moment everything changed. Danger took the place of security, poverty of wealth. Peace gave way to distress, disasters, and violence."[76] The Dendi people, formerly inhabitants of one of Songhay's main provinces, took over much of a beleaguered Songhay from the south. Ultimately, the French took Timbuktu in 1894, Gao in 1898 and the salt-mines of Tuareg in 1900.

Eighteenth & Nineteenth Century West Africa

The Volta States, the Yoruba States, as well as Benin, etc., were West African nations located farther south on the Niger and Volta rivers than the empires of Ghana, Mali and Songhay. Medieval Arab traders believed gold grew from the ground there, probably because middlemen traders of Ghana, Mali and Songhay protected their position by preventing the Arabs from actually reaching these places.

Peoples in these areas found themselves in precarious positions as Mali and Songhay became increasingly Islamic over the years, and European slavers began to impinge on the coastlines. These areas became raiding grounds for slavers. Statehood in these areas was most likely developed in response to external threats. "In the Voltaic area the presence of permanent threats of assault and pillage seems to have induced people to look for more effective protection and leadership. The increase in the political unity created by these circumstances was accompanied by the growth of a supra-village ideology. . . . Such forms of organization create a permanent need for regular supplies of food and other commodities for the maintenance of the armed forces, the remuneration of warriors, and the establishment of communications by means of roads, boats, spies, messengers, etc."[77]

The Voltaic states, which were located in and around what is present-day Ghana, were central governments that grouped villages into provinces and taxed them. The sovereign was the ultimate court of appeal over most cases, and the only one who could order capital punishment. The king and his court toured the state, taking census and collecting taxes. Special government officials were assigned the duty to collect them. Armed contingents of the king enforced his orders and decisions. Tax revenue supported not only the royalty but also the nobility, administrative officials, appointed village chiefs, priests, administrators of prisoner of war villages, and ambassadors. At some point, the Ashanti Empire incorporated at least some of the Voltaic states and required tribute from them.

Aside from traditional provincial taxes, international trade produced considerable revenue for the aristocracy and tax revenue for the central government of Voltaic states. Horses and salt from the north were traded for cotton, kola nuts, iron, spices and slaves from the south. Caravans paid road tolls and taxes to local and provincial officials. Each province had a specific official dedicated to tax collection. The central authority also organized and supervised markets, in which each merchant paid taxes or dues to the responsible provincial official. Taxes could be paid in cowries, cattle, or with agriculture or merchandise.

The ruler's wealth derived from the taxation of prisoner of war villages. Through this system, the king had control over large herds of cattle and horses. However, the traditional African duty of reciprocity was also present here: "Wealth constituted for the ruler no more than a sort of status symbol. . . . As Izard has put it for Yatenga: As the king possesses everything he need not possess anything . . ."[78] The power of the central monarch was also limited with respect to governance matters such as crime. Whereas in the majority of African states, the adjudication of murder lay with the central monarch, almost all crime in the Volta states was handled locally.

The Yoruba states also had a legal code, penal system and courts of appeal. Capital punishment, like elsewhere in Africa, was the prerogative of the Oba, the ruler. The Oba was not a despot, however, as he did not have the power to issue laws. Fines and punishment for crimes were specified. His authority was the final interpretation of laws already established. The limited nature of the Oba's power likely stems from the fact that these states were most likely confederated for defense purposes. The central government appointed a vice regent to govern each province, but the Oba's primary responsibility was in handling foreign affairs. His government was, as usual, supported by agricultural taxes, as well as other tributary gifts. All social categories were obliged to pay tax in kind, currency or service. Local rulers were required to travel to court once a year, to pay respects and deliver tax. The greatest of the Yoruba states was probably the Oyo Empire.

CENTRAL AND SOUTH AFRICA

Central and South Africa instituted tax systems much like the rest of Africa. These states represent examples of indigenously developed governments that were not appreciably influenced by Europeans or Arabs. Ankole, mentioned earlier, is considered a "pristine" state, meaning that no predecessor state has been acknowledged by anthropologists. And considering that almost all scholars on Africa believe that the Bantu migration went from north to south, it might be assumed that the Ankole model spread southward, throughout central and south Africa.

For instance, the Luba and Luanda, of eighteenth-century Angola, instituted the traditional internal requisition or tribute as a tax. As for excise taxes on trade, Jan Vansina contends that their markets were less sophisticated than other parts of Africa, with no set market days and no taxation. However, at some point in Angola, perhaps after Portuguese incursion, poll taxes and other land based taxes became the norm.

The Zande state was based primarily on agricultural production, and they followed the typical method of African economic organization and taxation, where each village had its own customs and kings, but groups of villages representing a particular ethnic group or community were governed by provincial officials selected by a central authority that required each province to pay their taxes to the state in the form of a mandated agricultural or craft product, the variety of which was collected and then redistributed by the central government back to the provinces. Provincial chiefs were intertwined with the ideological superstructure and derived revenue from it, as well as from court fees and raiding. The central authority also organized defense and maintained roads and dispensed justice, etc.

A unique characteristic of the Zande state was the fact that the aristocracy was punished more harshly than the commoners. This gives off the impression that the villages were largely autonomous, and that the central government's actual reach extended only as far as the exaction of taxes from provincial officials (i.e., a confederacy). Provincial chiefs could only terminate deputies "for cause"—which included but was probably not limited to sorcery, disloyalty, misappropriation of tribute, and adultery with wives of commoners. These chiefs taxed the labor of commoners for the maintenance of roads to the provincial capital, as well as the road from the provincial capital to the national capital.

Like elsewhere in Africa, the central government was under a duty of reciprocity, in theory at least. But there is a question whether the redistribution of collected tax actually occurred. While the ruler and his immediate family were forbidden from consuming the collected taxes, redistribution may have been limited to the military and clients of the king. The history of the Zande is important because they had little contact with "non-African" cultures.

Moreover, seventeenth-century Kuba was an exceptionally sophisticated state. The central authority appointed provincial chiefs who presided over county governors who collected taxes from numbers of villages. The central government included numerous officials, including tax collectors and traders representing the monarch. The monarch could also call upon a special police force. Tax and corvee labor supported this system.

Kuba's laws were made by councils rather than by edicts of the ruler. The laws were codified, and the judicial system employed judges and courts of appeal. Early Kuba had a tax system that was well-defined, "with a complex apparatus to ensure its regular flow."[79] Through taxation, the central government stimulated agricultural and craft surpluses which then required a complex governmental structure to redistribute these surpluses throughout the territory, based on some conception of merit. Provincial chiefs were required to collect taxes when the ordinary system failed. They kept a census and organized corvee labor for military or administrative purposes. Provincial chiefs also organized corvee labor for special or ritual purposes, gathering singers, drummers, smiths and carvers, as the needs arose.

Like elsewhere in Africa, taxation in kind was designed to foster a more complex economy. Each village, particularly conquered villages on the periphery or villages settled by prisoners of war were required to produce a specific product, like iron, salt, ivory, mats, hats, "even shrimps." The central authority received these products and redistributed them to provinces that could not produce these items. This system brought various ethnic groups, including the Twa (or Pygmies), under one central authority. "[T]he traders and artisans could bring in or manufacture prestige goods, either rare foreign items, or luxury goods. . . . They allowed the king to build up a treasure in commodities that would not perish to be used at his discretion as spoils for his supporters, when he wanted to reward them."[80]

In contrast with the Voltaic and Yoruba states, the Kuba state was not a "loose confederacy." The central monarch sometimes marshaled forces to attack recalcitrant provinces and keep them in the fold. He and his court also toured rebellious provinces and collected tribute from them personally. The state was responsible for addressing wrongs done to Kuba traders and for apprehending and punishing criminals. "Peace was a king's strongest weapon. It drew people. Personal safety was remarkable here, and over the decades and centuries had thus led to a sizeable emigration from the peripheral chiefdoms, which were always warring, to the peaceful core, and this despite the burden of taxation which may have been just a bit higher there."[81]

By the end of the nineteenth century, Kuba was an important trading territory. Their most lucrative product attracting outsiders was ivory and rubber. Caravans passing through bought these local products in exchange for salt, beads, cowrie shells, raffia cloth, brass, and copper—each of which might constitute a form of currency to be exchanged for something else later. Markets were well-developed, as government officials maintained law and order and collected taxes. Disputes were handled in courts located in or near the markets. "Common commercial usages existed, such as lending on credit, pawning, prescription, sale before witnesses and prescribed gestures to close a deal legally."[82]

East Africa

Taxation also constituted an important component of economic regulation in East Africa from the eleventh to the sixteenth century, for Africans there were involved in large-scale international trade with Asia. Also known as the Swahili Coast, states and city-states extended from present-day Ethiopia (Kilwa) down to the southern state of Great Zimbabwe and Monomotapa. Urban coastal cities aligned themselves with states in the interior, "levying taxes on caravans traversing their territory. Chiefdoms and states that failed to protect traders risked being excluded from the lucrative trade of the Afrasian world system."[83] Tons of African gold was traded for new plants, cowries, glass and cloths. We know that Ethiopian rulers taxed both imports and exports. In Kilwa, the majority of governmental revenues came from the tax on imported cotton.

Attiya Waris describes Islamic-styled taxation on the Swahili Coast, the city-states around and about present-day Kenya.[84] Indigenous communities prior to the seventh century appeared to pay taxes to the central authority as most other "typical" African states did. But in the seventh century, the Sultanate of Oman began to occupy and establish city states on islands off the coast of Kenya, from which the Arabs might dominate trade with the interior militarily. Similarly, the Portuguese would later use coastal islands in West and East Africa as forts in the service of slave trading. Unlike the Portuguese, Arab occupiers intermingled with indigenous communities, which led to the emergence of local rulers and a unique culture highlighted by its language, Swahili.

Like in Jimma Abba Jifar, when devout Muslim leaders were in control, there was no requirement to redistribute tax revenues. The fact that there was constant conflict over the collection and redistribution of taxes also helps reveal the syncretization process that lasted several centuries. Like in North Africa, Islamic styled taxation in East Africa included the *zakat*, *jizya*, *sadaqa*, and *khums*. According to Professor Waris:

> *Zakat* is a form of voluntary single capital tax levied on Muslims at a minimum rate of 2.5 percent on all savings and all cash assets annually accumulated. It is used specifically to finance among other things, poor relief, and emancipation of slavery, assistance to individuals serving Islam. However it does not fall within the control of the states. Despite *Sadaqa* is another form of voluntary tax for charitable purposes under no state control whatsoever. *Jizya* was a tax imposed on conquered non-Muslims in a Muslim nation under treaties signed between the two communities as a payment in lieu of compulsory military service, which could only be imposed on Muslims. *Khums* was a tax on assets redeemed by force and included spoils or war booty. It was considered

a state asset at the disposal of the leader or war booty for the commander in chief of his personal disposal.[85]

Of course, taxes on lucrative Indian Ocean trade enriched those with military power. Laws identified payment schedules for goods passing between East Africa and the Indian sub-continent. This is also around the time of the great pre-colonial civilizations of Southeast Asia. There were customs duties, as well as capitation taxes on the heads of captured slaves. Discriminatory taxes were levied on Indian merchants to discourage their presence. Gold was the preferred currency, and Waris reports that Zanzibar and some other wealthy city states produced their own coins.

Although Islam was a dominant power in West Asia and East Africa, it did not have a monopoly on Afrasian trade. Ethiopia remained largely a Christian territory, and trade from this region with Asia extended all the way to China. One thirteenth-century Ethiopian emperor was said to have under his rule ninety-nine kingdoms, including seven Muslim ones. As usual, payment of tribute signified allegiance to the emperor, and nonpayment tantamount to rebellion.

The Portuguese and their advanced weaponry arrived on the East African coast in the sixteenth century, imposing their own taxes, enslaving the people and setting off another mass migration toward the interior. The Portuguese subjugated states, forced them to pay tribute in exchange for "protection," waged war against uncooperative states, and sent punitive expeditions against states that defaulted on imposed tributes. Historians record an episode between King Ibrahim of Kilwa and the Portuguese explorer Vasco Da Gama that illustrates the ubiquitous nature of taxation in Africa, the wanton destruction of sophisticated African civilizations, and the mass migration of peoples and their culture toward the interior of the continent:

> King Ibrahim: Good friendship was to friends like brothers are, and that he would shelter the Portuguese in his city and harbor . . . to pay tribute each year in money or jewelry was not a way to a good friendship, it was tributary subjugation . . . to pay tribute was dishonor.
> Vasco Da Gama: Take it for certain that if I so decide your city would be grounded by fire in one single hour, and if your people wanted to extinguish the fire in town, they would all be burned, and when you see all this happen, you will regret all you are telling me now, and you will give much more than what I am asking you now, it will be too late for you. If you are still in doubt, it is up to you to see it.
> King Ibrahim: Sir, if I had known that you wanted to enslave me, I would not have come, and I would have fled in to the forest, for it is better for me to be a fox but free, than a dog locked up in a golden chain.[86]

King Ibrahim agreed to pay tribute, but that did not prevent the Portuguese from returning to destroy a once proud empire. A Portuguese eyewitness records the brutality as such:

> The Portuguese entered the city by force of arms, killed many Moors, and carried off great riches which their owners had not thought to save, in the belief they could defend the town. They could not even save their own women, very rich and beautiful with seven and eight bracelets on each arm and just as many thick and valuable on their legs. This was an occasion for severe cruelty, for the men, blinded by avarice rather than mercy, in order not to lose time, cut off the arms, the legs, and the ears which bore the jewelry without pity.[87]

The Portuguese forced many into their service, removed scores more as slaves destined for Europe, and instituted one-sided trading policies with the remaining free citizens. Many of the Ethiopians retreated to the hinterlands were they set up defensive fortresses and resisted Portuguese incursions. Rebels were impaled, hacked to death, quartered, and put to death by other cruel and inhuman means. Yet, the East Africans still managed to keep the Portuguese from the interior, and at least once in 1592 forced the Portuguese to pay tribute in exchange for protection.

According to Waris, the Portuguese signed treaties with Mombasa, Zanzibar and Kilwa. "All of them repeatedly failed to actually pay the tribute, despite repeated demands by the Portuguese . . . resulting in the continual failure to bring any money into the coffers of the Queen of Portugal."[88]

CONCLUSION

In the first chapter of this book we asked a philosophical question, does it matter what slaves thought "direct tax" meant in the U.S. Constitution? The point there was not really to determine the precise meaning any one or group of African slaves would attach to the words "direct tax," but to make the point that the legal interpretation of texts is often incomplete to the extent it does not include respect for black people as an interpretive community. In this chapter, the point is to show that sixteenth-, seventeenth-, and eighteenth-century Africans, or at least the elite amongst them, would indeed have sophisticated understandings of law, government, administration and taxes. By the eighteenth century AD, a West African society like Rahman's Futa Jalloh was equipped to institute inheritance, import, export, excise or poll taxes. Like everywhere else, payment of taxes signified allegiance, nonpayment of taxes signified rebellion, and tax expenditures were used by the government to secure loyalty. And so we conclude here with two very brief biographies of eighteenth-century black men from West Africa who were enslaved and transported to the United States, and who likely would have as sophisticated an understanding of taxes as anyone else. How the progeny of these men are treated in the United States is the subject of the next several chapters.

Olaudah Equiano

Olaudah Equiano (1745–1797) was an African who was captured, sold into slavery, purchased his freedom, and wrote an autobiography detailing his life prior to captivity, the dreadful Middle Passage, and the horrors of plantation life in Virginia. His journey demonstrates the availability of African intellectuals and aristocrats who could at the time of the United States' founding have provided an account of justice or law which would have been decidedly African in nature. Though Equiano himself may have been enslaved before receiving a tremendous amount of learning regarding his home nation's legal systems, he describes his father as a judge in his original village and would probably be familiar with at least some of the principles under which African legal disputes were decided.

Equiano, otherwise known as Gustavus Vassa, a name given to him by his first white slaveowner, was captured as a child by fellow Africans and sold in the Americas to a British Naval officer who lived in Virginia. While under the charge of his British master, Equiano learned to read and write and became a worthy seaman. When he was later sold in the Caribbean, plantation owners viewed him as too valuable for grueling plantation work, but also feared him because he could navigate a ship and might have lead an escape or insurrection. Equiano was sold to another master, this time a Philadelphia Quaker named Robert King who allowed Equiano to trade goods on his own account in addition to the wares of his master and purchase his freedom. Instead of accepting King's offer to partner with him in business, Equiano settled in England where he became prominent in the abolitionist movement.

In 1789, only two years after the Continental Congress, Equiano published his autobiography, becoming a cause célèbre. As an abolitionist writer Equiano described how slavers on the Zong tossed 133 slaves overboard for purposes of an insurance claim. His autobiography helped toward ending the slave trade in Great Britain in 1807. Equiano used the wealth derived from his autobiography to gain independence from his abolitionist benefactors. He spent parts of the rest of his life assisting former English slaves resettle in Sierre Leone. However, the sincerity of his commitment to opposing slavery can be questioned because a free Equiano also owned slaves, not unlike a few other wealthy free blacks of the time. In fact, Vincent Carretta questions Equiano's sincerity in all matters relating to his autobiography, believing that Equiano was born in South Carolina instead of Africa.[89]

Prince Abdur Rahman

Abdulrahman Ibrahim Ibn Sori is bettern known as Prince Abdur Rahman, the African prince who was enslaved in 1791, sold to a plantation owner in Natchez, Mississippi, freed at the behest of President John Quincy Adams and Secretary of State Henry Clay, and returned in 1829 with his wife but without his children to Liberia, West Africa. Andrew Jackson used Adams' well-treatment of Rahman against Adams in the presidential election. Rahman died within four months of his homecoming, without having reached the place of his birth, Futan Jalloh.

What's most interesting about Prince Rahman, relative to this piece anyway, is that he was in fact a member of an African royal family, and as such had studied at the universities in Jenne and Timbuktu. He was not taught to read and write by slave masters, as he was already schooled in liberal arts and could read and write in Arabic. An English/American doctor, John Cox, who had been the first European to visit Rahman's West African kingdom, and who Rahman had personally tended to while the former was ill, discovered Rahman's presence on the Mississippi plantation. Initially, his master in Natchez would not grant Rahman his freedom for almost any price, as indispensible as Rahman was to Foster's farming operation. It wasn't until 1826 when Rahman sent a letter received by the U.S. government that he was recognized as an African prince and plans for his repatriation developed. Clearly, Rahman can be counted as one of many Africans who, despite our modern conception of slaves as ignorant and lesser, were in fact knowledgeable of governmental systems and law.

Futan Jalloh was a Muslim kingdom formerly within the Malian Empire but at the time of Prince Rahman near the Songhay Empire, a federation of states most of which paid tribute in exchange for local autonomy. The Fulbe of Futan Jalloh were a minority and often in conflict with non-Muslims in the area, sometimes in control over the more populous Jalunke and at other times controlled by them. Futan Jalloh participated in the slave trade, selling prisoners of war and exiled criminals in exchange for European goods, especially guns. European traders would not accept any form of payment except slaves, including gold. Obviously, a kingdom that refused to trade with the Europeans left itself vulnerable to other kingdoms who would acquire guns, subdue them, sell them into slavery, and take over their lands. Selling prisoners of war and criminals to Europeans became an expeditious though shortsighted way for West African tribes to deal with both national rivals and crime. According to Rahman, his people appeased their own sensibilities regarding slavery by restricting their battles to non-Muslims (i.e., the Jalunkes). "We never go to war with people who do God Almighty service."[90] As this was a typical philosophy toward slavery, many kings and princes and other royalty were sold into American slavery.

In 1730, the Fulbe established Futan Jalloh as a theocracy but with a military head of state, the Almaami or "he who leads the community in prayer."[91] In 1748, Rahman's father, Sori, was elected (or appointed) Almaami. Sori's armies expanded the northern and eastern frontiers of Futan Jalloh. The Fulbe ruled subject to a constitution, and Sori sought to extend its protections to all citizens within the state. However, Sori's chosen ministers failed to support his endeavors, particularly by underreporting and embezzling significant tax revenue. In 1759, Sori exiled himself before a likely coup d'etat. However, his successor proved weak, eventually allowing an alliance of non-Muslim peoples, in 1763, led by the Wasulu, to raze the capitol of Timbo, destroying "the old mosque, where the constitution of the state and other historic papers were burned." A senate of the kingdom's elders reappointed Sori as head of state. After several initial defeats, his military campaigns again proved successful, restoring the country's prosperity, and those he conquered and captured were sold into slavery.

Terry Alford describes Prince Rahman's experiences in his homeland of Futan Jalloh as a somewhat unexceptional child of privilege, who as a member of the ruling clan, received a proper Muslim education before becoming a colonel in his father's army and eventually being captured in battle and sold into slavery. Rahman's hometown of Timbo had a population of about eight thousand lived in neatly arranged houses with hedges made tall so that pedestrians could not see within. The men wore white gowns and either turbans or skullcaps to cover their long braided hair. Consistent with Songhay culture, the Fulbe prized education and learning. Their schools taught reading, writing, arithmetic, and languages, and Islamic law as an advanced, elective subject. "Individual libraries on religion and jurisprudence were common, and books and writing paper were prized gifts."[92]

As was traditional, Rahman began his schooling at age seven, reading and writing the Qu'ran, hardly any different than would a privileged Moroccan or Egyptian child. At age twelve, Sori sent Rahman to further his education in two of the Songhay Empire's famous cities of learning, Djenne and Timbuktu. According to Thomas H. Gallaudet, Rahman learned geography, astronomy, calculations, and the laws of the country."[93] He returned to Timbo in 1778 to aid his father's final campaign against the Fulbe's opponents. Rahman helped Sori successfully lead a coalition of Fulbe fighters, allies and Muslim mercenaries, twice the size of George Washington's army. The Kingdom's elders again appointed Sori as Almaami, and Rahman became one of his colonels. Shortly thereafter, however, a military expedition led by Rahman to restore a vital trading route resulted in his capture. Despite offers of ransom, he was delivered to the coast and sold.

NOTES

1. P. G. Monateri, *Black Gaius: A Quest for the Multicultural Origins of the 'Western Legal Tradition,'* Hastings Law Journal (2000).
2. Naomi Zack, Philosophy of Race (2002).
3. Michal Tymowski, The Origins and Structures of Political Institutions in Pre-Colonial Black Africa (2009); Claessen & Skalnik, The Early State (1978); Claessen & Skalnik, The Study of the State (1981).
4. Osafo-Kwaako, Philip, and James A. Robinson, *Political Centralization in Pre-Colonial Africa.* Journal of Comparative Economics (2013).
5. Tommie Shelby, We Who are Dark (2007).
6. Hon. Richard Posner, Overcoming Law (2005).
7. The Afrocentric project, to the extent it is useful, is made that much more difficult by Posner and others who attempt to exclude its proponents from the resources at the best universities. Take into account W.E.B. Dubois' affection for one of the self-taught historians Posner criticizes: "I have learned much from James A. Rogers. Rogers is an untrained American Negro writer who had done his work under great difficulty without funds and at much personal sacrifice. But no man living has revealed so many important facts about the Negro race as has Rogers. His mistakes are many and his background narrow, but he is a true historical student." W.E.B. DuBois, The World and Africa (1979). Considering how many more great things J.A. Rogers might have done with the information available to academics today, this chapter is meant to honor him and David Walker and Martin Delaney and George Wells Parker and John Henrik Clarke and Frank Snowden and Chancellor Williams and Asa Hilliard and Yosef Ben-Jochanan.
8. Martin Bernal, Black Athena (1987).
9. Hon. Richard Posner, Overcoming Law (2005).
10. For example, some have claimed that there is a pattern of missing noses on sculptures and busts of historical figures believed to be African. Some suggest that the missing noses are proof that whites intentionally destroy evidence of the African character of antiquity. But according to Runoko Rashidi, there is no evidence that Napoleon blew off the nose of the Sphinx, nor is there any solid evidence of a conspiracy to remove or obliterate the noses on busts of Egyptian pharaohs. See Afrocentric mythbusters: Manu Ampin & Runoko Rashidi.
11. Toyin Folala, Africa, Volume 1 (2001).
12. Michal Tymowski, The Origins and Structures of Political Institutions in Pre-Colonial Black Africa (2009).
13. Ibid.
14. Ibid.
15. Ibid.
16. Letzion & Hopkins, Corpus of Early Arabic Sources for West African History (2000).
17. Michal Tymowski, The Origins and Structures of Political Institutions in Pre-Colonial Black Africa (2009).
18. Ibid.
19. Ibid.
20. Cheikh Ante Diop, The Cultural Unity of Black Africa (1990).
21. Michal Tymowski, The Origins and Structures of Political Institutions in Pre-Colonial Black Africa (2009).
22. Ibid.
23. Herbert Lewis, The Early State (1978).
24. Ibid.
25. Ibid. at 329.
26. Ibid. at 331.
27. Michal Tymowski, The Origins and Structures of Political Institutions in Pre-Colonial Black Africa (2009).

28. Anatolii M. Khazanov, The Early State (1978).
29. Claessan & Skaalnik, The Early State 641(1978).
30. See also Robin Einhorn, American Taxation, American Slavery (2006) (identifying ad valorem taxation as evidence of modernity).
31. Michal Tymowski, The Origins and Structures of Political Institutions in Pre-Colonial Black Africa (2009).
32. Ibid.
33. Ibid.
34. Ibid.
35. Ibid.
36. Ibid.
37. Ibid.
38. Ibid.
39. Ibid. ("Besides agricultural produce and the products of animal husbandry, the tax was also paid in uncommon items—in gold, . . . , cola nuts, salt or kauri shells—depending on the region of Africa and the availability of these precious goods.")
40. Ibid.
41. Ibid.
42. Robert Bauval, Thomas Brophy, Black Genesis: The Prehistoric Origins of Ancient Egypt (2011).
43. John A. Wilson, Authority and Law in Ancient Egypt (1954).
44. Aristide Theodorides, The Legacy of Egypt (1971).
45. But see Nell Irvin Painter, The History of White People (2009) (Claiming that race as we know it did not exist in Antiquity).
46. John A. Wilson, Authority and Law in Ancient Egypt (1954).
47. Richard Wilkinson, Tausret: Forgotten Queen and pharaoh of Egypt (2012); Shirley Jordan, Hatshepsut: First Female pharaoh (2007).
48. Aristide Theodorides, The Legacy of Egypt (1971).
49. John A. Wilson, Authority and Law in Ancient Egypt (1954).
50. Ibid.
51. Ibid.
52. Russ VerSteeg, Law in Ancient Egypt (2002).
53. Jac. J. Janssen, The Early State (1978).
54. Robin L. Einhorn, American Taxation, American Slavery (2006).
55. Anna Mancini, Maat Revealed, Philosophy of Justice in Ancient Egypt (2004).
56. A. Abu Bakr, *Pharaonic Egypt*, in UNESCO's General History of Africa II: Ancient Civilizations of Africa 78 (1990).
57. Stephanie Willbanks, Federal Taxation of Wealth Transfers (2004).
58. P.G. Monateri, *Black Gaius: A Quest for the Multicultural Origins of the 'Western Legal Tradition,'*Hastings Law Journal (2000).
59. Ibid.
60. W.E.B. Dubois, Black Folk Then and Now (2007).
61. Iurii Kobischanov, *Axum*, in The Early State (1978).
62. Ibid.
63. *The Importance of Nubia: a Link between Central Africa and the Mediterranean*, Ancient Civilizations of Africa, UNESCO General History of Africa 141 (1990).
64. Runoko Rashidi, *Iraq: The African Presence in Early Iraq*, in Encyclopedia of the African Diaspora (Ed. Carole Boyce Davies) (2008).
65. Cheikh Ante Diop, PreColonial Black Africa (1988).
66. Ibid.
67. D.T. Niani, *West Africa from the 12th to the 16th Century*, UNESCO General History of Africa (1990).
68. Ibid.
69. Letzion & Hopkins, Corpus of Early Arabic Sources for West African History (2000).
70. Cheikh Anta Diop, PreColonial Black Africa (1988).

71. Cheikh Anta Diop, African Origins of Civilization: Myth or Reality (1989).
72. Howard Zinn, A Peoples History of the United States (2005).
73. Molefi Asante, Classical Africa (1994).
74. Ibn Battuta, Letzion & Hopkins, Corpus of Early Arabic Sources for West African History (2000).
75. Molefi Asante, Classical Africa (1994).
76. Ibid.
77. Skaalnik & Claasen The Early State, 626.
78. Peter Skalnik, *Early States in the Voltaic Basin*, The Early State (1978).
79. Claessen & Skalnik, The Early State (1978); Claessen & Skalnik, The Study of the State (1981).
80. Jan Vansina, *The Kuba State*, The Early State (1978).
81. Ibid.
82. Ibid.
83. Ogundiran & Folala, Archaeology of Atlantic Africa and African Diaspora (2007).
84. Tax Justice and the Political Economy of Global Capitalism, 1945 to the Present (Eds. Jeremy Leaman, Attiya Waris).
85. Ibid.
86. Ogundiran & Folala, Archaeology of Atlantic Africa and African Diaspora (2007).
87. Ibid.
88. Tax Justice and the Political Economy of Global Capitalism, 1945 to the Present (Eds. Jeremy Leaman, Attiya Waris).
89. Vincent Carretta, Equiano, The African (2007).
90. Terry Alford, Prince Among Slaves (2007).
91. Ibid.
92. Ibid.
93. Ibid.

THREE

Taxes and the Rise of White Supremacy (1600–1900)

This chapter demonstrates how federal, state, and local taxes were used to establish and maintain social, political, and economic white supremacy in the United States by revealing many of the tax laws in this nation's history that redistributed wealth from blacks to whites, that foreclosed or discouraged the presence of blacks in lucrative markets during times of great national economic expansion, and that were otherwise designed to subordinate black people and establish a racial caste system in the United States.

Toward this showing, this chapter makes several claims, including: First, in the eighteenth and nineteenth centuries, states and localities in the South levied higher poll taxes on free blacks than on whites, levied discriminatory occupational taxes on free black laborers, required whites to hire other whites, and sometimes levied special taxes on whites who did business with blacks. Thus, the first examples of governments in the United States taking affirmative action toward the economic advancement of one race were tax laws designed specifically to encourage the presence of whites in lucrative markets, and exclude or discourage blacks from those opportunities.

Second, slavery was by itself a 100 percent tax on black labor that redistributed wealth from black laborers to white slaveowners and mercantilists in the south, north and England. Prior to the American Revolution, tax laws were often race neutral with respect to slavery. But antebellum tax laws clearly identify the institution as "negro" slavery. State, federal and local taxes then took a portion of the wealth which ought to have vested in those black laborers from slaveowners and mercantilists and re-redistributed it to anti-poverty programs designed exclusively for poor whites. Moreover, antebellum slaveowners complained bitterly that the Federal Tariff re-redistributed hundreds of millions of dollars of their ill-gotten gains to manufacturing interests and mercantilists in the North.[1]

Third, despite the fact that slavery was supposedly abolished by the Thirteenth Amendment, the 100 percent tax on black labor and its redistribution of black wealth continued in the form of Jim Crow apartheid and its sharecropper-convict peonage system, which the federal government chose not to deal with until at least World War II.[2]

Fourth, the only constitutional amendment achieved by the civil rights movement toward the struggle for racial equality is the Twenty-sixth Amendment abolishing poll taxes in all federal elections. The Twenty-sixth Amendment was followed shortly after by *Harper v. Virginia* (1966), in which the Supreme Court abolished poll taxes in state and local elections as well. The issue of poll taxes has resurfaced in the form of Twenty-first-century voter identification laws.

Fifth, a tax case, *Bob Jones University v. United States* (1983), is perhaps the most under-appreciated case in all of Supreme Court jurisprudence, at least from the perspective of critical race theory, because it stands for the proposition that federal statutes may not be interpreted toward the maintenance or exacerbation of racial subordination. Moreover, the combination of *Bob Jones v. U.S.* (1983) and another tax case *Allen v. Wright* (1984) exemplifies the Supreme Court's current doublespeak with respect to dismantling social, political and economic white supremacy. After the court in Bob Jones announced that anti-discrimination was a compelling national interest and established national policy, it turned around one year later and announced in *Allen v. Wright* that adversely affected blacks will typically not have standing in court to force the government to actually honor that commitment.

Making matters worse, the year after that, the court held in *Heckler v. Chaney* (1985) that even if a small group of exceptionally affected black people have standing to challenge government inaction, the court has no constitutional authority to force the executive branch of government to prosecute cases of discrimination or racial subordination. The court held similarly a century earlier, in the Reconstruction era civil rights cases, that slavery and racial subordination were illegal, but that the court had little to no authority to force states and localities to honor this national commitment toward a meritocratic ethos. The more things change, the more they stay the same.

Last, I contend that *Bob Jones v. United States* was the final straw before a long and sustained conservative attack on so-called judicial activism, beginning first with *Chevron v. NRDC* (1984) where the Supreme Court delegated its law interpreting function to the executive branch, precisely because the executive branch was more easily swayed by political whims rather than deep-seeded principles of fairness or justice. The lone dissenter in Bob Jones, William Rhenquist, was soon thereafter appointed chief judge of the Supreme Court. After that, the Reagan/Bush administrations packed the court with neo-formalists who would dismantle affirmative action and otherwise discourage the government from addressing racial subordination.

TAXING TOWARDS WHITE SUPREMACY

The absence of discriminatory taxation in the seventeenth century suggests that North America had not yet committed to a strict racial order. European settlers dealt with Native American nations on competitive and sometimes submissive terms. For examples, Puritans cooperated with the Massachusetts Indians, the Dutch in New York were forced to respect the Iroquois, and Virginia settlers warred against the Powhatan Confederacy. In terms of Africans, Eurocentric thinkers and philosophers had not yet established the myth of black inferiority.[3]

By the turn of that century, however, Native Americans had been entirely pushed off of North America's East Coast. European settlers tried first to enslave Native Americans, but with little success: "In the first decades of colonization in the 1600s, 'slave' and 'Negro' were not synonymous in the American colonies. Slaves were as likely to be Indians as Africans."[4] Native Americans knew the terrain better than the colonizers and were liable to escape. European settlers responded by selling Native Americans to slave operations in the Caribbean and South America where they would be unfamiliar with their surroundings. Thus, the first 100 percent tax on labor in the Americas was levied not on blacks, but Native Americans.

Moreover, slave labor was imported from Europe before it was imported from Africa. Formally, these individuals were designated indentured servants. But that term suggests willfulness to contract when in reality scores of Europeans were kidnapped and sold into American slavery as chattel: "Many indentured white servants were coerced into extending their labor contracts until death—effectively making them light-skinned slaves."[5]

Originally, African settlers were also likely to be indentured servants. The terms of their indentured servitude were initially respected, as they were typically freed from service after the contract term. Indentured servants were legally able to buy land once their terms ended. But as their terms were ending those who survived found the availability of land diminishing.

Bacon's Rebellion of 1676 demonstrates the absence of a strict racial order at that time. Indentured servants, poor whites and African slaves rose against Virginia's white elites who would not financially support a war against Native Americans to take their land for redistribution. Those seventeenth-century blacks who became free after completing their terms of service were enfranchised with the right to vote in places like early colonial Virginia. In addition, "[s]ome early owners of black slaves were themselves black."[6]

Despite this "egalitarian" beginning, racial hierarchy soon followed, as Virginians stripped free blacks of the right to vote before the American Revolution. After the Revolution, a racial order or white supremacy was established nationally. By the end of the nineteenth century, racial hegemony was global.

The institutionalization of racial hierarchy in the United States was slow and steady, and taxation was a prominent feature. By the end of the seventeenth century, Massachusetts for instance began to officially recognizing racial differences in public laws, including the tax codes.

In 1648, Massachusetts had no poll tax, only property and income taxes. It did not yet discriminate between its citizens by race. Nor did its property tax discriminate between indentured servants and slaves, using the phrase "servants and children as take not wages."[7] By 1692, though, Massachusetts expressly taxed "all negros, molattos and Indian servants, as well male or female."

Right before the American Revolution, in 1770, Massachusetts began sharing in the profits of slavery by taxing polls and estates, which included, among other things, slaves. By 1777, Massachusetts began to receive a greater share of the profits of slavery by taxing slaveowners at ad valorem rates, rather than flat rates by the poll. And, in 1778, Massachusetts ultimately settled on a new poll tax on slaves with an exemption for female slaves.

Yet, the tax laws of Massachusetts show that they were not absolutely and entirely committed to a racial order. The 1777 Massachusetts' law added a poll tax on free men with no distinction between free black and white men.

One might expect more racial tolerance out of Pennsylvania, home of the Quakers. Early colonial Pennsylvania did not share in the profits of slaveholding initially, since it had no property tax to speak of. Seventeenth-century Pennsylvanians instituted a poll tax only on unmarried men, plus import taxes and flat rate land taxes. And, like Massachusetts, Pennsylvania did not discriminate between unmarried white and black men. Moreover, representatives from Pennsylvania at the federal Constitutional Convention opposed slavery most openly and vehemently.

By 1764, however, even Pennsylvania taxed estates, which included the value of slaves held at the time of death.

Unsurprisingly, the southern colonies took early to distinguishing between its citizens on the basis of race. Virginians and South Carolinians, specifically, used their state and county tax laws indiscreetly toward establishing white social and economic supremacy: "Dispelling that confusion and ensuring the dominant position of whites in general—and Englishmen in particular—colonial legislatures, especially in Virginia, South

Carolina, and, later, Georgia, began in the 1650s to systematically define residents by color and lineage."

Virginia's first poll tax in 1624 did not distinguish between free adult males. But by 1680 their tax laws distinguished between "christian servants" and "African slaves." They were both taxed at the same rates. Thus, the distinction seems to have been designed strictly toward establishing a new social order.

Eventually, Virginians, at least the poor ones, came to prefer taxing slave holding and liquor (so-called sin taxes) over higher poll taxes on free whites: "The slave tax 'will be a great ease to the poorer sort of people, by lessening the levy by the poll.' 'It hath been found by experience' that taxes on tobacco, slaves and other items 'are easy to the people, and not so burdensome as a poll tax.'" For eight years, 1724–1732, taxes on slavery in Virginia were removed by England. After 1732, however, England reinstated taxes on slavery and demanded that Virginia tax slave traders "ad valorem"—taxes based on the appraised value of the subject property.

After a number of slave insurrections, landless Virginians without a direct interest in slavery wanted to increase the tax on slaves in order to discourage the importation of more Africans and, thus, the likelihood more revolts. To increase the white population and protect against insurrections and revolts, Virginia abolished its poll tax for white men in 1787. When Ira Katznelson claimed that "affirmative action" used to be white, he was right, but he did not go back far enough in time.[8]

Of all the colonies, South Carolina committed earliest and most stridently toward institutionalized white supremacy. Not only was slavery expressly sanctioned and supported by the government, it was expressly and publicly identified as negro slavery. In 1669, the South Carolina Constitution, written by John Locke, stated, "Every freeman shall have absolute power and authority over his negro slaves." A 100 percent tax on black labor was the official law of the land in South Carolina. Of course, the slaveowner collected and got to keep the bulk of the tax, otherwise a 100 percent tax on slavery would have ended the institution (i.e., confiscatory taxes). How much the slaveowner was allowed to keep would be the subject of political debates between poor whites and slaveowners in southern legislatures for the next two hundred years. John Locke and the South Carolina Constitution exhibited the paradox of American slavery, white men yearning to be free to own black people.

At first, white South Carolinians had a tenuous hold on their territory. In 1715, a coalition of Yamesees, Creeks and Cherokees almost destroyed the colony. But after the Cherokee broke the Native American coalition, white settlers regained control.

The next year, in 1716, South Carolina instituted a tax on property, including land and slaves. This first South Carolina tax distinguished between blacks and Native Americans, and exempted whites entirely. In fact, slave owners were taxed about 50 percent less for owning Native American slaves. For classification purposes, "mustees, mulattoes, & all such slaves as are not entirely Indian shall be accounted as negroe." Taxes on importing slaves were first set at 40 English Pounds but shortly thereafter reduced to 10L.

The colony of South Carolina levied no poll tax on white men, since their presence was needed and encouraged to provide security over what quickly became a majority black population. Plantation owners were often absent because of the extreme heat of South Carolina's low country, residing in England or in the North, and leaving slaves to toil under the watch of overseers. Still, slaves vastly outnumbered the overseers, who were sometimes black themselves. So, to discourage the further importation of more slaves, which might lead to insurrection and a reduction of the value of domestic slaves, South Carolina, in 1721, levied taxes on slave trading and in 1740 required that the tax be paid by the buyer (resident). Still, "as a white immigrant observed in 1737, it 'looks more like a negro country than like country settled by white people.'"

In 1739, South Carolina endured Stono's Rebellion, one of the first organized slave revolts in colonial history, in which "a group of about sixty blacks killed twenty whites, skirmished with militias, and marched toward the Florida border until the militias caught up and killed most of them."[9] In response, the legislature raised the tax on slave importations to confiscatory levels and instituted plans to increase the number of white settlers. In addition to the absence of poll taxes on white men, South Carolina required slaveowners to buy/hire one white servant for every six black slaves purchased. Furthermore, "they coped with the threat of slave revolts by deploying patrols and striving for political unity against their 'Domestic Enemy.'"[10]

In 1740, South Carolina passed the Negro Act, or "the Slave Code," which sought to clamp down on the movements and already limited freedom of slaves, as well as that of free blacks. All blacks were presumed to be slaves, and all slaves were prohibited from activities such as vending, retailing, traveling or owning guns outside the presence of a white adult, buying alcohol, etc. To make the tax on black labor as close to 100 percent as possible, the South Carolina legislature also made it illegal under certain circumstances to pay slaves for their labor or for slaves to hire themselves out (as had already become a growing practice) or even masters to provide slaves with fine clothing.

Furthermore, the Negro Act required plantation owners to hire at least one white person for every ten slaves. These are perhaps the first instance of affirmative action on American shores.

The South Carolina legislature temporarily raised the tax on imported slaves to 100L per head in 1740, and then again in 1760. Despite these efforts to increase the white population, by 1760 "slaves were over 90 percent of the population in three low country parishes, over 80 percent in another eight, and over 70 percent in another two. In 1774, slaves were 78 percent of the low country population overall."[11] In 1769, British merchants filed several petitions complaining that the tax on imported slaves was meant to preserve the value of slaves already in the colony.

Slaves in eighteenth-century South Carolina not only worked agriculture, they were deployed by their masters in various occupations and industries, including Charleston's urban economy as artisans, merchants and retailers. But black slave labor crowded out free white labor, and thus, the Charleston legislature imposed discriminatory taxes to help white laborers compete with white slaveowners who hired out their slaves as merchants and artisans in the cities. In 1789, the city of Charleston took further actions. According to George Ruble Woolfolk,

> [they] required white artisans to take on white apprentice for every two slaves taught or bought to learn a trade. . . . Charlestown owners of slaves for hire were permitted to buy badges for only the first six at the regular rate. . . . The taxes therefore reflect not only the concern of the whites for the effect of town or hired labor upon the slaves' spirits, but also skilled white labor's fear of the superior competitive advantage of slave labor.[12]

Whites in South Carolina discouraged or eliminated competition from free blacks as well as from slave labor. At times, they actively harassed free blacks and sought to discourage nonwhites from settling in South Carolina by instituting a poll tax on "all free negroes, mulattoes and mustees, from ten to sixty years of age, who pay no other part of the taxes imposed by this Act."[13] The tax was levied on both black men and black women, whereas white women were never taxed by the poll in any colony. Free blacks who could not pay their poll tax were sold into slavery.

Eighteenth-century free blacks in South Carolina continuously, yet unsuccessfully petitioned the state legislature to repeal the poll tax upon them, citing their loyalty to the state, the fact that they paid taxes, and that widows with children were being extorted by tax collectors. While they did not presume to be on equal footing with whites, black petitioners described themselves as "citizens"—which is not unimportant with regard to the question of whether blacks were in facts citizens of the United States at the time of its founding rather than incorporated into the United States by the Thirteenth, Fourteenth, and Fifteenth Amendments.

At that time, North Carolina's economy was nowhere close to the size of Virginia or South Carolina. They simply levied poll taxes on slaves of both sexes. North Carolina did not discriminate between free whites and free people of color for either revenue or regulatory purposes. But, like all of the other colonies, its legislature had no moral compunction against sharing in the profits from slavery through taxation of slaveowners and the rest of the slave industry.

SLAVERY AS A 100 PERCENT TAX ON BLACK LABOR

Colonial laws limiting slavery to blacks were the first example in the United States of discriminatory taxation and systematized redistribution of black wealth to Whites. Through slavery, wealth which should have vested in black laborers was redistributed directly from the slave to the slaveowner, then a portion was re-redistributed from the slaveowner to the government, and then the government re-re-redistributed a portion to poor whites in the form of anti-poverty projects that typically excluded blacks from receiving benefits.

Government sanctioned slavery is itself a tax, otherwise called a "corvee." Colonial laws limiting slavery to blacks were the first example in the United States of discriminatory taxation and systematized redistribution of black wealth to whites. The concept of slavery as tax is not novel. In "Taxation in the Bible," Professor Geoffrey Parsons Miller describes Egypt's exaction of forced labor from the Israelites as a corvee or tax.[14] Anthropologists also accept that taxation includes corvee labor, the requirement to render unpaid service.[15]

Slavery as a tax is also consistent with the aforementioned John Locke's ideal that one has a natural right to the fruits of one's labor. Slaves themselves, as written in their narratives, believed they had a natural right to what they produced which was then taken from them by the slaveowner. Henry Bibb, expressed his feelings about subverting the 100 percent labor tax thusly:

> I did not regard it as stealing then, I do not regard it as stealing now. I hold that the slave has a moral right to eat, drink, and wear all that he needs, and that it would be a sin on his part to suffer and starve in a country where there is plenty to eat and wear within his reach. I consider that I had a just right to what I took, because it was the labor of my own hands.[16]

Calling slavery a tax is not without conceptual difficulties, of course. One could argue that taxation is necessarily a governmental activity, and that American slavery was condoned or allowed by government, but not compelled by it. However, to the extent the mechanisms of government were captured and conscripted toward the maintenance of slavery, American slavery was a corvee, or a tax. Consider that the role of the "sheriff" in Europe up to that point had typically been that of tax collector. The sheriff collected taxes from the citizenry, then remitted a portion to the Crown. Although the 100 percent tax on black labor was not collected by a government official, the slaveowner can be described as a "sheriff" or tax collector who then remitted a percentage of the collection to the government for redistribution.

Now if the government instead of the slaveowner got to keep a greater percentage of the profits inuring from slavery, then a 100 percent tax on black labor would have been emancipatory rather than oppressive. Still, considering that a hallmark of American tax jurisprudence is the "substance over form" doctrine, where the refinements of formal characterizations yield to the actual substance of a transaction, the seventeenth, eighteenth, and nineteenth-century African slave would not find a meaningful distinction between the slave master, who collected the tax, and the government, who protected the slave master—especially since the government shared in their oppression through capitation and excise taxes. Substance over form also supports Douglas Blackmon's contention that Jim Crow peonage was tantamount to slavery, a continuation of the 100 percent tax on black labor up until World War II.[17]

Still, once we depart from statutes and other formal tax pronouncement, the definition of tax could devolve to mean anything "taxing" or burdensome, as in Jody Armour's *The Hidden Costs of Being black in America*. Moreover, calling slavery a tax marginalizes the various and myriad forms of physical and psychological torture that was common to maintaining racial, chattel slavery—as well as convict leasing and agricultural peonage.

Another conceptual difficulty with calling slavery itself a tax is that it might at first blush support those who contend that tax itself is slavery. If slavery is considered a tax, then is tax to be considered slavery?[18] At least some people think so. After contemplation, however, conceiving of slavery as a tax should produce the opposite effect: A -10, -20, even -50 percent tax on wages or capital hardly equates to the nearly 100 percent tax on black labor that slavery and peonage represented.

There were some black and Indian slave owners.[19] Thus, it cannot be said that slavery as a tax only distributed wealth from blacks to whites. In some cases, black owners were harsher on their slaves than white owners. In other cases, black ownership of slaves was a ruse to protect landless blacks who would be "really" re-enslaved and harshly treated by whites if they were not owned by someone (anyone). Native American slaveowners also believed they worked *with* their slaves, rather than lording above them. However, black ownership of slaves outside of Louisiana never became significant, especially since almost every other state enacted laws prohibiting free blacks from even owning slaves. To allow free blacks to own other blacks would have placed them on equal status with whites.

Some whites were enslaved, formally and informally. But neither black slave ownership nor instances of white slavery detract much from the enormous sums slavery as a tax redistributed from blacks to whites.

Slaves were sometimes allowed to keep a bit of their income for themselves. To incentivize greater productivity, some slaveowners allowed their more valuable slaves to sell goods on their own or hire themselves out for pay. A slave who was cognizant of his or her market worth could possibly negotiate their freedom from their master after a term of years.

But, there was nothing a slave could do to win freedom from some owners. For example, years after helping Lewis and Clark traverse the hostile Northwest, Clark beat his slave, York, for being "uppity" and enquiring about his freedom from Clark.[20] Notwithstanding, whatever amounts industrious slaves were able to keep, slavery was quite nearly a 100 percent tax on black labor.

Slavery as a tax supported white socio-economic-political supremacy in at least three ways: 1) it helped establish a racial order once it was restricted to blacks or people of color; 2) it redistributed wealth from the slave to the slaveowner, and then taxes on the slaveowner redistributed that portion of slave wealth to anti-poverty and public works programs designed to inure strictly to whites; and 3) it foreclosed lucrative markets to blacks and reserved those opportunities for whites, all the while simultaneously forcing blacks to remain in an oppressive market that did not serve them.

At first, American slavery was almost exclusively based on agricultural production, and the entire product of a slave's work was simply taken by the master. Quickly, slavery "matured" as a mode of production. Slaves became capital to deploy not only in agriculture, but also in myriad occupations from steelworkers to riverboat guides. John Hope Franklin estimated that by the 1850s, more than half of all slaves worked in non-agricultural professions. Regardless the endeavor, slaves were expected to remit all of the income derived from their service to their owners. Human peddlers taxed their black laborers both through direct ownership and supervision, as well as through distant investment and trust relationships. Consequently, income from black slave labor in the south was 100 percent taxed by their white owners regardless whether those owners actually lived in the South, North or even England.

REVOLUTION, CONSTITUTION, AND BURGEONING WHITE SUPREMACY

At least one author believes that the primary reason the South participated in the American Revolution was because a year before it started a court in Great Britain ruled in the Somerset case that a slave becomes free once he touches England's soil.[21] The extension of this doctrine to all English colonies may have pushed the southern colonies to war. It is not clear however that southern slaveowners took such a threat seriously. It was one thing to discourage the importation of Africans to England, and quite another to prevent the exploitation of slave labor in colonies that produced raw goods for manufacture in England. In fact, England did not abolish the 100 percent tax on black labor in Jamaica until 1834.

Regardless their primary motives, the freedom and liberty sought by American colonists was clearly inconsistent with the institution of slavery.[22] Conceiving of slavery as a tax further illustrates the paradox: slaveowners revolted against English taxation without representation, all the while forcibly, violently and unjustly instituting a 100 percent tax on black labor.

To pay for the French and Indian War of 1754, English Parliament passed a series of tax measures which angered the colonials, including the Sugar Act, the Stamp Act, and the Townshend Duties. Many colonists felt like the exploited "other." Oftentimes, they described their subjugation in terms of slavery. In 1776, they declared not only their independence from the crown but also that "all men were created equal." "No Taxation without Representation" was the well-known mantra of the American Revolution.

The Continental Congress scarcely provided for George Washington's troops during the revolution, leaving them to impress upon citizens' property in order to feed themselves. Congress attempted to pay its considerable war debts by requisitioning funds from the states, but the states performed miserably. "Requisitions" were direct taxes levied by the Congress upon the states. Congress determined first how much money it needed, then required each state to pay a share, like dues to a club. Congress had no means, however, of forcing the states to pay the demand. And so they didn't.[23]

Frustrated by the unwillingness of the states to pay requisitions, Congress sought alternatively to raise revenue by taxing imports, but New York and Rhode Island had the most lucrative ports to tax and used their powers under the Articles of Confederation to veto two attempts to enact a federal excise or impost tax. "No state could pay its soldiers, repay loans from its citizens at their par value, and meet the increasingly urgent pleas for money ("requisition") of the Continental Congress. Massachusetts tried and caused a rebellion. Most states did not try. The upshot was the US Constitution."[24] The Articles of Confederation, our first Constitution, was scrapped.

The principal difficulty in constructing a new Constitution that gave Congress the power to tax was in negotiating over whether and how to tax slavery. The southern slave states wanted to prohibit all federal excise taxes because they feared a northern dominated Congress would set the tax at confiscatory levels and end slavery. "At one point, [Patrick] Henry apparently summarized the threat with appalling clarity. He roared at the convention: 'They'll free your niggers!'"[25]

George Mason railed against giving the federal government the power to tax exports, because that would give Congress the power to end slavery by taxing the things that slavery produced. According to Paul Finkelman, John Rutledge of South Carolina equated a tax on exports with an attack on slavery.[26]

The South would not unite with the North against the British unless there was some guarantee that Congress would not repeal the 100 percent tax on black labor. They sought that guarantee in the form of greater representation in the House of Representatives, by including slaves as whole persons for purposes of voting rights. On the other hand, the South favored giving Congress the power to directly tax the states through requisitions only so long as slaves were not considered persons at all for this purpose. Governor Morris of Pennsylvania highlighted the inconsistency between counting slaves as persons when determining representation in the House of Representative but not counting them as persons when apportioning a direct tax between the states,

> that the inhabitant of Georgia and [South Carolina] who goes to the coast of Africa, and in defiance of the most sacred laws of humanity tears away his fellow creatures from their dearest connections & damns them to the most cruel bondages, shall have more votes in a Government instituted for protection of the rights of mankind, than the Citizen of [Pennsylvania] or [New Jersey] who views with a laudable horror, so nefarious a practice.[27]

In addition, Morris argued that consumption taxes would unfairly burden the North because slaveholders prevented their workers (slaves) from purchasing goods that would be taxed.

James Wilson, also of Pennsylvania, objected to slavery on different grounds. He knew that "Slavery crowded out free [white] labor, as slaveholding planters monopolized the land to 'prevent freemen cultivating a Country.'"[28] We will discuss later this tension between slaveowners and landless whites that would be at the center of tax debates in state legislatures throughout the South for as long as slavery was tolerated.

Abolitionists were divided over whether the federal government should profit from the slave trade by taxing it:

> Mr. T. Moore—I am astonished to hear gentlemen, who advocate the resolution now under consideration, reprobate a traffic as horrid and infamous, and yet wish to draw a revenue from infamy, if it is an infamy. I differ very widely in opinion from the honorable gentleman from Pennsylvania, who thinks that a tax of ten dollars per head will operate as a check to the growth of this horrid traffic. If I thought it would have that effect I would cheerfully vote for the resolution. I believe a tax of ten dollars will not prevent the importation of a single person of this description. . . . I hope this House will reject the resolution under consideration, and totally disapprove every measure which attempts to draw revenue from an act that rivets the chains of slavery on any of the human race.[29]

Ultimately, slaves were counted as three-fifths of a person for purposes of both direct taxation and representation, and the excise tax on the slave trade was limited to ten dollars. The Constitution also included the Fugitive Slave Clause which required free states to extradite runaway slaves. The combination of the power to raise armies against "domestic enemies" along with the "fugitive slave clause" meant the federal government and the northern states had to do more than tolerate the 100 percent tax on black labor, but also to support it. To further protect slavery, the Constitution prohibited federal taxation of domestic articles, the bulk of which was produced by slave labor.

Congress was not given the power to tax exports, it never levied the ten dollar tax on imported slaves, and it chose not to rely on directly taxing the states, as direct taxes had already proved ineffective and inspired the constitutional Convention in the first place. The power to tax imports was all that was needed to pay off the revolutionary war debts, and so the Constitution succeeded with respect to its original mission.

Of the provisions in the U.S. Constitution relating directly or indirectly to slavery, those giving slave states greater representation in Congress had by far the largest impact at the time. Curiously, however, once the South's protection of greater representation had waned because of the admission of new "free" states in the West, Abraham Lincoln and most others apparently believed that the Constitution prohibited Congress from abolishing slavery through regular legislation, even though the text and the history of its enactment suggest otherwise.

The Constitutional Convention of 1787 was squarely faced with the question of whether the United States was founded upon the principle of white racial supremacy. Instead of openly establishing a racial hierarchy in the Constitution by expressly levying the 100 percent tax on "negro slaves" (as South Carolina already had), the Framers wrote a constitution that accommodated white supremacy without requiring it. Confronted by the inconsistency of slavery with the principles espoused in the Declaration of Independence, the Framers of the U.S. Constitution failed to follow their moral principles and failed to outlaw the 100 percent tax on black labor. "[T]he Constitution was not perceived to be substantially pro- or anti-slavery at the time, even though by the judgment of eternal morality, the Constitution should have done better."[30]

Hardly any representative to the constitutional Convention, even those stridently in favor of slavery, offered a moral justification for it. They argued that the economics of the time, instituted by England they claimed, required cheap labor in order for an agricultural outfit to be profitable. Representatives of nonpropertied southern whites were fearful that abolishing slavery would result in large amounts of emancipated slaves who would be without land or employment. Referring to slave revolts, Benjamin Franklin declared, "Slavery rather weakens than strengthens the State."

It was not lost on some northern delegates that compromising on slavery was compromising their publicly espoused ideals regarding human liberty. Perhaps this is why negotiations over whether and how to tolerate slavery in the U.S. Constitution were held secretly:

> Unfortunately, it is not clear what, if anything, the New England delegates said about slavery. We can be sure that they did not make stirring speeches about human equality, but the delegates guaranteed that nobody else would ever know exactly what they said by voting to hold the entire finance debate in secret—so that they did not write letters describing it. Madison took notes, but while his notes resemble transcripts for other phases of the debate, they shift into a summary mode for March 28, the day Congress produced the three-fifths ratio.[31]

Ultimately, the Framers refused to expressly recognize race in the U.S. Constitution, at the same time the document clearly supports slavery. The new federal government was to return fugitive slaves and suppress slave insurrections, along with other internal rebellions. Slave holders were given extra votes in Congress due to the three-fifths compromise. And Congress was prohibited from taxing goods produced by slaves as exports.

Although the Constitution neither explicitly mentions race nor slavery, there should be no illusion that the majority of Framers, whether they supported slavery or not, operated under the notion that there exists a white race and that its newfound presence in the Americas formed the primary basis for creating private and public institutions and associations toward economic advancement and defense against "others." But, perhaps the Framers can be credited with rejecting explicit references to race because they hoped for a better day when the citizenry they were representing would not be so beholden to the concept of racial superiority. That seems to be the modern, post racial redux. But Derrick Bell's Interest Convergence Theory suggests that the Framers probably eschewed explicit references to race and slavery in the U.S. Constitution because it would have encouraged blacks, both free and enslaved, to support the British and their loyalists in the colonies.

No doubt the Framers were aware of the South Carolina Constitution and its explicit reference to negro slavery. They could have replicated it in the U.S. Constitution. But undoubtedly they were also aware that during the revolution the British Lord Dunmore marched troops through South Carolina with buttons reading, "Liberty to Negroes." They were no doubt aware that during the war, "African Americans abandoned the plantation in large numbers."[32]

FEDERAL TAXES ON SLAVERY

Profiteering from slavery was not limited to southern communities. The federal government taxed slavery and used the proceeds for war and otherwise protect or expand the United States of America. Congress thrice exercised its taxing power over slavery by 1817.[33] Direct taxes on slavery were levied in 1791, 1798, and 1813. These federal taxes were never intended to confiscate slaves from their masters, though they could have.

In 1794, Congress levied a tax on carriages. A tax on carriages does not relate to slavery directly. But a tax on carriages could have been extended to slavery as simply another species of property Congress could tax, and possibly tax out of existence. Thus, Congress' power under the Constitution to directly tax property owned by citizens was challenged in *Hylton v. United States* (1796).[34] The court held that a tax on carriages was not a direct tax that required uniformity and apportionment.

The court did not hold that only requisitions upon the states qualify as direct taxes. The court held that a tax on carriages is not a direct tax, yet a tax on land would be. The decision, issued seriatum with an opinion from each judge, left open the question whether Congress could tax the holding of slaves, but seemed to suggest that it could. According to Calvin Johnson:

> [T]he carriage tax opened a loophole and, as a tax on a form of property, created a dangerous precedent; for if Congress can assess or rate one species of property, it followed that they may assess or rate every species of property. . . . The real security against prohibitive slave taxes lay in the political arena. The real security lay in the South's extra seats in the House of Representatives and extra votes in the electoral college. The slave states kept this advantage until mass immigration increased the northern free populations enough to swamp the three-fifths representation of slaves.[35]

The court did not determine specifically what "direct tax" meant. It simply decided that a tax on personal property would be too complicated to apportion. Calvin Johnson interprets Hylton to mean that "direct taxes" in the Constitution only refers to requisitions levied by the federal government upon the states. If the constitutional limitations on direct taxes are limited strictly to requisitions as Professor Johnson contends, then the constitutional restriction of apportionment would not apply to federal property taxes, as is currently believed. This interpretation allows for more aggressive, progressive taxation, like a wealth tax, as proposed by Beverly Moran or Tomas Piketty.[36]

Despite the concern over Hylton, Congress never actually used taxes to confiscate slaves or end slavery. And by the time of Civil War, Congress and President Abraham Lincoln somehow came to believe that it could not end slavery through normal legislation, like taxation.

In 1797, a plan was introduced in Congress to increase national revenues by increasing the existing tariffs on foreign goods or by imposing a direct tax and dealing with the questions whether and how to tax the ownership of slaves. Many southern representatives were in favor of a plan proposed by George Wolcott which included a direct tax on the ownership of slaves, because it lessened the burden on poor free men in southern states. The tax was justified as a means for encouraging slaveowners to make their slaves more efficient. It would have also discouraged slaveowners from acquiring more slaves for the purpose of deploying them in urban occupations, which crowded out free white labor. Congress rejected the 1797 direct tax plan and simply increased the tariff rates on foreign imports

Even though "George Mason had argued in Philadelphia that slavery would bring the judgment of heaven upon the nation,"[37] Congress eventually committed the United States to profiting off of the slave trade rather than ending it. In 1798, Congress collected $2 million through a direct tax on land, houses and slaves. A flat rate of $.38 per slave was imposed. Between 1791 and 1802, Congress imposed a tax on distilled spirits, stills, wines, snuff, refined sugar, property sold at auction, legal instruments, real estate and slaves. It is unclear how much of the $6,758,764 collected during this time was attributable strictly to slaveholding.

Federal taxes on slavery were imposed again as a consequence of the War of 1812. In 1813, Congress levied excise taxes on sugar, carriages, distillers, sales at auctions . . . and slaves. Again, it is unclear how much of the $25,833,449 collected was attributable specifically to slaveholding:

> The 1813 tax . . . dropped the crucial features of the 1798 tax, the progressive house tax and the prior taxation of houses and slaves, and added new feature; assessments of the "value" of individual enslaved human beings. Except in states that assumed their quotas, the 1813, tax was levied on all tracts of land "with their improvement," all houses, and all slaves "at the rate each of them is worth in money."[38]

All federal property taxes were repealed in 1817. Thereafter, and until 1861, the federal government relied exclusively upon the Federal Tariff on foreign goods and the sale of newly conquered Indian lands in the Mississippi Valley.

Slaveowners hated the Federal Tariff for siphoning off their wealth from slave labor and redistributing it to the North. The tariff raised the price on British and other foreign goods and shipping, which forced slaveowners to pay higher prices to northern merchants, shippers and financiers. It quite effectively transferred the profits of slavery from black slaves to white slaveowners to northern merchants. Southern pro-slavery advocates estimated that the transfer of slave wealth from South to North due to the tariff amounted to hundreds of millions of dollars. Congress used revenue from the tariff and the sale of lands taken from Native Americans in the Mississippi Valley to completely pay off the federal debt and enjoy a budgetary surplus by 1837.[39]

STATE TAXES ON SLAVERY

In "Taxes and Slavery in the Antebellum South," George Ruble Woolfolk showed that state revenues directly from taxing slavery sometimes, perhaps regularly, exceeded half of a southern state's annual budget. His study does not include indirect taxes on slavery, such as taxes on "executors' and administrators' commissions; cotton brokers; cotton pickeries; probate; cotton presses; cotton warehouses; 'marriage contracts; mortgages; money loaned at interest; collateral inheritances, distributive shares, and legacies; suits at law; and probable effect of the institution upon land values for purposes of assessment."[40] According to Woolfolk, "Such an important source of public funds as taxes on slaves naturally became involved in public policy and led to definitive political issues."[41]

States taxed almost all transactions conceivably related to slave trading, including retail sales, brokerage, warehousing, registration, etc. In South Carolina, for example, taxes on slave holders and merchants provided almost 60 percent of that state's budget: "South Carolina's slave revenues in 1844 were $181,069 out of a total of $292, 427 and in 157 were $273,303 out of a total of $463,144."[42] Slavery via convict leasing and sharecropping was similarly lucrative. For example, the sale of convict slaves to local businesses in Alabama constituted nearly 25 percent of that state's budget. "By the end of 1890, the new slavery had generated nearly $4million, in current terms, for the state of Alabama over the previous two years."[43]

Direct state taxation of slaveholding extended all the way to estate taxes, as exemplified by State of *Maryland v. Charles W. Dorsey*, in which the legal question was whether to include in the decedent's gross estate a slave who was emancipated by the decedent's will. Often occurring at death, a decedent slaveholder might manumit or free a longtime loyal servant out of affection, guilt, or because of a contract with the slave. Black women in personal relationships with slaveholders and the children of such relationships were more likely to be manumitted than others, but still only at the death of the slaveowner. Moreover, taxing manumission, the voluntary freeing of a slave by the slaveholder, was prevalent in other American countries like Cuba and Brazil. Some communities prohibited manumission outright, while others restricted or regulated it, including taxing it. Similarly, some slaves in the United States had to pay "fees" for freedom papers.

STATE TAXES ON SLAVERY IN THE POST-COLONIAL SOUTH

After the revolutionary era, the U.S. economy became increasingly reliant on slavery. The 100 percent tax on black labor levied by the slaveowner and protected by the state reduced the cost of production for the agricultural economy, particularly cotton farming—which in conjunction with slavery inspired the greatest economic boom in U.S. history. Because of the 100 percent tax on black labor, blacks as a whole were almost entirely shut out from this economic expansion. The effects would last generations.

Moreover, state legislatures profited from slavery via taxation. The revenue from the 100 percent tax was re-redistributed by the state and county legislatures through a secondary series of state and local poll, capitation, excise, and property taxes. These taxes paid for infrastructure and anti-poverty programs designed exclusively for poor whites in the South.

According to Robin Einhorn, some of the early nineteenth-century's most contentious debates within white communities regarded the taxation of slaveholders and the slave industry.[44] Poor, landless whites sought to use taxation to extract some of the profits from slavery from slaveowners. Nonslaveholders wanted a "progressive" tax system, where the wealthy pay a greater percentage of their income than the poor. They also preferred that state taxes on slaves be levied ad valorem (as a percentage) on all property.

Slaveowners, on the other hand, sought to ensure that taxes on slaveholding never rose to confiscatory levels. They fought to maintain a regressive system, where a disproportionate burden falls on the poor via capitation and sales taxes. Slave-holders preferred that state taxes exclude certain species of property from property taxes and impose a flat rate on whatever property remained taxable. Einhorn contends that the "[h]ardest point of all for slaveholders to accept was their taxation beyond the ordinary purposes of government for such 'extraordinary' objects as building railroads, digging canals, and 'paying debts already contacted by the state for internal improvement.'"[45]

Whether to tax slaveholders a flat fee or a percentage of their property's value remained a point of contention up until the Civil War.

Northern states were less reliant on the 100 percent tax on black labor because their economies relied less on large scale agricultural production. They had less need for slaves and, consequently, had smaller black populations. In the eighteenth century, slavery in the North was most prominent in and around New York City. Merchants and artisans employed slave labor in Manhattan, and 40 percent of white households owned slaves in the surrounding counties (Kings, Queens, etc.). Although slaves in New York born after 1799 were to be freed at age twenty-eight for men and twenty-five for women, scurrilous owners sought to maximize their investment by selling them into slavery in the South before their emancipation date. In any case, New York chattel slavery, the center of the northern slave institution, was reduced to seventy-five slaves in 1830.

Still, the North profited greatly from slavery as well, since the cotton distribution system depended on brokers, financers and shippers from

New York and other parts north. Vast amounts of wealth were transferred northward to pay for these services. The Federal Tariff, which forced southern slave owners to pay higher prices for northern goods, re-redistributed vast amounts of wealth from slavery from the South to the North.

By contrast, 75 percent of citizens in the low country of South Carolina in 1774 were subject to the 100 percent tax on black labor. Virginia went from 7 percent African slave population in the 1690s to around 40 percent in 1750: "[W]hile gentry slaveholders and yeoman farmers disagreed about a range of issues and developed increasingly divergent lifestyles, they made the Revolution together-as slaveholders and as farmers who hoped to be able to buy slave s in the future."[46]

INDISCREETLY RACIST TAXATION IN THE ANTEBELLUM SOUTH

Virginia

After the American Revolution, Virginia committed even more firmly to a racial order. They repealed their poll tax on white men, and then repealed the ad valorem principle of taxing slave holders. Robin Einhorn contends that Virginia's refusal to tax slaves at ad valorem rates reflected the power of white elites to prevent poor whites from burdening slavery. Virginia's tax on slaveowners remained this way from 1787 until the 1840s: "Virginia continued to tax slaveholders 'by the poll.' In 1860, it charged $1.20 on every slave over age twelve, with unique anti-evasion provisions. Slaves were taxable at the state level regardless of county exemptions for 'bodily infirmity' or the otherwise tax-exempt status of the 'company, institution, or person owning or renting them.'"[47]

Moreover, Virginia, like most other states, taxed all ancillary aspects of the slave trade as well. Manumission, for example.[48]

Whites in Virginia feared that the ever increasing presence of black Africans would eventually lead to a revolution—like the 1803 Haitian Revolution, the greatest and most successful tax protest in history, greater in that regard than the American Revolution. As fear of similar insurrections spread amongst whites in the United States, there was a backlash against the presence of blacks, particularly against free blacks. In 1805, one Virginia petitioner asked that all blacks be removed entirely from the state. Another proposed that the state levy a tax for the purpose of buying slaves and shipping them out. That same petition would have also limited the freedoms and privileges of free blacks as well.[49]

Therefore, a white person petitioning for abolitionist taxation in Virginia in 1805 was not unheard of. But whites who petitioned state legislatures to tax slavery out of existence in their communities almost always petitioned the legislature to use the funds to ship former slaves out of the jurisdiction (to other states, South America, Africa, or just "out" or "away"). A striking exception is an 1817 petition from Tennessee calling for the emancipation of slaves and their resettlement in Tennessee free from poll taxes.

Undeterred by abolition movements, some in Virginia were even more committed to the 100 percent tax on black labor: "In the midst of the 1829–1830 Virginia constitutional convention, James Madison made an astonishing claim: that slaveholder power benefited enslaved African Americans."[50] Such ridiculousness by otherwise learned men could only mean that by this time the hegemony of white supremacy in the United States was nearly complete.

Then, in 1831, Nat Turner's Rebellion rocked Virginia. His revolt was a frightening national sensation for whites. Fearful citizens flooded the Virginia legislature with proposals for getting rid of all the blacks in the state of Virginia. Petitions for confiscatory taxes arrived in good number at various state legislatures. Multiple petitions proposed to levy an escalating tax on slaveowners until enough was raised to purchase them all and "send them away." Another proposed to tax all blacks, free and slave, for the purposes of their removal.[51] Another "more moderate" proposal sought merely to discourage the presence of free blacks by requiring them to pay a tax or fee for licenses to act as tradesmen—market foreclosure.

South Carolina

Like in Virginia, tax laws show that post-colonial South Carolina intensified its strategy to redistribute slave wealth to poor whites and to restrict the ability of free blacks to succeed in the marketplace. Since as early as 1801 South Carolinians imposed special levies on slaveowners to pay for the building of roads and causeways. However, the white citizens of South Carolina, especially residents of Charleston, used taxation to keep free blacks in their "proper place."

In 1822, South Carolinians stared down another slave rebellion, in which Denmark Vescey, a Caribbean-born, literate, and free member of the African Methodist Episcopal Church, organized over a thousand slaves to take the city of Charleston. The plot was thwarted days before regime change was to unfold. Responding to Vescey's plot, South Carolinians enacted more oppressive laws designed to restrict almost every remaining freedom and privilege enjoyed by slaves and free blacks. Free blacks in South Carolina were prohibited from assembling and were required to have a white guardian. South Carolina made it illegal to teach slaves to read. Similar measures were enacted in other states.

To discourage the presence of free blacks, the South Carolina legislature enacted an additional poll tax on slaves of $.75, and a tax on free blacks of $2. By contrast, there remained no poll tax on white women in

South Carolina (which was typical of the southern states), and no poll tax on white men (which was not). Free blacks delinquent on this or any other tax, like James Walker, who was past due $215 on his acreage tax, were sold into slavery.

In addition to state capitation taxes, counties and cities, such as Charleston, levied additional taxes on free blacks. In fact, responding to Vescey's rebellion, the city of Charleston taxed almost anyone who dealt commercially with blacks, free or enslaved. Charleston imposed a ten dollar tax on all houses owned by blacks, as well as on all landlords who leased units to black tenants, regardless whether free or hired out slaves. Furthermore, there was a ten dollar tax on every "free man of color" who worked as a mechanic. Of course, violations were ultimately punishable by a 100 percent tax on labor their labor (i.e., re-enslavement).

The proceeds from these 1822 taxes were redistributed to poor whites in the form of jobs and public services. A portion was earmarked to pay for an all-white municipal guard.

By 1824, owners of rental real estate (presumably white ones, but one can't be sure) began petitioning the State to repeal the tax on black residency. In addition, by 1825 guardians of free blacks were petitioning to repeal the head tax on free blacks. Attempts to repeal the poll tax on free blacks continued unsuccessfully for decades. In 1840, a petition citing the hardships of poor black women pled again for the repeal of the special poll tax, to no avail. South Carolinians practiced openly discriminatory taxation well into the 1850s, including, for example, levying another tax on free black mechanics, so that whites could enjoy more of the marketplace.

North Carolina

As for post-revolution North Carolina, its first tax on slaveownership was established in 1777. It was levied at ad valorem rates initially, but quickly changed to a flat fee, which favored slaveowners over poor whites. According to Einhorn, North Carolina "emerged from the Revolution with the most primitive (and idiosyncratic) tax structure in the nation," with a flat tax per acre of land and a poll tax on free men and slaves of both sexes.[52]

North Carolina tax assessors were required to use slaves as a unit of measurement: "A 1780 law directed assessors to value other kinds of property 'in proportion to what the negroes were valued.'"[53] This language reveals that North Carolina slaveowners were perhaps the first to develop "uniformity clauses" which prevented yeoman legislatures from passing legislation designed to confiscate and expel slaves and slavery. Uniformity clauses mandated that taxes on slaves could not exceed the tax on other property, like real estate. This way, legislatures could not tax slavery out of business without damaging other important parts of the economy.

By the 1850s, North Carolina's tax laws and tax law petitions show that the benefits of slavery were waning considerably, at least from the perspective of whites who didn't own any or many. More and more landless whites sought to expel all blacks from the state, regardless whether enslaved or free, because the changing nature of slavery from agricultural peonage to full-blown occupational leasing crowded out even more white labor. In 1848, a North Carolina petitioner proposed a poll tax on free blacks so that the proceeds could be used to ship all blacks to Liberia. More petitions proposing the same reached the legislature in 1850. And an 1852 petitioner requested "such caustic laws as to compel [free blacks] to emigrate, or by raising a fund by taxing them, to be appropriated to their colonization in Africa."[54]

To further discourage the presence of blacks in North Carolina, petitions proposed taxing slaves who owned dogs, since blacks who could not own weapons used them for protection. One petition sought to "prohibit free people of color from owning more than one dog, possessing firearms, from filing suit, from declaring insolvency, and to enslave and sell free blacks who are unable to pay debts or the poll tax."[55] The proffered excuse was that slaves allowed their dogs to ruin farm animals.

Upper South

Slavery in the Upper South (Maryland, Kentucky, Tennessee, and Delaware) was significant, but not as prevalent as it was in Virginia and North Carolina. "Slaves were 30 percent of the Maryland population in 1776, but 16 percent in Kentucky and 13 in Tennessee in the 1790s."[56] The tax issues, however, were roughly the same: less-propertied whites sought to share in the profits of slavery by raising taxes on slave-holders, while slave-holders sought uniformity clauses that prevented legislatures from raising the tax on slaves to confiscatory levels.

Kentucky

Slaveholding elites in Kentucky took various steps to ensure that state legislatures could not be captured by landless and otherwise nonpropertied whites who might tax slavery out of existence. The first Kentucky Constitution, adopted in 1792, explicitly protected slavery and the 100 percent tax on black labor. According to the original Kentucky Constitution, "the legislature shall have no power to pass laws for the emancipation of slaves without the consent of their owners, previous to such emancipation, and a full equivalent in money for the slave so emancipated." Like South Carolina before it, Kentucky constitutionalized its 100 percent tax on black labor and made white supremacy the official racial order of the state. And, like every other southern state, the slaveholders "collected" the tax from their black laborers, and then Kentucky also taxed slaveholders within their jurisdiction and redistributed those proceeds to anti-poverty programs designed strictly for whites.

Maryland

Maryland's colonial tax system was more sophisticated than Virginia, South Carolina or North Carolina's, because their legislature was not captured by slaveowners.[57] Very early, Maryland abolished poll taxes on both free men and slaves. However, they did tax the ownership of slaves on an ad valorem basis. The rate applied to slaves was set equal to the rates imposed on all other property (i.e., uniformity clauses), so that legislatures could not confiscate slaves through taxation. But Maryland farmers reduced their dependence on slavery fairly early after they switched from tobacco to wheat, which required less intensive labor.

Ad valorem taxation requires the government to assess the value of the property, and the appraisal is often controversial of course. To reduce controversy over the assessment of so-called unproductive slaves, Maryland amended their property tax schedules to place flat fees on child slaves and the elderly. Further guidance was provided for the assessment of productive slaves: "Assessors were to raise the valuations of skilled male slaves according to 'their respective trades and their proficiency therein'; and to reduce the valuations of slaves who 'shall not be perfect in their limbs or sight, or from the want of health or any visible infirmity are rendered incapable to perform their usual and proper labour.'"[58]

Maryland's occupational schedule for the assessment of slave value gives further proof that by the mid-nineteenth century perhaps a majority of slaves, at least in the Upper South, were often deployed as skilled professionals who were forced to redistribute the fruits of their labor to their owners, which was then redistributed by the state, county and local governments to poor whites in the form of public services and commercial protectionism.

Tennessee

Tennessee was considered quite inhospitable for large-scale agricultural production, since much of Tennessee (along with parts of Georgia and West Virginia, etc.) relates to the Appalachia's. Therefore, slavery was not a natural fit. However, the new and growing demand for coal and iron could be satisfied in Tennessee. With slaves or without was the question.

Early nineteenth-century tax laws and tax law petitions in Tennessee show a serious power struggle between slaveowners seeking to expand to new lands, on one hand, and poor whites on the other who knew that permitting slavery in the "West," which Tennessee represented at this time, was against their interest because it crowded out both their labor and available farmable land. From 1817 to 1819, the Tennessee state legislature received a number of petitions requesting that slaveowners be allowed to manumit or free their slaves, and, further, that those emancipated slaves be allowed to resettle in western Tennessee exempt from poll taxes for a specified period.[59]

But the tide changed quickly. By 1825, multiple petitions were filed to tax "free people of colour" as high as slaves. At least one petitioner requested that "they be prohibited from voting in any election whatever and that they ought to have a guardian to direct their conduct."[60]

Then, like most other places in the South, things got mean in Tennessee after Nat Turner's 1831 rebellion in neighboring Virginia. For the purpose of forming vigilant patrols to prevent slave insurrections, citizens petitioned the state to tax slaveholders with a special levy of $.50 from the owner of any runaway slave caught. Other 1831 petitions called for taxes on slaveowners to pay for patrols. Others sought to prohibit the importation of slaves from North Carolina or Virginia, fearing the probability that those blacks would be influenced or aligned with Turner's revolt.

Soon after, in 1834, the Tennessee Constitution was at stake. "[Y]eoman delegates spent three weeks reading out petitions (thirty in all) for a gradual abolition of slavery. Then, incredibly, they wrote a report attacking all laws that 'assign to men their rights according to the different shades of color.'" Without some form of protection, Tennessee slave owners were faced with the very real possibility that poor white majorities would confiscate their slaves through taxation. "Faced with this yeomen revolt, planters demanded security."[61]

Ultimately, the 1834 Tennessee Constitution, like Maryland's, instituted an ad valorem tax on slaves, but with a uniformity clause guaranteeing that the rates on slaveowners would not exceed that of other property taxes. These clauses prevented legislatures from taxing slavery out of business. Then to reduce the political influence of poor whites, "A tax on white polls shall be laid, in such manner and of such amount as may be prescribed by law." By the 1840s, petitioners to the Tennessee state legislature expressed no emancipatory sentiments at all and, instead, sought new tax laws for the purpose of excluding free blacks and hired slaves from competitive markets, and spending the tax revenue on public works projects inuring to whites, like free bridges and roads, or to pay for the execution of rebellious slaves.[62]

TAXES, SLAVERY, AND THE DEEP SOUTH

The 100 percent tax on black labor expanded along with the economic development of the "Deep South" or "Mississippi Valley"—Louisiana,

Alabama, Mississippi, Florida, Georgia, and Arkansas. After the cotton gin was invented in 1792, cotton production skyrocketed. This boom industry profited southern agriculturalists and New York mercantilists alike. Around 85 percent of cotton produced in the United States was shipped through the port of New York to Great Britain (mostly to Liverpool): "Contemporary estimates were that shippers, insurers, bankers, and merchants of New York receive forty cents of every dollar spent in the cotton market."[63]

The astounding breadth of the cotton trade provided the federal, state, county and local governments in the South and the North with the opportunity to profit from slavery indirectly by taxing the cotton industry at some point either in the production pipeline or on its return as a tariffed manufacture. "High prices for cotton, especially in the early 1830s, produced the greatest economic boom in the nation's history. The Depression of 1837 destroyed value throughout the Mississippi Valley, but by the 1850s the economy was booming again."[64]

In the first half of the nineteenth century, slavers transferred over one million black people to the Deep South because of 1) the cotton boom, 2) the fear of Nat Turner type insurrections from large and sometimes majority black populations in Maryland, Virginia and the Carolinas, and 3) a reduced dependence on slavery in Maryland and Virginia tobacco farming. Around the same time a superior strain of cotton was invented in Mississippi in 1820. Native Americans were forcibly removed by Andrew Jackson and the U.S. military, and white homesteaders converted the entire Mississippi Valley to cotton farming.

> The census of 1820 recorded 69,064 slaves in Louisiana and 32,814 in Mississippi. Twenty years later, the respective numbers were 168,452 and 195,211. And twenty years after that, there were 331,726 slaves in Louisiana and 436,631 in Mississippi. In the years 1820–1860, a sevenfold increase in the Valley's slave population produced a forty fold increasing in its production of cotton. Divided out in aggregate, this was the 600 percent increase in productivity that slaveholders could so proudly record in their individual copies of Affleck's Cotton Plantation Record and Account Book.[65]

The seizure of Indian lands, removal of its inhabitants, and sale of those lands strictly to white farmers and speculators provided the federal government with a huge budgetary surplus, and, therefore, the federal government did not levy any internal taxes from 1817 to 1860. federal revenues from the sale of Indian lands to homesteaders were returned to the states in the "Distribution Bill," allowing those states to provide traditional government services and anti-poverty programs for whites only.[66]

So much land in the Deep South was cleared for cotton production that slaveowners had to import food and other goods for themselves and their slaves from other places. This dependence on goods from outside the South rendered slaveholders vulnerable to the Federal Tariff, which became a wildly effective way to indirectly transfer the profits of slavery from the South to the North. With a high federal tax on British and other foreign goods, northern merchants could extract huge rents from slaveholders by charging higher prices for domestic goods.

Black people weren't just property, they were capital. Through credit and investment transactions, plenty of northerners owned all or parts of slave operations in the Deep South:

> Slaveholders stored their savings in slaves, and those slaves thus stood security for those who owned them. In the antebellum period, the vast majority of collateralized loans in East Feliciana Parish, Louisiana, involved mortgages on human beings. . . . Even when they had not been legally pledged—even though their name may not have been recorded on the same piece of paper as their owner's promise to pay and the legal rate of interest—slaves served as ultimate guarantors of the loans that banks made to merchants and that merchants made to planters.[67]

Taxing credit transactions and other tertiary business dealings relating to slavery became a normal part of the regulatory environment of the Deep South. In fact, cotton industry financing depended on slaves as pledged security. According to Walter Johnson:

> In the years 1820–1860 . . . The port of New Orleans was the largest in the South. Every year the city exported millions of pounds of cotton that fed the global economy of the nineteenth century, and imported millions of dollars of credit that created liquidity in the Mississippi Valley and in the United States as a whole. Both the cotton trade and credit market were founded upon the labor and assigned value of enslaved people.[68]

In the 1850s, racism in the United States had become entirely indiscreet. There was nowhere in the United States where a black person could be free from the specter of the 100 percent tax. The Fugitive Slave Act of 1850 and the Supreme Court's decision in *Dred Scott v. Sanford* combined for the proposition that no black person had rights that a white man was bound to respect. Free blacks could simply be captured and sold "down river" to the Cotton Belt without any right to due process or habeas corpus.*Dred Scott*and the Fugitive Slave Act set the stage for a national economy based on slave-leasing, a national 100 percent tax on black labor.

Attempts to prevent the 100 percent tax on black labor from expanding into the Northwest failed. Courts allowed blacks to be bound by indentured servant contracts with terms of fifty, sometimes ninety years. These contracts could be assigned to anyone at any time. Illinois, for one, awarded "specific performance" for breaches of these contracts. Moreover, specific performance awards in Illinois bound the laborer and their "children hereafter born."[69]

Northwestern states and territories enacted "uniformity" requirements, preventing poor whites from dominating a legislature and taxing slavery out of business, whatever its form. Of course, no serious aggregate of poor whites in any state ever used taxes to confiscate the state's slave population. Ultimately, uniformity clauses simply limited the extent to which poor whites shared in the profits of slavery.

TAXING THE SLAVE LEASING INDUSTRY

A tax history of slavery reveals how much the institution had transformed into a modern industry, including the right to lease or rent slaves, along with the concomitant responsibility to buy insurance on them. Legislatures taxed slave leasing transactions, and they also taxed derivative transactions like insurance contracts on leased slaves. In fact, one petitioner asked the Virginia state legislatures to lessen taxes on out of state insurance companies, so that slaveowners might keep more of the wealth which ought to have vested in black laborers.[70]

Even before the revolution, slaves in South Carolina were often hired out by their masters. Because of the small white population there at the time, slaves sometimes enjoyed a bit of autonomy and hired themselves out with the expectation that they remit all payments to their masters. By the 1850s, agricultural slavery all over the South was supplemented with a lucrative slave leasing industry. Slaveowners assigned their rights to control a slave to others for a fee. For example, a slaveowner might help a distant, infirm relative by sending them a slave who would hire himself out and remit all of his pay either to the owner or the relative as assignee. With certain restrictions, the assignee could deal with the slave as the master would. And of course, state legislatures taxed these transactions.

> Leased slave laborers typically cost $120 a year near the beginning of the [Civil War], but their cost more than doubled by the crisis years of 1864 and 1865. Slaves with a particularly useful skill, such as carpentry or prior iron-making experience, fetched $500 or more per year.[71]

Slave leasing contracts became more sophisticated, sometimes stipulating what type of clothing, how much food and what types of punishments the rented slave was to receive. "[S]laves with wives still living back at the plantations from which they had come were allowed to return home periodically, sometimes several times a year."[72]

Owners were reluctant to hire out their slaves (property) to the same lessee if the slave was returned damaged: "Slaves who at Christmas reported to their owners that the managers of the iron works had abused them often were not made available to the company again."[73] Or, the owner could protect against the abuses of a lessee simply by buying term property insurance on their slave. In fact, a Virginia petitioner in 1854 asked the state to reduce the tax on out of state life insurance companies in order to reduce the cost of insuring leased slaves.[74]

Slave leasing provided at least a small opportunity for slaves to reduce the tax on their labor. As a means of promoting good work habits and securing submissive conduct, owners sometimes allowed slaves in these arrangements to keep a portion of their pay for themselves. Similarly, agricultural slaves were sometimes allowed on Sundays to sell produce they grew on the side. "As an incentive to work hard and follow rules, slaves were permitted to earn small amounts of cash for themselves—typically less than $5 a month—by agreeing to perform extra tasks such as tending the furnace at night, cutting extra wood, or digging additional ore."[75] Of course, not all slaveowners allowed these privileges.

Because of the cotton boom and the advancement of the slave leasing system, slavery in 1860 was as profitable and redistributed more black wealth than ever. Folks like J.M. Brown openly touted his occupation as a "negro raiser" who bred blacks solely for the purpose of leasing and selling them to others. "25 percent of the white households [in the South] owned slaves." In fact, "More wealth was owned in the form of enslaved African Americans in 1860 ($3billion) than in railroads and manufacturing assets combined ($2.2billion). Even counting land, as well as livestock, railroads, factories, and bank capital, slaves comprised 20 percent of ALL American wealth."[76]

Legislatures extracted even more revenue from the slaving industry by raising taxes on almost every type of transaction imaginable, including leasing. An 1847 South Carolina petition proposed to tax slave owners who leased their slaves for more than a month. In 1860, Mississippi raised its slave tax to 75 cents. Virginia added a levy of $1.20 on every slave over twelve years old. Louisiana imposed a $300 tax on slave traders and a $30 tax on slave brokers. Legislatures taxed nearly everyone who fed at the trough of the cotton-slave market bubble, levying on cotton factors, commissioner merchants, wholesalers, warehouses, cotton pressers, brokers of real estate, freight, notes, produce and merchandise and others in support of the cotton industry.[77]

Despite this innovation in slave labor production, not even propertied whites were guaranteed success at this time. Even with laws making slaves the very last species of property to be sold to extinguish tax debts, "Bibb county sheriffs routinely held slave auctions to pay off the unpaid taxes of local landowners."[78]

REDISTRIBUTING REVENUES FROM SLAVERY

Collecting tax revenue from slaveowners and businesses that dealt in slavery was but one side of establishing socio-political-economic white supremacy in the United States. Redistribution was another. Governments redistributed to their white citizens wealth generated by and rightfully belonging to black slaves. Cities, counties and states compensated thousands of public agents in order to maintain the slave system, including militias to fight insurrections, slave patrols, slave catchers, judges, sheriffs, tax assessors, inspectors, etc.

Moreover, antebellum states spent their public funds on anti-poverty programs designed specifically for white citizens, including "literary, library, and poor funds." The common exceptions to these affirmative action programs for whites were taxes dedicated to exporting slaves and free blacks to Africa, South America, or simply out of the state. Of course, these emancipatory or abolitionist taxes were not designed for the purpose of improving the lives of blacks, but to exclude them from a marketplace reserved almost exclusively for whites. Somewhere near 93 percent of all blacks in the United States lived in the South during the Ante-Bellum period and the Jim Crow era and were almost completely shut out of the game economically and politically.

States used public funds derived from slavery and later from convict slave leasing to provide free public education for whites, while depriving blacks of the same under the concept of "separate but equal." And by the time "real" slavery ended after World War II, "millions of white southerners had been raised from profound poverty, illiteracy, and ignorance to at least modest middle class status. Free public schools, consistent medical care, passable roads, clean tap water, electricity, even the concept of regular hourly wage work . . . were promulgated upon millions of the most dispossessed of Americans with a speed and efficacy that in hindsight made the Great Society initiatives of the 1960s appear timid and indolent."[79]

RE-REDISTRIBUTION OF SLAVE WEALTH VIA FEDERAL TARIFFS ON FOREIGN GOODS

By way of taxation, a substantial percentage of profits from slavery ended up in the North. Although the federal government did not tax slavery directly after 1817, southern slaveowners describe in detail how the Federal Tariff indirectly redistributed wealth from slave owners in the South to mercantilists in the North. This considerable redistribution of wealth via the Federal Tariff supports reparations and equal protection scholars who contend that the benefits of past discrimination and subordination were distributed to every corner of the United States.

By taxing foreign imports to the point where they exceeded the prices of northern domestic products, the tariff forced southerners to pay higher prices to northern manufacturers and mercantilists than without the tariff. Perhaps it is just desserts that the South could not hold on to the profits of slavery, which they would have deployed in service of greater white solidarity. On the other hand, the clear effect of the Tariff makes it harder for northerners to deny that their economic fortunes were tainted by slavery.

Slaveowners could not circumvent the tariff by establishing large scale manufacturing operations in the South, because such operations could not possibly turn a profit when the majority of people in the South at that time had no disposable income because of the 100 percent tax on their labor. Consequently, southern slavers bought their goods from the North and were resigned to complain that the majority of profits from slavery ended up there one way or another. "[T]he American Tariff is neither more or less than a system by which the slave states are plundered for the benefit of those states which do not tolerate slavery."[80]

Slaveowners did not mind of course that the tariff they endured was much less onerous than the tax they levied on their black laborers. Nor did they recognize that federal tariffs on foriegn goods also favored the Louisiana sugar industry. Still, their complaints demonstrate that wealth which should have vested in slaves was redistributed to slaveowners, which was then taxed and redistributed both to southern governments and northern industrialists, which was then taxed by their governments who redistributed the wealth to their citizenry, and so on. . . .

Prominent southerners who protested against the tariff claimed at first only to be "sectionalists." To them, the Federal Tariff was not unlike British taxes that siphoned off profits from American industries during the revolutionary period. Some tariff protestors proposed that southern states levy taxes on northern made goods specifically to make them more expensive than foreign goods (particularly British). They proposed that each southern state levy an ad valorem tax on out of state merchandise, "other than that imported from foreign countries."[81]

The southern free tax movement of the antebellum South was "specifically concerned with three aspects of federal trade regulation, which they believed redistributed wealth and trade from South to North: Federal Tariffs that protected Northern Manufactures from European competition and thus raised prices for those who purchased manufactured goods; duties on foreign shipping that supported domestic shippers by keeping "foreign" ships out of the coastal trade—regulations known as the American Navigation Acts; and federal spending on maritime improvements in the North and bounties paid to New England cod fishermen—expenditures that used tax revenue to support a localized sector of the economy."[82]

Now if the South had gotten its way, the 100 percent tax on black labor would have stretched across the entire Western Hemisphere. The most avid southern secessionist, like Admiral Maury, hoped the South would ultimately become the major trading port between the Pacific and Atlantic oceans, with New Orleans and Havana as their major ports. If this grand fantasy were carried out to its fullest, Maury's plan would then transfer all blacks in the United States to South America, particularly Brazil. The entire southern continent was to become one ginormous plantation (similar to how the French converted all of Haiti to sugar production, such that it eventually could not and still cannot sustain other vegetation.)[83]

The southern economy was declining because of the tariff, and also because the steamboat industry, which had been transporting the produce of the West to the manufacturing and population hubs of the Northeast, particularly New York, had been losing business to the east-west railroads. New Orleans had also been losing business to railroads from Tennessee and Alabama to South Carolina. Thus, escaping the U.S. tariff and circumventing the railroads by seceding and annexing Cuba became the new strategy to revitalize a floundering Mississippi Valley economy. Regime change in Cuba was thought to be worth over $25 million. Canalling through Nicaragua would have been next.[84]

Regime change in Cuba might also have protected the value of domestic slaves owned by U.S. traders and slave leasers, which was falling due to the illicit international slave trade in Cuba. Spain prohibited the importation of slaves to Cuba. But the well-known illicit importation of slaves to Cuba and then to the United States continued. This bootleg trading in slaves devalued the worth of slaves held in the United States. According to Johnson, "Because of the illegal slave trade going on in Cuba 'A Negro who could have been purchased for $500 eight year ago is at present time to be had for $300.'"[85]

Annexing Cuba would have protected the 100 percent tax on black labor, there and in the United States. Contrary to contemporary popular belief, slaves of the Deep South tended to escape toward Cuba rather than Canada. Because of this, whites in the Deep South were petrified of a black Cuban republic separated by only a few nautical miles from the vastly majority black southern counties of Alabama, Mississippi, and Louisiana. Spain had already threatened Cuban slaveowners that if they revolted against the crown, they would arm Cuban slaves against their masters. According to the "direct trade" movement, Cuban slaveowners were under tyranny because of the taxes they paid to Spain along with the tariffs they had to pay on goods like sugar to the United States. Southerners feared that emancipated Cuban slaves would then propagate a Haitian-style revolution throughout the Caribbean and in the Deep South. Annexing Cuba would have removed the threat of the Spanish to arm the slaves there. It would also prevent Great Britain from buying Cuba from the Spanish and abolishing its slave industry.[86] Thus, according to Walter Johnson, "Prices would be emancipated that people might remain enslaved."[87]

Annexing Cuba was no mere pipe dream. Before the Civil War, wealthy planters in the South who dreamt of annexing Cuba and protecting its status as a slave nation sponsored several private invasions, hoping to liberate it from Spain. Despite the fact that the U.S. Neutrality Act of 1801 prohibited private persons from waging war on nations with which the United States was at peace, personalities like Narciso Lopez tried on multiple occasions to overthrow the Spanish-Cuban government, though unsuccessful each time.[88]

MORE THAN JUST A TAX ON WEALTH

Calling slavery a tax may be fairly criticized for trivializing the violence and degradation accompanying that brutal relationship. It is important to recognize that slavery "taxed" some blacks to death, including children. Infant mortality amongst slave children was as high as 75 percent.

Wherever and whenever they could, slave owners seeking to make their slaves ever more productive increased their work rate and reduced their provisions. Torture was prevalent, and sometimes for mere amusement. Of course, more intelligent owners favored those punishments that allowed the slave to return to work more quickly. They were more concerned with greater efficiency and productivity, rather than abject humiliation and subordination. For instance, overseers discovered that waterboarding slaves allowed them to return to work quicker than whippings: "I favor good and fair work, yet not overworked so as to tax the animal economy, that the woman cannot rear healthy children, nor should the father be overtaxed, that his vital powers be at all infringed upon."[89] There may be some who doubt that businessmen would abuse their valuable property, but not only does such a belief unduly assume a level of rationality amongst individuals (of any time or place) that is inconsistent with the various degrees of care with which people actually treat property they own, it also concedes that slaves who were unproductive due to age or infirmity were especially vulnerable.

Slavery was most certainly more than just a tax on a person's right to property as it related to black women: according to Douglas Blackmon, "White men openly forced black slaves into their beds for two centuries before the Civil War, and sexual access to local black women remained a running point of confrontation between white landowners and their black laborers deep into the twentieth century. . . . Black women faced the double jeopardy of being required to submit both to the cotton fields and kitchens as well as the beds of the white men obtaining them."[90] Even after chattel slavery, white men took advantage of black women almost without recourse. This era included numerous state laws prohibiting blacks from testifying in court, so it is perhaps no surprise that government officials openly doubted whether it was legally possible for a black girl to be raped.

A preacher who encouraged black women to resist the advances of overseers, owners, and others was stripped naked and whipped in the streets:

> Rev. Williams began preaching that black women should resist the sexual advances of the dominant white men of the community. . . . The mob . . . went upon him without warning and taken him out of the parsons aide . . . and stripped him naked and one sat upon his head and each by turns with a buggy whip, whipped him until his back was raw from head to foot and after whipping him they told him that they whipped him because he was controlling colored women.[91]

Black people did not fail to resist the imposition of the 100 percent tax on labor, to which the preacher's tragic story attests. John Hope Franklin, in *Runaway Slave: Rebels on the Plantation*, detailed hundreds, perhaps thousands of incidents where slaves ran away, attacked their masters and overseers, organized revolts, and sometimes all three.[92] Everyday sabotage and resistance were just as important a means of combating slavery and the 100 percent tax on black labor as Nat Turner, John Brown, and Denmark Vescey's plans for insurrection.[93]

MAINTAINING THE 100 PERCENT TAX ON BLACK LABOR THROUGH PEONAGE SHARECROPPING AND CONVICT LEASING

The Thirteenth Amendment was intended to repeal slavery. But the convict leasing/sharecropping system of the Jim Crow South was tantamount to slavery, and thus the 100 percent tax on black labor did not end until around 1945. This is the thesis of Douglas Blackmon's 2009 Pulitizer Prize winner, *Slavery By Another Name: The Re-Enslavement of African Americans from the Civil War to World War II*. Not unlike chattel slavery before it, the convict leasing/sharecropping system, as a nearly 100 percent tax on labor, redistributed wealth from blacks to whites, foreclosed or discouraged the presence of blacks in lucrative markets, and contributed to the establishment of our loose racial caste system in the United States.

> [T]he specter that former slaves, with their huge mathematical majorities in Louisiana, Mississippi, southern Alabama, south Georgia, and South Carolina would soon vote and rule government and perhaps take their masters' lands. This vision was a horror almost beyond contemplation . . .[94]

Immediately after the Civil War, newly emancipated, majority black populations in the South were in control of economies in shambles. In Alabama, for example, all the banks had collapsed and the aggregate value of the state's farm property had depreciated by around 60 percent. Intellectual, political and financial capital was sorely lacking, since slaves had legally been prohibited from learning to read. Up to that point, even free blacks had been restricted from participating in civil governance. Still, myths about uncontrollably rapacious and immoral black majorities, presented to northern white audiences by movies such as *Birth of a Nation* were just that, myths to defend the retrenchment of black peoples' civil rights.

Despite these obstacles, numbers of slaves filed "tax refund" suits against their former masters: "[H]undreds of former slaves filed suit against white landowners in 1868 demanding that the former slave masters be compelled to pay wages earned during the prior season's work." A famous newspaper article recounts the demand of one Jordan Anderson of Ohio who demanded $11,000 in back pay for he and his family before he would consider returning to Tennessee to work for his old masters. Of course, southern whites clinging to the remnants of their wealth and social position responded negatively to lawsuits for back pay, "by burning down the courthouse, and with it all 1,800 lawsuits . . ."[95]

Under pressure to devise new ways to resubjugate their black populations if they were to maintain their social and economic position, whites signed newly emancipated blacks to lifetime labor contracts. Instead of providing emancipated blacks with forty acres and a mule, the federal Freedmen's Bureau "and northern military commanders stationed in the South encouraged blacks to enter into labor contracts with whites. Whites signed black farmhands to contracts filled with provisions aimed at restoring the subjugated state of African Americans."[96]

Initially, the contracts offered to newly emancipated blacks were for life. If they could make it to a court, the contract stood a decent chance of being dissolved by a Union military officer. But, the threat of violence led to the existence of many such agreements, both formally and informally: "In one South Carolina case in 1865, when four freedmen refused such agreements, two were killed and a third, a woman, was tortured."[97]

After courts prohibited these lifetime contracts, "employers" began writing contracts with a definite term that could be extended *indefinitely*—for any breach determined by the employer. These newer contracts were extended to the extent the employer furnished anything to the laborer, such as medical care, clothing or food. "The contracts further authorized 'that should the said Pace advance me anything over and above what he had already furnished me, I agree to work for him under this contract until I have paid for same in full.'" The contract was also extended if the farmer incurred costs relating to the recapture of an escaped worker. And, "[a]ny effort to escape the slave farm risked not just the laborer who attempted to flee but any black person he or she encountered."[98] Regardless the name by which it is called, this was no less than a continuation of the 100 percent tax on black labor and the maintenance of white supremacy.

Employers almost always found ways to extend the contract of exceptionally talented workers: "In the case of highly productive laborers, Pace nearly always asserted a basis for keeping them far long than the original term."[99] In a 1920s movie exposing the convict labor system, one inmate informs another that if they like you, they will never let you leave. Perhaps more than anything else in U.S. history, slavery, convict leasing and slave labor contacts such as these perverted black culture because hard work not only went unrewarded, it was penalized.

Some contracts even authorized farmers to lock up their laborers in cells at night, like slaves. "Under the documents, the blacks Pace acquired 'agreed to be locked up in the cell at night' and submit to 'such treatment as other convicts.'" Some contracts required the "employee" to accept "whatever punishment the farmer deemed necessary—including the lash." Workers could not leave the farm without a pass and were required to speak to the owner "in a servile manner."[100] Meanwhile, whites reserved more lucrative occupations for other whites.

> Off the farms, only the most menial work could be awarded to African American—a convention that both blacks and whites violated only at risk to their own physical well-being. Black public behavior beyond the "bumbling Negro" caricature acceptable to whites—whether in attitude, dress, or visible aspirations—also invited economic ostracism by whites, at best, and physical injury at worst. The possibility of mob violence against any African American who blatantly rejected the unwritten code lingered in the background of black life, a relatively infrequent but omnipresent threat.[101]

Two year contracts often extended to ten. "Most of the early contracts adopted in the South in 1865 and 1866 were dissolved by commanders of the occupying Union troops. But they framed a strategy that southern whites would return to again and again."[102]

Again, the 100 percent tax on black labor cannot be discounted as a purely private affair. With the help of state legislatures, a would-be "free" market had been returned to a state of slave production. In Mississippi, blacks were required to accept slave labor contracts by January 1st of each year or face arrest and convict slavery. In other states, like Florida and Georgia, blacks could not be hired legally without the permission of or a discharge from the previous employer. blacks in the South were faced with the choice of accepting slave labor contracts, or being convicted of a crime which would render them a convict slave. In either case, their labor was taxed at nearly 100 percent, the only difference being the slightly greater potential for brutality, torture and death in the convict leasing system.

Like hired and leased slaves before the war, these contracts were assignable, so that employers could maximize their investment by selling or leasing their slaveworkers to others: "[T]he document allowed Pace to 'hire me out to any person, firm or corporation in the state of Alabama—at such sum as he may be able to hire me out for a term sufficient to pay him all that I may owe him.' For all practical purposes, Pace owned John Davis."[103]

Children could be resubjected to the 100 percent tax without even having signed a contract. The state bound children in Alabama to their former slave masters if their parents were "deemed inadequate." "[T]he Alabama legislature swiftly passed a measure under which the orphans of freed slaves, or the children of blacks deemed inadequate parents, were to be 'apprenticed' to their former masters"[104]

After courts deemed lifetime contracts illegal, southerners switched to criminalizing all aspects of black life and reenslaving "bad" blacks through the criminal justice system and reenslaving the "good" ones through sharecropping contracts which were only slight improvements over the Reconstruction era slave labor contracts: "[T]he misdemeanor convict leasing system solved two critical problems for southern whites. It terrorized the larger black population into compliance with a social order in which they willingly submitted to complete domination by whites, and it significantly funded the operations of government by converting black forced labor into funds for the counties and states."[105]

Plessy v. Ferguson basically stood for the proposition that whites could legally conscript government institutions toward white supremacy so long as they did not outwardly reveal the intended purpose. It seems perverse to say that it actually represented forward progress, because if *Dred Scott* had not been superseded by the Thirteenth Amendment, whites would be able to conscript government institutions with any pretext at all. Of course, the court in *Plessy* and thereafter cared little if separate services were actually provided on equal terms. *Brown v. Board of Education* has come to stand for the laudable proposition that almost any outward avocation for white supremacy is at least taboo. *Washington v. Davis* reverses course and allows whites again to conscript government institutions toward the maintenance of white supremacy so long as that purpose goes unstated. Almost the entire Prison Industrial Complex, as described by Michelle Alexander in *The New Jim Crow,* relies on the court's unwillingness to credit statistical evidence proving disparate treatment.

Because the Thirteenth Amendment prohibits involuntary servitude, except with respect to the duly convicted, the 100 percent tax could be applied to criminals. Consequently, whites in the South criminalized all manners of conduct so that any black person who threatened the system could be reenslaved as a prisoner. Meanwhile, to avoid that fate, "good" black people submitted to the same farmers, merchants and industrialists for whom they had labored prior to the war, under more or less the same terms. "Forcing convicts to work as part of punishment for an ostensible crime was clearly legal too; the Thirteenth Amendment of the Constitution, adopted in 1865 to formally abolish slavery, specifically permitted involuntary servitude as a punishment for "duly convicted criminals."[106]

Failure to sign a slave labor contract routinely led to the convict leasing system.

Not only did convict slavery keep the cost of labor on private farms low, it was an effective means for controlling subversive blacks: "[T]rumped up legal charges and forced labor as punishment created both a desirable business proposition and an incredibly effective tool for intimidating rank and file emancipated African Americans and doing away with their most effective leaders."[107]

Federal courts initially found many of these state laws unconstitutional. But, in 1883, the Supreme Court held that most local racial matters were outside the purview of Congress, and that enforcement of the Civil War amendments was primarily a state matter:

> [T]he US Supreme Court ruled that the Civil Rights Act of 1875, the one federal law forcing whites to comply with the provisions of the Fourteenth and Fifteenth amendments—awarding voting and legal rights to blacks—could be enforced only under the most rare circumstances. Civil rights was a local, not federal issue, the court found. The effect was to open the flood gates for laws throughout the South specifically aimed at eliminating those new rights for former slaves and their descendants.[108]

Southern legislatures enacted laws regarding what had been trivial matters up til then. Even though statistics show that crime had not increased in most places, states filled their books with laws designed to subjugate newly-emancipated blacks.[109] Outlawing vagrancy was a favorite of southern legislatures. Since legislatures understood they could not explicitly discriminate with respect to race in their statutes, they entrusted the subordination of blacks and other minorities to the executive and enforcement branches of government who could exploit neutral but vague and ambiguous statutory terms, which of course gave law enforcement officials discretion to prosecute those they wished. "Every southern state except Arkansas and Tennessee had passed laws by the end of 1865 outlawing vagrancy and so vaguely defining it that virtually any freed slave not under the protection of a white man could be arrested for the crime."[110]

Whereas the 100 percent tax on black labor prior to the Civil War had been primarily a private endeavor dependent upon the support of government, through convict leasing southern states became slave owners themselves after the Civil War. Between 1865 and 1870, Alabama, Texas, Georgia, and Mississippi sold or leased black convicts to railroads, iron works, coal mines and cotton planters—including several hundred in Mississippi to Nathan Bedford Forrest, the founder of the Klu Klux Klan. Florida, North and South Carolina and Tennessee also participated. Not just state government, but counties and localities who had previously punished misdemeanors with a fine of one dollar, began selling and leasing their prisoners as well. By the 1880s, sales and leases of county prisoners exceeded that by states. Buyers or renters of convict labor extended the convict's term by tacking on costs such as medical care, clothing, housing, and for any damage they were accused of causing. By 1902, "the seizure of black men on the back roads of the South was no longer even a brazen act."[111]

By developing the concept of the "plea bargain," southern officials circumvented the Thirteenth Amendment requirement that one be "duly convicted." Governments placed the costs of trial on the accused, and captured blacks understood that fighting the system meant a longer sentence. Therefore, defendants were expected to "plea bargain" or "confess judgment" in order to lower the costs of the trial. State and local judicial systems gradually lessened the amount of process due, until there was none. After some years, the charade of trial or even a courthouse became unnecessary, not unlike non-violent drug prosecutions today. Some prisoners were held without any records indicating why or for how long. "[T]he South's judicial system had been wholly reconfigured to make one of its primary purposes the coercion of African Americans to comply with the social customs and labor demands of whites. . . . It was not coincidental that 1901 also marked the final full disenfranchisement of nearly all blacks throughout the South."[112]

Still, convict slavery was much more than a 100 percent tax on property rights. The prison camps were cramped and filthy, and the convicts tortured and malnourished. The young, the physically weak, and the women who dared to visit or try to extricate a loved one, were routinely sexually abused. "At the lumber camps in southern Alabama, women seeking the freedom of their men were simply arrested when they arrived, chained into their cells, and kept to serve the physical desires of the men running the camps. The slave camps and mines produced scores of babies—nearly all of them with white fathers."[113] Death was common.

Convict slave labor crowded out free white labor just as chattel slavery had. Employers used convict leasing not only to resubjugate black labor, but also to break white labor strikes: "Rather than relent to the strikers demand, the company leased the mines to Comer, who filled them with legions of convicts at his disposal. The strike was crushed. The same year, Alabama collected $50,000 in revenue from the slave of convict leases."[114] But, unlike chattel slavery, the 100 percent tax on blacks through convict-leasing inured to a wider distribution of whites: "[A]lmost any white person who become involved in the resolution of a black man's legal situation could casually add his own 'costs' to the balance of a prisoner's debt and compel him to labor for an even longer period."[115]

More efficient than chattel slavery, during seasons when intensive labor was unnecessary, employers could simply return their slaves and not have to "care" for them during unproductive periods of the year.

Thus, in 1900, small farmers who would not have had capital or credit to buy a slave outright during the antebellum period, could simply rent slaves from the state, county or local jail and tax them . . . to death. This system proved more efficient than chattel slavery, since leasing slaves from the state or county also meant that small farmers did not have to "rear children" or suffer the expense of caring for the old or sickly. Ironically and perversely, leased convict slaves may have been treated worse than leased chattel slaves because acquiring more convict slaves was actually cheaper and, furthermore, no one with legal rights, like an owner or insurance company, had much interest in them. Generations of free blacks were keen always to be in the favor of at least one white man of substance who could vouch for them if they were ever "captured."

> Nearly every sheriff and town marshal in southern Alabama made his primary living in some variation of this trade in human labor. . . . Others limited themselves to the less organized, clandestine capture and sale of black men along the railroads or back roads. . . . Even more men acted as 'special constables' or temporary deputies appointed to serve arrest warrants concocted to justify the capture of a particular black man. . . . Vulgar whites like Franklin could rob or harm a black man with impunity, against which he had no recourse. . . . "When are you going to pay me the money you owe me" Franklin pressed. "I don't owe you anything," Davis said. The two men stood facing each other in silence for a moment. John Davis had been snared in the web.[116]

Northerners were largely unconcerned. The new slavery of the South, the new 100 percent tax on black labor, received far less attention and opposition from northerners and poor southern whites than did chattel slavery: "In the eyes of the vast majority of white America, the refusal of the southern states to fully free or enfranchise former slaves and their descendants was not an issue worthy of any further disruption to the civil stability of the United States."[117]

It is a mistake to think that only convict slaves were subject to the 100 percent tax on labor, since the cost of hiring peonage sharecroppers eventually fell below the cost of buying or renting prison laborers from the state. The supply of black laborers available to white farmers increased because blacks unattached to a white farming operation were subject to arrest for vagrancy or some other trumped up charge. Moreover, blacks who "voluntarily" hired themselves out to white farming operations knew that complaining about wages or working conditions invited the landlord or farmer to press any type of charge against them and convert their status from sharecropper to convict. Soon, there was hardly any economic difference between a sharecropper or a convict slave, even if there were significant distinctions in liberty: "[B]lack tenant farmers and sharecroppers often returned as uncompensated convict laborers, subject to imprisonment, shackles, and the lash, to the same fields where a few days earlier they had worked as independent, free men."[118]

Sharecroppers were supposed to receive wages, but landlords tacked on more costs than the laborer could pay, leaving them in debt to the farmer: "Of nearly 2.5 million farms in the eleven states of the old Confederacy, the owners of almost one-million farms reported giving some form of compensation to workers during the previous year. On most of the farms a total of more than 850,000—the entire compensation to 'laborers' for the year was less than seventy nine dollars."[119]

Customarily, black peonage workers received only a Christmas bonus, which was often paid in kind rather than in money: "Landowners, acutely aware that any worker fully clear of his debts might then attempt to relocate to a friendlier or more generous white property holder, routinely exaggerated costs and interest so that virtually no sharecroppers could ever fully extinguish their obligations. Instead, African Americans typically left the transactions with a small cash 'bonus' or loan to use for a few weeks."[120]

Because convict slaves could just as easily be put out on chain gangs or sent basically to die in the coal mines, blacks chose the frying pan instead of the fire, signing private labor contracts that allowed their employers to beat them and lock them up at night. They knew they were caught in catch-22: "We had sold ourselves into slavery—and what could we do about it? The black man asked, 'the white folks had all the courts, all the guns, all the hounds, all the railroads, all the telegraph wires, all the newspapers, all the money, and nearly all the land."[121]

After the price for leased convicts fell below the price of hiring sharecroppers, Texas, South Carolina, Louisiana, Mississippi and Arkansas stopped selling prisoners to private employers. Still, the low cost of private peonage couldn't be maintained without the threat of convict slavery. So, despite the fact that states stopped, counties continued to sell county prisoners to private employers: "[T]he harsher reality of the South was that the new post-Civil War slavery was evolving—not disappearing." In 1910, 93 percent of all African Americans lived in the South and the overwhelming majority of which were subject to a nearly 100 percent tax on their labor.

What is also inescapable is the fact that the employers who took advantage of these situations for commercial game were then taxed by the local, county and state authorities, the proceeds of which were redistributed in the form of government services to which blacks were largely excluded.

IMPLICATIONS OF UNJUST REDISTRIBUTION VIA TAXATION

Unfortunately, the tax history of race relations in the United States has been unappreciated by those who defend African American claims to reparations for slavery and Jim Crow-era apartheid (neo-slavery), particularly those who rely on theories of "unjust enrichment." Slavery was a tax that unjustly extracted wealth from the laborer to the slaveowner. Then, formal taxation of slaveowners, as well as taxation of all aspects of the slave trade, re-redistributed those ill-gotten gains to anti-poverty programs in the South dedicated strictly for Whites. It was not uncommon in the antebellum south for the proceeds from taxes on slavery to exceed well over half of a state government's annual budget. And yet, the tax history of race offers even more to the story.

First, acknowledging that the sharecropping/convict leasing system was actually "slavery by another name," acknowledging that it was a continuation of the 100 percent tax on black labor also buttresses Carlton Waterhouse's position that reparations are due for Jim Crow-apartheid era, as well as for chattel slavery. Conceiving of slavery as a 100 percent tax on black labor demonstrates the magnitude of material deprivation experienced by African Americans before and after the Civil War, and helps better frame the conversation around how much is owed to the descendants of slaves.

Next, the argument that reparations are not due because most whites did not own slaves is defeated by the ubiquitous redistribution of slave wealth via taxation. Not only did southern states profit off of slavery and redistribute that tax revenue primarily to their white citizens, the federal Tariff, the chief source of income for the United States from the War of 1812 until the Civil War, indirectly re-redistributed hundreds of millions of dollars from slavery to mercantilists in the North, which was then re-re-redistributed to nonpropertied whites by northern states who taxed those merchants who supplied the southern agricultural economy with almost all of the goods upon which the South needed to live since almost every acre of land in the Mississippi was dedicated to cotton production.

In addition to the vast redistributions of wealth that was slavery and the taxation of slavery, racist taxes on free blacks also redistributed wealth to whites. Consider that discriminatory excise taxes excluded blacks from lucrative markets, and poll taxes disenfranchised blacks so that they could be burdened disproportionately with societal externalities, like criminal prosecutions and environmental waste, for examples. In this way, the tax history of race in the United States, particularly racially discriminatory occupational taxes and poll taxes designed to disenfranchise blacks, also demonstrates how whites conscripted government toward the installation of institutionalized white supremacy, and the benefits thereof were distributed widely.

Some critics of reparations argue that "the people currently asked to pay had nothing to do with the injustices of the past." Even if tax redistributed wealth from blacks to whites, opponents of reparations contend that such an unjust redistribution in the past is irrelevant to the liability of whites today. A tax history of race in the United States shows how, as Daria Roithmayr might put it, unremedied market exclusion from the past has led to economic subordination in the present. In her early work, Roithmayr showed how housing discrimination and segregation as official policy of early twentieth-century private and public market institutions restricted much if not most of the financial benefits of homeownership to whites.[122] Whites then used the equity in their homes to fund education and entrepreneurial opportunities. Meanwhile, blacks were forced in large part to stand to the side of this game of Monopoly, waiting to be allowed to roll the die after the only available properties left are the cheap blue and purple ones. In this way, racial market exclusion, wealth redistribution and racial ordering via racist and discriminatory taxation locked in segregation and inequality, and extended black material subordination into the twenty-first century (even if one recognizes that we are in the nascent stages of the demise of white supremacy). So even if whites today express shock and regret about the horrors of slavery, releasing or foregoing the privileges that come along with white supremacy has been a more difficult task.

Also consider that third parties are sometimes liable for the intentional actions of others to the extent they ratify the unjust behavior of the actual perpetrator by accepting the benefits that derive from the immoral or unlawful act. Ubiquitous redistribution of black wealth via slavery as a tax, taxes on slavery, discriminatory occupational taxes on free blacks, and poll taxes also helps proponents of affirmative action and other remedial programs answer liberal whites when they ask "Why should 'innocent' whites pay the costs for remedying racial discrimination for which they were not responsible?" The tax history of race is not just about tax, it helps demonstrate how racism of all forms and types distributes material benefits (so-called white privilege) to all who can claim white as a racial category, how racist taxation contributed to the value of "whiteness as property."[123]

Despite the central focus of this piece being tax law, the pervasiveness and invidiousness of racism is the central lesson of this article.[124] Moreover, like Charles Lawrence's *The Id, the Ego, and Equal Protection,* this analysis of the historical intersections of tax and race is "most concerned with exploring how white supremacy is maintained not only through the intentional deployment of coercive power, but also through the creation, interpretation, and assimilation of racial text."[125] It attempts to demonstrate how racist taxation in the past redistributed wealth from blacks to whites and helped to perpetuate economic inequality to this day by "locking in" segregation and material disadvantage.[126] Showing how both outwardly discriminatory and neutrally worded tax laws with invidious unexpressed intentions helped establish socio-economic-political supremacy, a tax history of racism attempts to show that the Court's hyper-focus on 'discriminatory purpose' makes "no sense if equality was our goal."[127]

Therefore, examining the use of neutrally worded tax laws toward the maintenance of white supremacy is intended to support the work of those who encourage the court to alter its equal protection jurisprudence as it relates to race. According to Lawrence, the Supreme Court's Equal Protection Clause jurisprudence evinces this country's commitment to white supremacy, "even as it requires that we not speak 'out loud' about race and racism." The court 's approach to Equal Protection today is strikingly similar to its now discredited approach to poll taxes. In *Williams v. Mississippi* (1898), the court held that poll taxes designed to disenfranchise blacks of the right to vote were not unconstitutional because the text was neutral on its face and that application of the statute had not been shown to be discriminatory. Black voting went from an astounding 98 percent in 1885 to less than 10 percent by 1905. Similarly, in *Washington v. Davis* (1976), the court held that "because the defendants were not intentional racists, no constitutional violation had occurred, even though the facts showed dramatic racial inequality."[128] More to the point, no statistical or empirical showing seems to be enough, as the court in *McCleskey v. Kemp* (1987) rejected a regression analysis showing that those who kill whites are 4.3 times more likely to receive the death penalty as those who kill blacks.[129] A tax history of race further criticizes the court's requirement that plaintiffs produce a defendant who outwardly advocates for white supremacy, and attempts to show how this wild goose chase leads, not unintentionally, to a racial socio-economic and political caste system.

For Chief Justice Roberts and the majority of the Supreme Court, on the other hand, the Thirteenth, Fourteenth, and Fifteenth Amendments to the U.S. Constitution (the Civil War Amendments) establish nothing more than a principle against overt racial discrimination. Only under this assumption does it make sense for Roberts to cite *Brown v. Board of Education* for the proposition that, "The way to stop discrimination on the basis of race is to stop discrimination on the basis of race."[130] But if "the Thirteenth, Fourteenth, and Fifteenth Amendments embody a moral and constitutional duty to act affirmatively to disestablish the practices, institutional structures, and ideology of slavery and white-supremacy," then the court cannot prohibit any and all uses of race, only those that injure "through the production and reproduction of hierarchy, power, and material conditions of subordination determined by race."[131]

Professor Lawrence demanded that the court analyze the "cultural meaning" of racial events to determine whether they are invidious in fact. "I believe the Equal Protection Clause does more than require that every individual have equal access to the democratic process and does more than grant blacks the right to treatment free of invidious racial motives. Rather, it creates a new substantive value of "non-slavery" and anti-subordination to replace the old values of slavery and white supremacy."[132] Similarly, I have suggested that law and courts ought to recognize, as a subset of cultural meaning, racism beyond individual discrimination as asymmetrical market imperfections relating to race, that is to consider whether and the extent to which any circumstance asymmetrically distributes transaction costs like taxes, environmental waste and drug violence, or disproportionately distributes information or capital or any other prerequisite to free and fair competition in the national marketplace.[133]

Alas, Lawrence acknowledges that "an increasingly conservative Supreme Court majority has not only ignored my scholarly intervention but has marched relentlessly and radically, not to mention intentionally, in the opposite direction of my call to give attention to the meaning of racial text."[134] Ever since the court refused to consider racially disparate impacts in *Washington v. Davis*, and in *McCleskey v. Kemp*, the court, in the name of colorblindness, invalidates racial classifications designed to reduce racial inequalities while simultaneously validating laws that exacerbate racial inequalities so long as that purpose is not outwardly expressed. "[T]he Supreme Court majority's refusal to see society's racism is quite intentional."[135]

In such an environment, it is incumbent on critical race tax scholars, to recognize when neutrally worded tax laws, like poll taxes for one historical instance, are clearly designed to promote racial inequalities. And yet, even if the Supreme Court refuses to see it, critical race tax scholars must continue to expose these disparate impacts relating to taxation, because appeal to the court are but one way to protest racial injustice and blacks must always be willing to engage in private protest when public responses are inadequate. Moreover in the "public choice" legal environment which we find ourselves in the twenty-first century, where political factions are expected to compete and negotiate over the content of law, critical race tax theorists properly seek legislative and administrative remedies as much as they try to influence judicial opinions.

NOTES

1. Walter Johnson, River of Dark Dreams (2013).
2. Douglas Blackmon, Slavery by Another Name (2008).
3. Martin Bernal, black Athena (1987).
4. Douglas Blackmon, Slavery by Another Name (2008).
5. Douglas Blackmon, Slavery by Another Name (2008); Jordan & Walsh, Race and Economics (2008).
6. Douglas Blackmon, Slavery by Another Name (2008).
7. Robin L. Einhorn, American Taxation, American Slavery (2006).

8. Ira Katznelson, When Affirmative Action Was White (2005).
9. Robin Einhorn, American Taxation, American Slavery, page 97.
10. Robin Einhorn, American Taxation, American Slavery, page 95.
11. Robin Einhorn, American Taxation, American Slavery, page 94.
12. George Ruble Woolfolk, *Slavery and Taxation in the AnteBellum South*, Journal of Southern History (1960), 186–87
13. Thomas Cooper, The Statutes at Large Of South Carolina 54 (1838).
14. Geoffrey Parsons Miller, *The Corporate Law Background of the Necessary and Proper Clause*, in the Origins of the Necessary and Proper Clause (2013).
15. Claessen & Skalnik, The Early State (1978); Claessen & Skalnik, The Study of the State (1981).
16. Bibb (1850). Black slaves certainly did not need a lecture or treatise from Locke to understand that they were denied the fruits of their labor: "As Frederick Law Olmsted Traveled in the South, he was told 'that everywhere on the plantations the agrarian notion has become a fixed point of the Negro system of ethics: that the great result of labour belongs to the right of the labourer, and on this ground even the religious feel justified in using 'massa's' property for their own temporal benefit. This they term 'taking' and it is never admitted to be a reproach to a man among them that he is charged with it, though 'stealing,' or taking from another than their master, and particularly from one another, is so."
17. Douglas Blackmon, Slavery by Another Name (2008).
18. Robert Nozick, Anarchy, State and Utopia (1974).
19. Martin R. Delaney, The Huts of America (1859).
20. Some report that Clark eventually freed York, while others contend that York escaped.
21. Blumrosen & Blumrosen, Slave Nation: How Slavery United the Colonies and Sparked the American Revolution (2006).
22. David Brian Davis, The Problem of Slavery in the Age of Emancipation (2006).
23. Calvin H. Johnson, Righteous Anger at the Wicked states: The Meaning of the Founders' Constitution (2009).
24. Ibid.
25. Robin L. Einhorn, American Taxation, American Slavery (2006).
26. Paul Finkelman Slavery and the Founders: Race and Liberty in the Age of Jefferson (2014).
27. Ibid.
28. Robin L. Einhorn, American Taxation, American Slavery (2006).
29. Abridgment of the Debates of Congress, from 1789 to 1856: March 31, 1830-July 16, 1832 (Ed. Thomas Hart Benton, 1856).
30. Calvin H. Johnson, Righteous Anger at the Wicked states: The Meaning of the Founders' Constitution 186 (2009).
31. Robin L. Einhorn, American Taxation, American Slavery (2006).
32. Douglas Blackmon, Slavery by Another Name (2008).
33. federal Income Taxation, Eds. Freeland, Lathrope, Lind & Stephens (2014).
34. *Hylton v. United States*, 3 US 171 (1796).
35. Calvin H. Johnson, Righteous Anger at the Wicked states: The Meaning of the Founders' Constitution (2009).
36. Beverly Moran, *Wealth Redistribution and the Income Tax*, 35 Howard Law Journal 319 (2010).
37. Paul Finkelman, Slavery and the Founders: Race and Liberty in the Age of Jefferson (2014).
38. federal Income Taxation, Eds. Freeland, Lathrope, Lind & Stephens (2014).
39. Walter Johnson, River of Dark Dreams (2013).
40. George Ruble Woolfolk, *Taxes and Slavery in the Antebellum South*, Journal of Southern History (1960).
41. Ibid.
42. Ibid.

43. Ibid.
44. Robin L. Einhorn, American Taxation, American Slavery (2006).
45. Ibid.
46. Ibid.
47. Robin Einhorn, American Taxation, American Slavery, 228.
48. In 1782, the Virginia legislature received petitions objecting to laws providing for manumission. According to the petitioners, manumission tends "to depreciate that part of our property and the revenues arising therefrom would be 'greatly lessened' and that 'many would likely become chargeable and increase the demand on the people who are already highly taxed for other purposes." In 1782, the petitioners were worried that free blacks would support the British enemy. Fear of free blacks would increase after the revolution in St. Domingue (Haiti) in 1803.
49. Digital Library on American Slavery (2014).
50. Robin L. Einhorn, American Taxation, American Slavery (2006).
51. Digital Library on American Slavery (2014).
52. Robin L. Einhorn, American Taxation, American Slavery (2006).
53. Ibid.
54. Digital Library on American Slavery (2014).
55. Ibid.
56. Robin L. Einhorn, American Taxation, American Slavery (2006).
57. Ibid.
58. Ibid.
59. Digital Library on American Slavery (2014).
60. Ibid.
61. Walter Johnson, River of Dark Dreams (2013).
62. Digital Library on American Slavery (2014).
63. Walter Johnson, River of Dark Dreams (2013).
64. Ibid.
65. Ibid.
66. "By 1836, the sale of Western lands had provided the federal government with a vast budgetary surplus, which Congress, in the so-called Distribution Bill passed in June of that year, voted to disburse to the states for spending." Walter Johnson, River of Dark Dreams (2013).
67. Ibid.
68. Walter Johnson, River of Dark Dreams (2013).
69. Robin L. Einhorn, American Taxation, American Slavery (2006).
70. Digital Library on American Slavery (2014).
71. Walter Johnson, River of Dark Dreams (2013).
72. Douglas Blackmon, Slavery by Another Name (2008).
73. Ibid.
74. Digital Library on American Slavery.
75. Walter Johnson, River of Dark Dreams (2013).
76. Robin L. Einhorn, American Taxation, American Slavery (2006); Tomas Piketty, Capital in the 21st Century (2014).
77. George Ruble Woolfolk, *Slavery and Taxation in the AnteBellum South,* Journal of Southern History (1960).
78. Douglas Blackmon, Slavery by Another Name (2008).
79. Ibid.
80. Walter Johnson, River of Dark Dreams (2013).
81. Ibid.
82. Ibid.
83. Ibid.
84. Ibid.
85. Ibid.
86. Ibid.
87. Ibid.

88. Ibid.
89. Ibid.
90. Douglas Blackmon, Slavery by Another Name (2008).
91. Ibid.
92. Franklin & Shweninger, Runaway Slaves: Rebels on the Plantation (2000).
93. Alex Lichtenstein, Twice the Work of Free Labor (2006).
94. Douglas Blackmon, Slavery by Another Name (2008).
95. Ibid.
96. Ibid.
97. Ibid.
98. Ibid.
99. Ibid.
100. Ibid.
101. Ibid.
102. Douglas A. Blackmon, Slavery By Another Name, 27.
103. Ibid.
104. Ibid.
105. Ibid.
106. Ibid.
107. Ibid.
108. Ibid.
109. "Beginning in the late 1860s, and accelerating after the return of white political control in 1877, every southern state enacted an array of interlocking laws essentially intended to criminalize black life." Ibid.
110. Ibid.
111. Ibid.
112. Ibid.
113. Ibid.
114. Ibid.
115. Ibid.
116. Ibid.
117. Ibid.
118. Douglas A. Blackmon, Slavery By Another Name, 67–68.
119. Ibid.
120. Ibid.
121. Ibid.
122. Daria Roithmayr, *Locked In Segregation*, 12 Virginia Journal of Social Policy and the Law 197 (2004); *Locked In Inequality: The Persistence of Discrimination*, 9 Michigan Journal of Race and Law 31 (2003).
123. Cheryl Harris, *Whiteness as Property*, 106 Harvard Law Review 1709–1791 (1993).
124. Charles Lawrence, *Unconscious Racism Revisited: Reflections on the Impact and Origins of The Id, the Ego, and Equal Protection*, 40 Conn. L. Rev. 931, (2008).
125. Charles Lawrence, *Unconscious Racism Revisited: Reflections on the Impact and Origins of the Id, the Ego, and Equal Protection*, 40 Conn. L. Rev. 931, 939 (2008).
126. Daria Roithmayr, *Locked In Segregation*, 12 Virginia Journal of Social Policy and the Law 197 (2004); *Locked In Inequality: The Persistence of Discrimination*, 9 Michigan Journal of Race and Law 31 (2003).
127. Charles Lawrence, *Unconscious Racism Revisited: Reflections on the Impact and Origins of The Id, the Ego, and Equal Protection*, 40 Conn. L. Rev. 931, (2008).
128. *Washington v. Davis*, 426 U.S. 229 (1976).
129. McCleskey v. Kemp, 481 U.S. 279 (1987).
130. *Parents Involved in Community Schools v. Seattle School District No. 1*, 551 U.S. 701 (2007).
131. Charles Lawrence, *Unconscious Racism Revisited: Reflections on the Impact and Origins of The Id, the Ego, and Equal Protection*, 40 Conn. L. Rev. 931, (2008).

132. Ibid.

133. Andre L. Smith, *Boycotts, Interest Convergence, and Asymmetrical Market Failures Relating to Race*, 56 Howard Law Journal 891 (2013) (Wiley A. Branton Symposium Issue); *Race, Law, and the Free Market: A Critical Law and Economics Conception of Racism as Asymmetrical Market Failures*, 4 Georgetown Journal of Law & Modern Critical Race Perspectives 39 (2012).

134. Charles Lawrence, *Unconscious Racism Revisited: Reflections on the Impact and Origins of The Id, the Ego, and Equal Protection*, 40 Conn. L. Rev. 931, 940 (2008).

135. Ibid.

FOUR

Interlude: "No Reparation Without Taxation"

THE INTERNAL REVENUE CODE AND REPARATIONS FOR SLAVERY AND SEGREGATION[1]

Carlton: Andre, if you don't mind terribly, I'd like your opinion on the relationship between taxes and the concept of reparations generally and reparations to blacks for slavery and segregation specifically. As you know, I have done considerable research and writing on the subject of reparations for slavery and segregation.[2] Most scholarship explores its justifications and likelihood or its scope, form and administration.[3] But, reparations scholars have neither explored the implications of federal tax statutes to reparations schemes nor the possibility of using federal tax statutes as an instrumental part of a reparations program.[4] I am hoping our correspondence can fill some of this gap.

Andre: Sure, Carlton. I assume anyone interested in the relationship between federal taxes and reparations for slavery and segregation wants to know whether the IRS will tax amounts received by individuals under a reparations scheme.

Carlton: The answer, I'm sure, is probably complicated and political.

Andre: Somewhat. I would certainly need to know what form of reparations you envision and why blacks are entitled to them. Federal tax consequences depend on what is received and the justifications for it.

Carlton: Well, some suggest that reparations are compensation for past economic, physical, or emotional injuries,[5] while others propose reparations as a means of apology, punishment or atonement for past wrongs.[6] Similarly, some scholars propose reparations as a means to redress slavery, others as a means to redress segregation, or both slavery and segregation, and still others as a means to redress the government's role instituting or helping to institute and maintain white supremacy.

Andre: Hmm. Well, I think it will definitely help advocates for reparations to know if the IRS will treat reparations differently depending on the theory reparations are founded upon. So let's start there.

Carlton: Okay. Well, reparations commentators generally take three primary approaches to black reparations for slavery and segregation. We can label these approaches remediation, reconciliation, and reconciliatory-remediation.[7] Each approach represents a distinct justification for reparations and corresponding program types.

That said, I am also interested in ways in which federal taxation can be used as a means to support a reparations program. In my work "A Series of Unfortunate Legal Events," I propose that black communities develop organizations and institutions that are dedicated to remediating lingering harms from segregation and slavery.[8] Ultimately, my question for you is: In what ways will federal taxation affect such an endeavor, and may federal taxation in the form of charitable exemptions be used indirectly to support organizations dedicated to a reparative purpose?

Andre: Wow, Carlton. I've read with great interest your papers on reparations to black people for slavery and segregation, so much so that I also sought others with whom I am sure you are familiar, like *Getting Reparations for Slavery Right* by Roy Brooks, Jr.[9] The case for reparations is, I believe, compelling, though I am skeptical that "the forces that be" will ever see it that way.

Carlton: This is why I propose that reparations were best given by black people to black institutions who are committed to repairing the black community, as opposed to reparations given by white people to individual black people who can prove their enslaved African ancestry.

Andre: I like your approach, Carlton. Not because the traditional approach to reparations lacks adequate justification with respect to blacks, but because of the unlikelihood that it will be done, and if done, the unlikelihood that it will be done well. I'd like to contribute to your project by analyzing: the tax implications of traditional models of reparations should they be implemented; the ways in which federal income taxation can provide an alternative reparative model; and how the law of tax exemption relates specifically to your proposal that blacks remedy the harms of slavery and segregation themselves.

A SURVEY OF REPARATIONS PROPOSALS

Reparations toward Remediation

Carlton: Andre, as I mentioned, reparations commentators take three primary approaches to black reparations for slavery and segregation: remediation, reconciliation, and reconciliatory-remediation.[10] As presented, each approach represents a distinct justification for reparations and corresponding program types. Remediation, expounded by Robert Wesley, Charles Ogletree, and Randall Robinson and others, calls for remediation of the damage done to blacks individually and collectively through centuries of mistreatment.[11] The result they seek is substantive equality for blacks, complete elimination or at least substantial reduction of the material inequities created by America's legacy of slavery and segregation.

Andre: So they are calling for monetary awards as compensation and restitution? Kind of like contract damages.

Carlton: Yes. Commentators argue that reparations represent compensation for past economic, physical, or emotional injuries and restitution for the extortion of labor from enslaved blacks in addition to the panoply of social harms suffered across centuries of discrimination. While most proponents of this approach focus on the government, private corporations and other financial beneficiaries of slavery and subsequent discrimination against blacks may also be subject to claims under this approach.

Andre: So, the remediation approach ultimately focuses on monetary awards for individual and collective benefit, paid by the government or some other entity.

Carlton: Some, like Robert Wesley, favor collective reparations through a trust over individual payments.[12] But, direct cash payments to individuals, payment for black student college tuition, and a trust fund for community development all fit within the remediation approach.

Andre: I see.

Reparations toward Reconciliation

Carlton: Another approach to reparations rejects compensation and restitution in favor of reconciliation and social healing. Eric Yamamoto, Maxine Burkett and others have argued that reparations should focus on social healing and racial reconciliation.[13]

Andre: The purpose is to benefit the country as a whole, is that it?

Carlton: That's it. These commentators discuss reparations from a broader social framework. While they recognize and acknowledge the harm caused by slavery and segregation they see social healing and national reconciliation across racial groups as forward-looking and, thus, the proper goal of reparations.

Andre: So who gets paid under a reconciliation scheme?

Carlton: Reconciliation advocates share the concern for the most disadvantaged blacks, but tend to reject racial based programs in favor of a progressive commitment to eliminating poverty and improving education for all Americans. Reconciliation advocates propose reparations programs that enrich the most disadvantaged of the society regardless of race. America's historic mistreatment of blacks and other racial groups provides a motivation and justification for their approach

Andre: Economically disadvantaged whites could also be beneficiaries of reparations programs?

Carlton: Indirectly, yes. In most cases, they propose governmental programs based on economic need rather than racial identity.

Andre: But doesn't this approach mean that private corporations and other beneficiaries of past wrongs hold no responsibility or obligation?

Carlton: This approach is not primarily concerned with assigning blame and punishing wrongdoers. Also, through this approach, commentators expect that reparations would receive a broader coalition of support across racial lines and serve as a progressive commitment to social justice, appealing to the interest of people of color and whites alike.

Atonement

Carlton: Roy Brooks has advanced a hybrid model incorporating elements of both the remedial and the reconciliation approach to reparations. His approach, "the atonement model," calls for a governmental apology for slavery and segregation and concrete action that makes the apology believable.[14] The concrete action constitutes an effort to "make amends" for the wrong that was done. As a consequence blacks would then provide forgiveness for the nation's past and all parties would move forward.

Andre: Sounds like the idea of atonement is to convince blacks that slavery and segregation will never happen again, after which we should redirect our energies and resources away from civil rights toward, say, greater economic activity.

Carlton: I think it has deeper meaning than that, but blacks finally being able to let their guard down, so to speak, may also be a significant consequence of atonement. Under Brooks' approach, the government must take actions toward remedying the harms caused by its past conduct.

Andre: Some of the programs can be similar to those under the remediation approach, I assume.

Carlton: Yes. The use of a trust fund to enhance blacks' educational and economic opportunities represents one aspect of Brooks approach. A national slavery museum and other programs that address the social understanding of slavery and promote greater racial reconciliation provide the other key aspect of Brooks' approach.[15] While the remedial funds would be limited to blacks, broader social programs focused on collective social understanding of slavery and racial discrimination would benefit everyone and move the nation forward on these racial issues.

Existing Government Benefits as Reparations

Carlton: Beyond the three approaches just mentioned—remediation, reconciliation, and atonement—reparations detractors typically identify any private or governmental benefit that blacks have received in the United States as reparations.

Andre: Even those government programs which are generally available to all?

Carlton: As strange as it may seem, David Horowitz and John McWhorter in their writing on the subject argue that any welfare benefit received by a black individual should be viewed as reparations, along with affirmative action, antipoverty programs developed by

President Lyndon B. Johnson, and civil rights laws prohibiting racial discrimination.[16]

Andre: I'm not sure if I understand how these programs are reparations rather than typical governmental methods for making the marketplace more equal, irrespective of whether there had been slavery or segregation. Which begs the question, aside from the justification for it, how does one define reparations? Or does the justification itself determine whether it is reparations?

Carlton: Al Brophy provides a much broader definition in his survey of reparations theory, *Reparations Pro and Con*. He maintains, "Programs that are justified on the basis of past harm and that are also designed to assess and correct that harm and/or improve the lives of victims into the future," are reparations programs.[17] Although this is pretty broad in scope it should help set some parameters on the kinds of programs that would qualify as "reparations" for our purposes.

Andre: Under this definition, some of the programs discussed by Horowitz and McWhorter would qualify as reparations, with the major exception of public welfare programs like public housing, school lunch, and direct payment programs. Many of these were originally designed to aide poor whites and intentionally excluded blacks from participation. Allowing blacks to access benefits already available to whites should not be considered reparations.

Carlton: I agree. I also think civil rights laws are less clear than Brophy suggests because they equally protect blacks, whites, and everyone else from racial discrimination. Affirmative action, on the other hand, loosely fits the definition when used to remedy past discrimination against blacks—but not so much when justified on the grounds of diversity, as in *Grutter v. Bollinger*.

Institutional Development and Reparations

Carlton: As I mentioned before, I advocate a different approach to reparations. First, I believe reparations are due for both slavery and segregation. And, to repair the longstanding harms from slavery and segregation, I propose the creation of new and the reformation of existing black political, economic, and educational institutions.[18] I propose that blacks create three independent trust funds: the Economic Fund, the Educational Fund, and the Political Fund. Each of these funds will support organizations and institutions committed to the reparative goal of building up black communities.[19]

Andre: Under your approach, it seems irrelevant whether whites or the government accept the responsibility of remedying a past wrong. It also seems irrelevant whether blacks and whites reconcile their past.

Carlton: My approach is designed toward black people taking primary responsibility for repairing the harms suffered and being the sole guarantors that blacks never suffer either slavery or segregation happen again. I think the government should provide the funding, but even if they do not, blacks need to create and operationalize these trusts.

The Economic Fund

Carlton: I propose an Economic Trust Fund that supports the development of new and existing black businesses who demonstrate a commitment to the goals of reparations.

Andre: Towards remediation, reconciliation and atonement? How so?

Carlton: By enhancing the quality and number of black businesses, the Economic Fund provides jobs and it increases the availability of goods and services to community members. Further, I suggest that the Economic Fund support specifically identified businesses such as a national newspaper and a major production studio for the creation of television and cinema productions. I also propose collaborative business ventures with the Caribbean and African nations and development programs focused on training black youth for future business ownership and management.

The Education Fund

Carlton: I propose an Educational Fund that focuses on improving the education provided to the youth in black communities. The fund would incorporate programs designed to support public schools, charter schools, private schools, as well as colleges and universities. It would provide grants to aide in the establishment of charter schools in black communities. These schools would be open to all children, but their curriculum would be geared toward meeting the educational needs of black children.

Andre: Do any individuals receive payments under either the Economic or Education Fund?

Carlton: Not unless it is as a scholarship. Trust sponsored schools would retain their freedom to design their charters in different ways as long as the values of the education trust are included. School types should vary widely to include diverse educational foci such as math and science, performing arts, international language and culture, public service and others. Beyond charter schools, I also propose that the educational trust provide targeted funding to public schools in black communities. These resources would be used to improve curriculum and staffing in addition to supporting special programs around black history, culture, and identity. Along with charter and traditional public school support, the Educational Fund would enable the creation and expansion of private academies open to all students but dedicated to meeting the educational needs of black youth. Private schools and academies enhance the limited options now available to most black students. Like the charter and traditional public schools these academies would focus on the educational needs of black children and addressing the educational consequences of America's legacy of slavery and segregation.

Andre: Sounds like a better approach to helping public school children than the "Leave Most Children Behind" attitude of voucher program advocates.

Carlton: Substantial funding for targeted programming by historically black colleges and universities represents another component of my proposal. The Educational trust would provide grants to cover scholarships and fellowships for students, endowed chairs for faculty, and reparations related research. The Educational Fund would also make scholarships and fellowships available to undergraduate, graduate, and professional students at majority institutions who commit to black institutional service.

The Political Fund

Carlton: I propose a Political Fund for the purpose of creating and developing black political institutions.

Andre: How do black political institutions serve the purpose of reparations?

Carlton: The goal of reparations should be to repair communities that would have thrived if not for slavery and segregation as a political mechanism to inhibit their growth. The goal of the fund, then, would be to fund institutions and organizations that enhance the political awareness of black community members and increasing their political influence.

Andre: That's a huge undertaking, perhaps a greater one than either the Education or Economic Fund.

Carlton: While sponsored organizations would demonstrate a commitment to the communal and other values proffered by the Political Fund, they could use a variety of means and approaches tailored to their constituencies. Black political institutions would likely begin with a local and regional focus by organizing the black electorate in the southern states and a selection of large cities with substantial black populations. In my proposal, sponsored institutions develop constituent support by designing local and regional goals and objectives in light of the political ideologies of black communities.

Andre: Would the fund be designed toward supporting black candidates or black issues?

Carlton: I propose a nonpartisan issue oriented membership organization that would operate through local chapters and a national policy office. It will conduct grass roots organizing to inform residents about the political process and then support their involvement around local and regional issues. Young adult involvement, education, and organizing should be a fundamental strategy of this organization. By training and involving youth, the organization furthers two critical objectives: 1) strengthening its volunteer workforce; and 2) building a foundation for future political organizing. In this regard the group fosters political engagement and sophistication within black communities; two vital qualities of democracy intentionally denied the vast majority of blacks across three centuries of American history.

Andre: What about a think tank?

Carlton: Indeed. I propose the creation of a Bethune Washington Institute to support scholarship that furthers the goals of reparations. The institute would operate as a nonpartisan organization committed to supporting the research of a wide range of scholars related to questions of reparations. Scholars with full-time commitments to other institutions would serve as affiliates working along with Institute fellows in conducting research, publishing findings and making policy recommendations based on that research. Beyond government policy questions, institute scholarship would address the economic, educational, legal, and political policies of private groups and individuals as well. Through its work, black economic, political, and educational institutions committed to reparations would receive meaningful insights into effective ways to fulfill their objectives. Furthermore, fellows would address relevant questions regarding cultural, medical, and familial reparations through research, publication and the use of developed networks of dissemination.

Andre: I think developing the think tank is of utmost importance, because it seems to me that your proposal requires a precise definition of "reparative," such that reparative organizations or programs designed to repair black communities can be readily distinguished from existing civil rights organizations.

Carlton: As you can see, I have outlined a few components of a communal approach to reparations rooted in the formation and reformation of black institutions. This approach differs from remediation, reconciliation and atonement. While it shares the remedial goal with the first and third approaches it moves forward with or without governmental support. In light of the significant impediments to black substantive equality in society, black communities need to embrace an affirmative role in remedying the diverse and outstanding harms that remain.

TAXING TRADITIONAL REPARATIONS MODELS

Andre: Carlton, you have given me with enough information to begin discussing the tax consequences of these differing reparations proposals. You have described the actors who might pay reparations, the government, corporations and black people committed to remedying the harms of slavery and segregation themselves. You have identified the goals scholars have for reparations programs, whether remediation, reconciliation, institutional development, or combinations thereof. Relatedly, you have discussed the justifications some have advanced for reparations, including restitution, remediation of past harms, and restoration of dignity, among others. And you have described different forms for receiving reparations, including, but not limited to, monetary payments, scholarships, grants, and the funding of organizations dedicated to reparative activities.

Carlton: Andre, it would be most beneficial to me if you were to begin by describing the federal income tax consequences of traditional reparations programs.

In Kind Reparations as Imputed Income

Andre: Reparations in the form of nonmonetary payments, are, as a general rule, nontaxable to the extent such nonmonetary payments don't have any significant market value. I have often joked that socially prohibiting white people from using the word "nigger" is nontaxable reparations. The older I have gotten the more I think it is not a joke and is the only reparations we will receive.

Carlton: Andre, I hope this project inspires you to think otherwise, especially if we provide reparations to ourselves.

Andre: Well, regardless of who gives it (blacks, the government, whites, corporations), if the in-kind payment has an ascertainable market value and is received by an individual, it will be considered income and included in gross income unless there is an express legislative exclusion.[20] For example, the IRS would be statutorily and judicially authorized to tax the receipt of forty acres and a mule. They may, however, choose not to prosecute the case, but that is a dangerous assumption to make . . . criminal even.[21]

Carlton: A congressional apology for slavery, I would imagine, is a nontaxable in- kind payment.

Andre: Correct. To the extent Horowitz or McWhorter include as reparations anything the offender does to ameliorate or atone for past injustice, the *Brown v. Board of Education,*[22] the Civil Rights Acts,[23] Affirmative Action[24] and Hate Crimes legislation[25] would all be forms of reparations irreducible to a taxable event.[26]

Carlton: None of those governmental forays into race relations "cost" white people or some white persons anything commercially significant. They only take away the privilege of using one's market and social power to stigmatize, discriminate, disassociate or subordinate.

Andre: Yes, but the focus on taxation is not the burden on the transferor, it's about the welfare of the transferee. Since the benefits of civil rights legislation can neither be precisely quantified nor properly traced to specific individuals, then income in the form of market benefits attributable to civil rights legislation cannot be imputed to any particular person and taxed. In the framework of Glenshaw Glass, the benefits of civil rights legislation are either not accessions to wealth, not realized, or not under any particular taxpayer's dominion or control.[27]

Carlton: However, in-kind reparations having an ascertainable market value and relating to specific individuals may be taxed?

Andre: Right. Receipt of cash is not the sole trigger for a taxable event.[28] Receipt of any tangible or intangible property with an ascertainable market value is subject to federal taxation. Consider General William Sherman's field order distributing land during the Civil War in forty acre tracts to "negroes now made free by the acts of war."[29] This unfulfilled promise would be an "accession to wealth" under current law because forty acres and a mule have an ascertainable market value, receipt of which must be included in gross income to the extent it exceeds any unrecovered investment in acquiring same.

Carlton: And this is cut and dried?

Andre: This is the law, after all, so there are arguments to be made. At the time there was no federal income tax,[30] so receipt today of it or its equivalent could conceivably be excluded from income to the extent it "relates back" to a time when such proceeds could not be taxed for lack of the Sixteenth Amendment.[31] It's a huge stretch, though . . .

Taxing Monetary Reparations Models

Andre: Under current federal income taxation, traditional models for reparations, those involving cash payments to victims, also produce income. But the crucial question in federal taxation is whether amounts received as income are to be included in "gross income." Section 61 of the Internal Revenue Code defines gross income, an individual's tax base, as income from whatever source derived.[32] However, there are numerous exceptions.

Carlton: How broadly has the Supreme Court interpreted these terms?

Andre: "Whatever source derived" is meant to encompass all of Congress' taxing power over income, and is construed extremely broadly.[33] Glenshaw Glass concludes that income includes "accessions to wealth, clearly realized over which the taxpayer has dominion and control."[34] Receiving reparations proceeds would therefore be an accession to wealth, just from a very peculiar but taxable source.

Carlton: But, Andre, if reparations were paid by the government, how could the Court allow the same government to take the money back? Wouldn't that constitute a forfeiture of some of the proceeds from the victims back to the victimizer? Clearly, the law does not compel such a result. What about the case of the child who kills their parents to get their inheritance? The law did not stand pat for that; the child does not receive.

Andre: It is unlikely, I think, that an Article III court would prevent the IRS from taxing reparations proceeds. One reason for interpreting income in its broadest sense relates to horizontal equity, the principle suggesting that similarly situated taxpayers should be taxed similarly, such that anything significantly good happening to anybody is almost always taxable.[35] Another reason for interpreting income broadly relates to keeping tax rates low, in that when a particular sum is to be raised a wider tax base requires a lower rate than does a narrow tax base.[36] For these reasons, it is unlikely a court would allow monetary reparations proceeds to escape taxation.

Carlton: So there's nothing in the Constitution to prevent the federal taxation of reparations proceeds?

Andre: Without delving too deeply in constitutional interpretation, I doubt it. So-called tax protestors seeking to get out of paying federal taxes invoke the Constitution and lose in court all the time. Now, there was recently a case in front of the federal Court of Appeals for the D.C. Circuit, *Murphy v. U.S.*, where the court held initially that damages from some types of lawsuits were not understood by the people of the United States in 1916 to be income, and thus outside of section 61.[37] That court came to its decision relying on an approach to interpreting the Constitution called Scalian Textualism.[38] However, sitting en banc, the D.C. Circuit reversed itself.[39]

Carlton: After *Murphy*, the constitutional argument might be that reparations receipts are outside the concept of income as contemplated by the people of 1916. But to succeed it needs either more judges who utilize textualist-originalism or more convincing evidence that such items were not to most peoples' thinking properly considered income. While both are possible, it would be unwise for reparations advocates to rely on either development.

Return of Capital

Andre: If courts construed reparations as a return of capital, it would not be taxable. Monetary reparations received as a return of capital will not be subject to federal income tax because a return of one's own capital is not an "accession to wealth."[40] The return of capital theory is why section 61 does not reach the return of money an individual has lent, invested or was unlawfully divested of. To be effective, though, the return of capital theory requires first requires a narrative where capital earned by slaves was divested by Americans or America generally, and that such capital has been held in constructive trust and is just now being returned.

Carlton: Some scholars deploy the legal concept of restitution as a justification for reparations.[41] Doesn't this justification suggest a return of capital?

Andre: To the extent restitution implies that the victim held property but was divested and is now being restored, reparations based on this principle may pass the first hurdle toward being considered a return of capital. The return of capital theory requires however that scholars deal with the intergenerational circumstance of the return—that the capital is being returned to someone other than who lost it.[42] For example, the point was made in an earlier chapter that John Locke's theory of natural rights to property supports the notion that slaves had vested rights in that which was taken from them by slave masters and redistributed by local, state and the federal government via taxation.

Carlton: To the extent it is available in respect of reparations for slavery, Douglass blackmon's *Slavery By Another Name* supports this narrative in respect of reparations for Jim Crow segregation.

Section 102

Andre: Reparations advocates also might suggest that proceeds received as restitution (or for any other reason) could be excluded pursuant to section 102, which excludes from gross income amounts received due to bequests, devises and inheritances.[43]

Section 104

Carlton: What about the tax code section personal injury lawyers rely upon to shield their client's lawsuit proceeds from taxation? If reparations compensate for injuries and pain and suffering, shouldn't they be non-taxable for that reason?

Andre: Section 104(a) excludes from gross income amounts received on account of physical sickness or physical injury.[44] Reparations under this section would be excludable only if receipt of proceeds were due on account of the physical abuse endured by slaves. It would not apply if reparations were distributed on account of being economically exploited, personally stigmatized and traumatized, or culturally dehumanized.

Carlton: Can the amount relating only to physical injury be received tax-free?

Andre: If reparations proceeds are received "on account" of physical injuries, then all amounts except for punitive damages are received tax-free. But, again, the idea that a specific percentage of whatever reparations proceeds can be tied to any one type of harm, physical injury or sickness in this case, requires a strong narrative—and a nuanced at that, because for tax purposes it must take care not to make reparations punitive.

Carlton: It seems to require an intricate narrative at that; one that characterizes reparations as primarily justified due to the physical injuries caused by slavery.

Andre: Yes. Important thing about section 104(a) though is that if there was a physical injury or physical sickness, then all damages paid on account of it are also excluded even if by themselves they would be taxable. For instance, although an award for back wages is generally taxable, an award for back wages on account of physical injury or physical sickness is excluded by section 104(a)(2). Obviously, this involves quite a bit of word play with respect to the word "on account of." If, then, reparations are awarded on account of physical injury, then the amount of reparations dedicated to economic exploitation, stigmatization and dehumanization as well as physical injury would be excludable.

Carlton: Since section 104(a)'s exclusion depends on the justification for reparations, it would seem that the tort model of reparations is superior in this regard to the atonement model, contract model, pension claim model, or restitution model. They are all inconsistent with section 104's requirements that damages be received on account of physical injury or physical sickness.

Andre: Punitive damages, however, are never excluded from income pursuant to section 104(a).[45] Therefore, reparations proceeds will not be excluded under section 104(a) to the extent they are designed to punish America for its involvement in slavery or the establishment of white supremacy through slavery and segregation.

Carlton: All that must be done, then, is not to label them as punitive damages, right?

Andre: As always, narrative matters. Or in tax, we say "substance over form."[46] Reparations proceeds need not be labeled as punitive damages for them to fall outside section 104(a)'s exclusion. Thus, reparations may be deemed punitive damages to the extent they exceed an amount necessary to compensate for contractual or quasi-contract expectations, or compensation for physical injury, or return of capital, etc.

Section 117

Carlton: Are there other tax code sections I've not heard of or considered?

Andre: You mentioned a scholarship fund. Reparations in the form of scholarships may be excluded from gross income in whole or in part depending on whether it satisfies the provisions of section 117.[47] Taxpayers may exclude from gross income amounts used as a scholarship toward tuition and fees at qualified educational institutions. However, amounts used toward room and board and some types of classes are not excludable. Also, to the extent a recipient must perform services to receive a scholarship used for tuition and fees, the fair market value of the taxpayer's services will be included in gross income.

Relation Back Doctrine

Carlton: You mentioned judges in tax cases sometimes invoke jurisprudential doctrines relating to fairness. Wouldn't taxes on reparations proceeds fit the bill of unfair?

Andre: The "relation back" doctrine is an equitable doctrine available to the courts should they care to exclude reparations proceeds from gross income.[48] Courts may, in the name of equity, disavow the formal date of a transfer in favor of the date upon which a substantive act inspired the transaction.[49] It is deployed when the formal approach to legal decision making produces consequences which make a judge or panel of judges uncomfortable. The relation back doctrine is one of many equitable tools used by courts to elevate substance over form, whenever form produces unseemly results.

Carlton: Some judges might be troubled by the idea that the government would take back in taxes that which it owed as reparations.

Andre: True. However, other judges may not be so troubled by it for several reasons, one of which perhaps being disagreement with the idea that blacks ought to receive reparations in the first place. Pardon my cynicism, but in my opinion, it would be at least naïve if not quixotic under the current mainstream cultural ethos and composition of the Supreme Court for reparations advocates to rely on the judiciary to make equitable decisions in favor of blacks.

Presidential/Executive Intervention

Carlton: Is it possible that the the IRS could choose not to tax reparations proceeds? You know, let it slide? Isn't it true that Treasury long ago decided not to tax reparations received by European Jews who suffered at the hands of the German government, or the $20,000 in reparations paid to Japanese Internees?

Andre: The IRS, like other governmental agencies, is entitled to a considerable degree of deference to their prosecutorial discretion. According to *Heckler v. Chaney*, this is the highest degree of discretion in law. When it comes to agency decisions of who or what to prosecute, such decisions are committed to agency discretion because there is no law to apply.[50] The IRS has ultimate discretion on which individuals it pursues for tax, and how vigorously.

It may decide, though it rarely does, not to tax items that it otherwise could. For example, the IRS does not tax lawyers or doctors who receive proceeds while working for a legal aid society or hospital, even though technically they earned it.[51] These lawyers and doctors, or even an undercover cop posing as a drug dealer, must turn over the amounts to their "employer" or to a legal aid society or hospital. But reparations proceeds, however constructed or justified, are different because the reparations recipient keeps the money.

There is at least one other recent instance in federal income tax where the taxpayer gets to keep the benefit without being burdened by taxation. The IRS decided not to tax certain types of the receipt of so-called frequent flyer miles, particularly those used personally after being accumulated while traveling on business.[52] A political uproar led the IRS to capitulate.[53] The case of reparations may be the opposite in that it would probably be politically unpalatable for the IRS not to tax reparations proceeds from tax law scholars complaining of inefficiency and horizontal inequity to political opponents complaining of wealth redistribution.

Carlton: But if the IRS has chosen not to prosecute the case of reparations in the case of Holocaust survivors and Japanese internees, musn't they hold to that?

Andre: The case of reparations for Japanese internees may be instructive, as there is no provision in the United States Code excluding reparations paid to them from gross income yet several legal sources suggest that those amounts are excludable as "on account of physical injuries." Support for this notion is found in the legislative history of the bill which was passed by Congress providing for reparations to Japanese internees.

Carlton: But since such a provision was not duly enacted by Congress, if Treasury were not to extend this "moral rule" to reparations for slavery, would an Article III court bind the IRS to this informal administrative decision?

Legislative Intervention

Andre: Instead, reparations advocates might include in their proposals a statute excluding reparations proceeds from gross income. Congress has for a variety of reasons excluded certain items from gross income, whether it be to encourage a mobile workforce, to relieve taxpayers of administrative burdens; and sometimes the reasons are unknown, speculative or just plain unconvincing.[54]

Carlton: Congress could amend section 104 to include reparations as an item of income properly excluded from gross income. Congress need not limit the exclusion to reparations for African American slavery and segregation. It could clarify that reparations generally are not taxable.

TAX BENEFITS AS REPARATIONS

Carlton: Andre, can tax relief itself be part and parcel of a reparations proposal?

Andre: Yes. Taxation can be used in lieu of a direct expenditure program, though many scholars caution against it. Giving someone a tax benefit is hardly different than a direct cash subsidy.[55] It matters little to most individuals whether they receive x amount of dollars or are relieved of paying out x amount of dollars, the result is the same, a benefit of x amount. Stanley Surrey makes this point in his famous article on Tax Expenditures.[56]

Carlton: I've heard that real estate and farming are large sectors of our economy that enjoy tremendous subsidies in the form of tax benefits.[57]

Andre: The list is long, as the elderly, the sick, those seeking better education, all are subsidized in some manner by way of reduced taxation. Ultimately, I would suggest that a reparations program would probably be better served by extraordinary tax credits or tax exemptions for reparative-based charities then by extraordinary deductions or exclusions from income.

Stanley Surrey's Tax Expenditures

Andre: Another of the stronger reasons for not using tax expenditures as subsidies concerns what's called vertical equity, the idea that higher income taxpayers should pay a higher percentage than lower income earners.[58] Tax subsidies in the form of exclusions from income or deductions from income have differing values depending on which tax bracket the receiving taxpayer happens to be in that year. A $1 deduction is typically worthless to someone who either has no income for the year, or has so little that they fall under the bare minimal threshold. On the other hand, to a taxpayer in the highest tax bracket, say 35 percent, a $1 deduction is worth 35 cents. If you are in the 25 percent tax bracket, a $1 deduction is worth 25 cents. And so on. Surrey makes the point that a HUD Secretary would certainly lose his job after proposing to invigorate the real estate market by subsidizing most those who would be encouraged the least, and subsidizing least those who would be encouraged the most.

Andre: Beverly Moran and Bill Whitford seized upon this concern for vertical equity when they asked whether the Internal Revenue Code was racist.[59]

Carlton:Is it?

Andre: Although the provisions of the Code are race-neutral in their text, Moran and Whitford point to several provisions effectively subsidizing whites more than blacks, including the home mortgage deduction, joint returns, et. al., Some disparate effects with respect to race are just as much disparate effects with respect to class (i.e., vertical inequity).

Carlton: But since blacks are disproportionally found in the less wealthy classes, enlarging vertical inequity has an acute bearing on racial subordination.

Andre: Also, Dorothy Brown points out that rhetoric surrounding whether a government grant is a subsidy as opposed to "welfare" depends quite a bit on race.[60] She shows how the Earned Income Tax Credit is viewed negatively as welfare because a significant percentage of its recipients are black, whereas farm subsidies are viewed positively because most of the recipients are white and, thanks to the Department of Agriculture, almost none of them are black.[61]

Carlton: This means a proposal for reparations using taxation as an integral part of dispensing benefits probably raises particular questions with respect to legislative willingness, fairness within the class of recipients, and efficiency toward any goal reparations through the tax code are designed to achieve.

Andre: A reparations proposal relying exclusively or primarily on extraordinary deductions would also skew that program toward more economically well-to-do blacks, like affirmative action.[62]

Tax Deductions

Carlton: Where race is concerned, Equal Protection Clause scrutiny is triggered.[63] The Supreme Court would likely prevent Congress from providing for a deduction expressly available only to black people. The Equal Protection Clause prevents Congress from discriminating based on race unless there are compelling reasons for doing so, and the use of race is narrowly tailored to address those compelling reasons. The Supreme Court has found that remedying general societal discrimination is not a compelling reason to pass laws expressly for the benefit of racial minorities, and it has found most remedies for blacks to be too loosely tailored toward remedying the specific consequences of past discrimination.[64] Congress may be able to address this through detailed findings of past governmental discrimination against blacks.[65] But as with the Voting Rights Act, the Supreme Court sets a very high standard.

Andre: If the Court barred race specific deductions, Congress would instead have to provide a deduction for an activity engaged in only or primarily by black people. For example, nineteenth-century North Carolina used a neutrally worded tax law on dog-owners to discourage blacks who were not allowed to have guns from using dogs as protection. Of course, those taxes were not designed to benefit black people. They show instead that tax can be used to impact a specific group by focusing on activities that they disproportionately engage in.

Carlton: It is difficult to imagine an extraordinary deduction from income that relates to an activity only engaged in by black people. And if there were an activity a majority of black people engage in, and Congress sought to incentivize it by providing a deduction from income for expenditures relating to such activity, those blacks who do not engage in the activity would complain of the government determining what it means essentially to be black (i.e., stereotyping or essentializing black identity).[66]

Andre: There would also be no way to prevent nonblacks from engaging in the activity and utilizing the tax deductions.[67]

Carlton: A third problem with using tax deductions as reparations relates to the moral duty of fair representation by black leaders lobbying for reparations. Being that reparations based on deductions from income benefit the wealthy more than the poor, this prospect would encourage black leaders negotiating for reparations to sell-out the lower classes that have less influence with politicians and civil rights leaders.[68]

Tax Credits

Andre: Tax credits are a much better option than extraordinary deductions or exclusions as part of a tax-based reparations proposal.

Carlton: Why?

Andre: A tax credit equally reduces every person's tax liability. Each dollar of a tax credit is worth exactly one dollar to each and every taxpayer.

Carlton: What if the person has no income?

Andre: If the tax credit is refundable, as opposed to nonrefundable, it does not matter whether the taxpayer has taxable income for the year.[69] For example, research and development tax credits are nonrefundable and carry over to successive years where they can be deployed against that year's tax owed, but the earned income tax credit is refundable and requires the federal government to issue refunds to those who owe no tax.

Carlton: I see that the EITC targets people whose salaries leave them below the poverty line while the research and development incentivizes certain activities.[70]

Andre: As a matter of caution, reparations scholars should also consider the controversy involving the so-called Reparations Tax Credit, where several tax protestors and scammers "sold" the idea to naïve blacks that the federal government had indeed absolved them of the responsibility to pay taxes because of slavery.[71]

Carlton: I heard something about that. What's so interesting is that so many black people believed it was deserved and that so few whites people militated against it, which suggests that Stanley Surrey was correct: crafting a legitimate reparations proposal through taxation is more likely to pass the legislature than one depending on the direct distribution of funds.

Andre: However, after that debacle, it might take extra convincing for many people to believe that a real black tax credit is available. One important thing we have not discussed is how information about a tax reparations program will be distributed, an important concern in matters of taxation generally.

Tax Exemptions

Carlton: What about Robert Wesley's proposal, that reparations proceeds should be distributed to a trust which would then carry on certain activities?

Andre: Tax exempt status for an organization dedicated to racial reconciliation or remediation of harms suffered by black communities due to slavery and segregation may be the form of tax expenditure most likely available for inclusion in a reparations package. Section 501 of the Internal Revenue Code lists several different types of organizations that Congress has relieved from federal income taxes.[72]

Carlton: Could the Economic Fund I propose operate a newspaper and still keep its tax-exempt status?

Andre: Yes. Some nonprofit tax-exempt organizations produce gains from commercial activities in line with their mission. Even if a nonprofit sponsors a commercial activity that is not in line with its mission, the organization does not lose its tax-exemption. It must simply pay the unrelated business income tax, or UBIT.

Carlton: What about private donations to a reparations trust fund? You know my proposal is for black people to pay reparations to themselves. Does the donor get a tax deduction?

Andre: In order for a donor to get a tax deduction, tax exemption must be coupled with a designation that the organization's mission is deemed by the IRS to be "charitable." Entities organized and operated strictly toward a charitable mission qualify as tax exempt pursuant to section 501(c)(3) of the Code, while section 170 determines the extent which the donor may deduct the donation from gross income.[73] Deduction from the gross income of the donor is also a contingent expenditure, in that the donor may not have sufficient income to utilize the deduction.

Carlton: In effect, then, a charitable nonprofit dedicated to repairing the black community creates the potential for a double subsidy, and places this tax attribute on par or beyond tax credits.

Andre: So long as Congress, the IRS or the courts declared that organizations dedicated to racial reconciliation or reparative activities are deemed tax-exempt charities pursuant to section 501(c)(3).

Carlton: Yet, I'm not sure if an ordinary tax exemption for an organization can be considered "reparations," if Professor Brophy's definition is used. If, under current law, an organization dedicated toward racial reconciliation or remediating harms to the black community stemming from slavery and segregation may already receive a section 501(c)(3) status as a tax-exempt charity, then no reparations proposal is needed.[74] In terms of taxation generally and tax exemption specifically, the concept of reparations requires Congress to provide to blacks something extraordinary, something otherwise unavailable.

Andre: Then, the question regarding the relationship between tax exemption and reparations is "what type of organization relating to reparations and racial reconciliation would not receive a section 501(c)(3) tax exemption but for a newly conceived and enacted reparations package?" Tax exemption already exists for organizations like the NAACP, whose mission is toward the "advancement of colored people."[75] Perhaps the benefit a reparations package could seek is for Congress to intervene into the way a charity may be organized or operated and still retain its charitable status.[76] For instance, under current law, it might violate governmental regulations for a charity whose main function is to dole out grants for reparative projects to limit its grant recipient pool to only black people, or that only black people are hired for certain positions within the charity. It is not clear, constitutionally or legislatively, whether these attributes prevent an entity from being a charity or both a charity and a tax exempt organization.

Carlton: In my works, I have suggested the "development of organizations and institutions that focus upon the needs of blacks but which remain open for others' participation."[77] These organizations would engage in a wide array of activities, requiring the establishment of many parent and affiliated organizations, each of which possibly operating as a tax exempt organization.

I suggest that blacks establish a Reparations Trust Fund designed toward the establishment of three separate but interrelated organizations, an Economic Reparations Trust, an Education Reparations Trust, and a Political Reparations Trust.

These trusts would direct funds both to established and newly-created organizations engaging in reparative activities relating to economics, education and politics. The Economic Fund would provide financing for black businesses, provide business expertise and consulting to black businesses, promote international black business development, and help establish youth business clubs. The Education Fund would provide grants to public charter schools and independent schools designed to meet the needs of black children (especially with regard to advancement in science and technology), help strengthen historically black colleges and universities, and establish educational collaborative promoting black cooperation on a global scale. The Political Fund will seek to provide black communities with a meaningful voice in the American political system by, among other things, supporting a nonpartisan issue-oriented membership organization, disseminating accurate information on political decisions from local to state to national, supporting black news media, establishing and training youth in political organization and mobilization, establishing a scholarly institute dedicated to evaluating political proposals and programs, and establishing both a Political Action Committee and a Candidate Fund for the purpose of influencing legislation and elections.

Andre: You have explained that these organizations represent black people committed to remedying the harms of slavery and segregation themselves. Yet, to my mind, it begs the question what, in terms of racial reparations, distinguishes these organizations from current organizations dedicated to the advancement of black people?

Carlton: The Reparation Trust Funds would be dedicated to "reparative" projects, rather than, say, civil rights projects. I propose that a think tank be established to identify through scholarship the appropriate distinction between a reparative project and a civil rights project.

Andre: This must be further explored as we discuss whether the IRS would deem such an organization's mission charitable.

Carlton: However, to the extent reparative projects either toward atonement or racial reconciliation are already encompassed within the term charitable, the government in granting tax exempt charity status has done no more or less than what it is already required to do. Something extraordinary is required, I think.

Andre: Well, there are several opportunities within nonprofit tax law for the federal government to provide tax exemption for reparative organizations in an extraordinary way.

Ordinary Charitable Tax Exemption

Andre: Ordinary tax exemptions are designed to subsidize entities and activities in two distinct ways. First the organization is exempt from income tax. Second, individuals get personal deductions from income for donations to a tax exempt organization.[78] If a one dollar deduction for someone in a 35 percent tax bracket is worth 35 cents to that person, then a one dollar donation to charity that also nets a tax deduction actually only costs the donor 65 cents, ($1 - $.35 = $.65).

There are also ancillary benefits arising from certain forms of tax exemption, such as "relief from the requirement to pay federal unemployment taxes, access to tax-exempt government bonds, and eligibility for preferred postal rates" and "indirect economic benefits granted by state and local governments." Entities organized and operated pursuant to section 501(c)(3) of the IRC, public charities, are entitled to all of these benefits. Other organizations, particularly mutual benefit societies, less so.

Carlton: What's the difference between a charity and a mutual benefit society?

Andre: If organizations dedicated to reparative activities exist primarily for the mutual benefit of its members, it may still operate tax free, but donations to it will be nondeductible. A charity must have a public mission. So the theory goes, Congress more efficiently fulfills its duty to provide aid to human suffering by encouraging and incentivizing private giving to charities, than by providing the charity itself. Congress should support charity without actually giving it out themselves, because Congress simply cannot be trusted to accurately, legitimately or efficiently determine which causes to support and the appropriate amounts of time, money and energy to devote.

Carlton: So, rather than drawing arbitrary or lobbied-for lines in the sand, a tax deduction for charitable donations serves as a means for Congress to supplement individual giving without having to make choices as to who shall receive.

Andre: On the other hand, a mutual benefit society's mission "is one that is focused on primarily benefiting a particular group of persons who are oftentimes members."[79] For instance, even though historically black-greek letter organizations, which are tax exempt as mutual benefit societies, perform large amounts of charity work, they are not organized and operated strictly toward a charitable mission, and thus, donations to them are not tax deductible.

Carlton: So a tax exempt mutual benefit organization will likely receive less donations than if it were a charitable organization and its donors subsidized by the Federal government.

Andre: In addition to having a charitable mission, an organization qualifying under section 501(c)(3) must be organized and operated exclusively toward their charitable purpose, such that no significant benefit may inure to private persons. As a good example of the width and breadth of this principle, the entity's organizing documents must dictate that upon dissolution of the organization all of its assets must be distributed to other tax-exempt charities. It must be operated in a manner such that neither its assets nor activities unduly benefit private individuals. Excessive salaries, private use of charity assets like computers, cell phones and cars are examples of private inurement which could result in revocation of the organization's tax exempt status.

Carlton: Nothing we've discussed so far endangers the Reparations Trust Fund.

Andre: Along with the prohibition against private inurement, a tax exempt charity cannot "campaign on behalf of (or in opposition to) any candidate for public office." It may involve itself in elections in a charitable way, by promoting issues rather than candidates or promoting voter registration, education and mobilization (turn out). Furthermore, it may not dedicate a substantial part of its activities toward lobbying, or "carrying on propaganda, or otherwise attempting, to influence legislation."

Carlton: Aspects of the Political Trust may violate these rules and might be ineligible for section 501(c)(3) treatment.

Andre: Another code section, section 501(c)(4) may allow for certain aspects of the Political Trust to be organized and operated in a tax-exempt manner (without the benefit of deductible donations). But the Candidate Fund could not be recognized as tax-exempt even under section 501(c)(4).

Opportunities for Extraordinary Tax Exemption

Carlton: If reparative organizations organized toward atonement or racial reconciliation already qualify for tax exempt charity status, and if there is no affirmative requirement for the whites generally or the government specifically to fund such organizations, it is unclear how these reparative organizations can be considered reparations.

Andre: Well, it might be reparations for Congress to provide tax exemption and charitable status to organizations dedicated to atonement and racial reconciliation who would otherwise not receive it due to a controversial component of its organization or operation. David Brennen, in *Race and Equality Across the Law School Curriculum*, explores several issues relating to race which impact on your proposal for organizations dedicated to reparations.[80] At the center of his discussion and ours is *Bob Jones v. United States*, where the Supreme Court held that the term charitable does not include organizations that are racially discriminatory.[81] While I think it is clear from a black or critical race perspective why any mission legitimately concerning racial atonement or racial reconciliation has a significant public benefit, it is not out of the question that an organization whose avowed mission expressly relates only to black people would be suspected of not furthering a public mission.[82]

Carlton: Of course, there are race neutral ways of describing a reparative organization, and surely there is the argument that such organizations benefit all Americans with greater domestic tranquility.[83] Being that there already exists scores of charitable organizations dedicated to the "advancement of colored people" and the like that expressing reparations in terms of a charitable mission should not be hard.

Andre: Another issue relates to organizational structure, specifically hiring. Current law requires the board of directors of a public charity to represent a cross-section of the public.[84] While this requirement is loosely styled it might be argued that a board whose members are exclusively black may violate this requirement. Moreover, an organization endeavoring to hire only black people may be even closer to violating the principal espoused in *Bob Jones University*. On the other hand, the IRS under the Bush administration approved of charitable status for a religious organization that expressly restricts its hiring to those of the faith.[85] This ruling militates in favor of "mission hiring."

Carlton: To the extent current law does not permit mission hiring, however, congressional fiat in favor of it in the case of a Reparations Trust would be an extraordinary tax subsidy, and thus reparations.

Andre: The third issue relates to organizational activities, specifically grant making. A charitable organization may operate strictly by doling out grants to others, sometimes as a means to alleviate individual poverty, other times as a means of supporting individuals or entities who will use the grants to further a specific charitable mission.[86]

Carlton: I guess, here, the question relates to whether a charitable grant making process can rely on race, can it exclude those potential grantees who are not black?[87] If it is declared that affirmative action in grant making is uncharitable, a congressional reversal would constitute an extraordinary tax exemption and qualify as reparations.

CONCLUSION

Carlton: I will give greater thought to your concern that my proposal that blacks pay reparations to ourselves will fit a more universal concept of reparations even better if the government makes an extraordinary tax subsidy or expenditure to support it. Because most of my proposed programs avoid racial discrimination, they should fit within the charitable purposes established by Congress. Support for black owned businesses, however, will need some legislative accommodation to allow the Economic Trust to maintain a tax exempt status despite race conscious support for black owned businesses. This cannot be readily avoided through race neutral criteria, since the goal is to remedy the dearth of black businesses resulting from the substantial discrimination in lending and the provision of goods and services during the Jim Crow Era.

As a result of this discussion I also think that reparations commentators need to provide more consideration to the use of tax credits as a delivery mechanism. It addresses some of the important concerns raised about the challenges associated with implementing a reparations scheme. I still believe that the use of trust funds for institutional development or to cover health care or educational costs will better remediate lingering harms from segregation facing black communities. Individual compensation, however, cannot be summarily ruled out. And despite the fiasco of the fraudulent and unauthorized "black Tax Credit" of 2001, tax credits as part of a reparations program may be one of the more effective mechanisms for the delivery of individual benefits.

NOTES

1. This chapter originally appeared as an article with Dr. Carlton P. Waterhouse in Reparations and Taxation, 7 Pittsburgh Tax Review 159 (2010).

2. Carlton Waterhouse, *Avoiding Another Step In A Series of Unfortunate Legal Events*, 26 B.C. Third World L.J. 207, 262–65 (2006).

3. See Roy L. Brooks, *Rehabilitative Reparations for the Judicial Process*, 58 N.Y.U. Ann. Surv. Am. L. 475 (2003); Alfred Brophy, *Some Conceptual and Legal Problems in Reparations for Slavery*, 58 N.Y.U. Ann. Surv. Am. L. 497 (2003); Boris K. Bittker, The Case of black Reparations (1973). Cf. Richard A. Epstein, *The Case Against black Reparations*, 84 B.U. L. Rev. 1177 (2004); Eric A. Posner & Adrian Vermeule, *Reparations for Slavery and Other Historical Injustices*, 103 Colum. L. Rev. 689, 692 (2003). For a response directly toward Posner and Vermeule, see Roy L. Brooks, *Getting Reparations for Slavery Right—A Response to Posner and Vermeule*, 80 Notre Dame L. Rev. 251 (2004).

4. An exception is Harold Peckern's *Reparation Payments—An Exclusion Revisited*, 34 U.S.F. L.Rev. 705 (2000). In it, Professor Peckern analyzes some tax consequences relating to reparations paid to Jews by the German government for the atrocities of the Holocaust. He suggests taxation of reparations should be excluded on moral grounds. He does not examine whether tax benefits can be used as a reparations program.

5. Alfred L. Brophy, *Reconsidering Reparations*, 81 Ind. L.J. 811 (2006).
6. Roy L. Brooks, *Getting Reparations for Slavery Right—A Response to Posner and Vermeule*, 80 Notre Dame L. Rev. 251 (2004).
7. Carlton Waterhouse, *Avoiding Another Step In A Series of Unfortunate Legal Events*, 26 B.C. Third World L.J. 207, 262–65 (2006).
8. Ibid.
9. Roy L. Brooks, *Getting Reparations for Slavery Right—A Response to Posner and Vermeule*, 80 Notre Dame L. Rev. 251 (2004).
10. Alfred L. Brophy, Reparations Pro and Con (2006).
11. See Robert Wesley, *Many Billions Gone: Is it Time to Reconsider the Case for black Reparations?*, 40 B.C. L. Rev. 429 (1998); Charles J. Ogletree, Jr., *Repairing the Past: New Efforts in the Reparations Debate in America*, 38 HARV. C.R.-C.L. L. REV. 279 (2003); Randall Robinson, The Debt: What America Owes to blacks (2000).
12. Robert Wesley, *Many Billions Gone: Is it Time to Reconsider the Case for black Reparations?*, 40 B.C. L. Rev. 429 (1998).
13. Eric K. Yamamoto, Sandra Hye Yun Kim and Abigail M. Holden, *American Reparations Theory and Practice at the Crossroads*, 44 Cal. W.L. Rev. 1 (2007); Maxine Burkett, *Reconciliation and Nonrepetition: A New Paradigm for African-American Reparations*, 86 Or. L. Rev. 99 (2007).
14. Roy L. Brooks, Atonement and Forgiveness: A New Model For black Reparations (2004).
15. Id.
16. David Horowitz, Uncivil Wars: The Controversy Over Reparations For Slavery (2002). Cf. Alfred L. Brophy, *Losing the (Understanding of the Importance Of) Race: Evaluating the Significance of Race and the Utility of Reparations*, 80 Tex. L. Rev. 911 (2002).
17. Alfred L. Brophy, Reparations Pro and Con (2006).
18. Carlton Waterhouse, *Avoiding Another Step In A Series of Unfortunate Legal Events*, 26 B.C. Third World L.J. 207, 262–65 (2006).
19. The values anchoring the charters of the three trusts emanate from the African American holiday of Kwanzaa. Unity, Purpose, Collective Work and Responsibility, Cooperative Economics, Faith, Creativity, and Self Determination serve as communal values to guide trust operations. Id.
20. *Commissioner v. Glenshaw Glass Co.*, 348 U.S. 426, (1955) (holding that income includes accessions to wealth, clearly realized, over which the taxpayer has dominion and control).
21. *Heckler v. Chaney* (1986).
22. *Brown V. Board of Education*, 347 U.S. 483 (1954).
23. See Robert P. Green, Jr. Equal Protection and the African American Constitutional Experience (2000).
24. See Phillip F. Rubio, A History of Affirmative Action (2001).
25. See Nathan Hall, Hate Crimes (2005).
26. See Alfred L. Brophy, Reparations Pro and Con, 10-18 (2006) (discussing different modes of reparations).
27. *Commissioner v. Glenshaw Glass Co.*, 348 U.S. 426, (1955).
28. *Old Colony Trust Co. v. Commissioner*, 279 U.S. 716 (1929).
29. Special Field Order No. 15 (1865). Michael T. Martin and Marilyn Yaquinto, Redress for Historical Injustices in the United States, 490 (2007).
30. Our current income tax scheme was enacted in 1913 and its constitutionality approved in 1916, Brushaber v. Union Pacific Railroad Co., 240 U.S. 1 (1916). See also 157 U.S. 429 (1895) (invalidating the income tax of 1894 as against the Apportionment requirement of the U.S. Constitution). But see *Springer v. United States*, 102 U.S. 586 (1881) (permitting an income tax during the Civil War as an indirect tax which need not be apportioned).
31. U.S.C.A. Const. Amend. XVI.
32. IRC Sec. 61.
33. *Helvering v. Clifford*, 309 U.S. 331, 334 (1940).

34. *Commissioner v. Glenshaw Glass Co.*, 348 U.S. 426, (1955).
35. Nagel & Murphy, The Myth of Ownership (2002).
36. Calvin Johnson, Shelf Project.
37. *US v. Murphy*, 460 F.3d 79, 92 (D.C. Cir. 2006).
38. Antonin J. Scalia, A Matter of Interpretation (1997).
39. *US v. Murphy*, 460 F.3d 79, 92 (D.C. Cir. 2006).
40. *Burnet v. Logan*, 283 U.S. 404 (1931).
41. See, e.g., Anthony Sebok, *Two Concepts of Injustice in Restitution for Slavery*, 84 B.U. L. Rev. 1405,1432–433 (2004).
42. Eric A. Posner & Adrian Vermeule, Reparations for Slavery and Other Historical Injustices, 103 Colum. L. Rev. 689, 692 (2003); but see Roy L. Brooks, *Getting Reparations for Slavery Right—A Response to Posner and Vermeule*, 80 Notre Dame L. Rev. 251 (2004).
43. IRC Sec. 102.
44. IRC Sec. 104(a)(2).
45. IRC Sec. 104(a).
46. Joseph Bankman, *The New Market In Corporate Tax Shelters*, 83 Tax Notes 1775 (1999).
47. IRC Sec. 117.
48. See Mark R. Siegel, *The Relation-Back Doctrine: Towards a Consistent Tax Rule for Gifts by Check*, 52 Rutgers L. Rev. 185 (1999).
49. *Estate of Metzger v. Commissioner*, 100 T.C. 204 (1993), aff'd, 38 F.3d 118 (4th Cir. 1994).
50. *Heckler v. Chaney*, 470 U.S. 821(1985).
51. Rev. Rul. 65–282, 1965-2 C.B. 21.
52. 2002-18 IRB 621.
53. Dominic L. Daher, *The Proposed Federal Taxation of Frequent Flyer Miles Received from Employers: Good Tax Policy But Bad Politics*, 16 Akron Tax J. 1 (2001).
54. Stanley S. Surrey, *Tax Incentives as a Device for Implementing Government Policy: A Comparison with Direct Government Expenditures*, 83 Harv. L. Rev. 705 (1970). Stanley S. Surrey & Paul R. McDaniel, Tax Expenditures (1985).
55. Stanley S. Surrey, *Tax Incentives as a Device for Implementing Government Policy: A Comparison with Direct Government Expenditures*, 83 Harv. L. Rev. 705 (1970). Stanley S. Surrey & Paul R. McDaniel, Tax Expenditures (Cambridge, Mass., 1985).
56. Id.
57. IRC Sec. 108, IRC Sec. 1031, IRC Sec. 121.
58. Richard Wood, *Supreme Court Jurisprudence of Tax Fairness*, 36 Seton Hall L. J. 421 (2006).
59. Beverly I. Moran & William Whitford, *A black Critique of the Internal Revenue Code*, 1996 Wis. L. Rev. 751.
60. Dorothy A. Brown, *Race and Class Matters in Tax Policy*, 107 Colum. L. Rev. 790 (2007).
61. Id.
62. Tamiko Brown-Nagin, *Elites, Social Movements, and the Law: The Case of Affirmative Action*, 15 Colum. L. Rev. 1436, 1472 (2004) ("Current and future beneficiaries of affirmative action policies at selective law schools are elites, certainly when compared to the typical minority student.")
63. See *Grutter v. Bollinger*, 539 U.S. 306 (2003), Parents Involved v. Seattle School District No. 1, 127S.Ct. 2738 (2007).
64. Darren Hutchison *"Preventing Balkanization or Facilitating Racial Domination"*; Juan F. Perea, *"Doctrines of Delusion: Bakke, Fisher and the Case for a New Affirmative Action"*, http://papers.ssrn.com/sol3/papers.cfm?abstract_id=2312630.
65. The first chapter of this work was designed to aid that effort.
66. See e.g., Dorothy A. Brown, *Race, Class, and Gender Essentialism in Tax Literature: The Joint Return*, 54 Wash. & Lee L. Rev. 1469 (1997). See also Richard Delgado and Jean Stefancic, Critical Race Theory (2001).

67. Maureen B. Cavanaugh, *On the Road to Incoherence: Congress, Economics and Taxes*, 49 UCLA L. Rev. 685 (2002).

68. E. Franklin Frazier, black Bourgeoisie (1997).

69. Dorothy A. Brown, *Race and Class Matters in Tax Policy*, 107 Colum. L. Rev. 790 (2007).

70. Ibid.

71. Andre L. Smith, *The IRS Don't Care About Poor black People*, in Katrina: America's Unnatural Disaster (2008).

72. IRC Sec. 501.

73. IRC Sec. 170.

74. IRC Sec. 501(c)(3).

75. The NAACP's tax exempt status was recently subject to a challenge. See Kara Backus, *All Saints Church and the Argument for a Goal-Driven Application of Internal Revenue Service Rules for Tax- Exempt Organizations*, 17 S. Cal. Interdisc. L.J. 301, 302 (2008).

76. David A. Brennen, *Race and Equality Across the Law School Curriculum: The Law of Tax Exemption*,54 J. Legal Educ. 336 (2004).

77. Carlton Waterhouse, *Avoiding Another Step In A Series of Unfortunate Legal Events*, 26 B.C. ThirdWorld L.J. 207, 262–65 (2006).

78. David A. Brennen, *A Diversity Theory of Charitable Tax Exemption—Beyond Efficiency, ThroughCritical Race Theory, Toward Diversity*, 4 Pitt. Tax Rev. 1, 26 (2006).

79. Ibid.

80. Ibid.

81. *Bob Jones Univ. v. United States*, 461 U.S. 574 (1983).

82. David A. Brennen, *Race and Equality Across the Law School Curriculum: The Law of Tax Exemption*, 54 J. Legal Educ. 336, 341–50 (2004).

83. Preamble to the United States Constitution.

84. David A. Brennen, *Race and Equality Across the Law School Curriculum: The Law of Tax Exemption*, 54 J. Legal Educ. 336, 340–51 (2004).

85. http://www.usdoj.gov/olc/2007/worldvision.pdf.

86. Darryl K. Jones et al., The Tax Law of Charities and Other Exempt Organizations: Cases, Materials, Questions and Activities (St. Paul, 2003).

87. David A. Brennen, *Race and Equality Across the Law School Curriculum: The Law of Tax Exemption*, 54 J. Legal Educ. 336 (2004).

FIVE

Taxes and the Demise of white Supremacy (1900–2015)

The year 1900 probably represents the apogee of indiscreet, express white supremacy in the United States and around the world. By this time, Europe and the United States had colonized the rest of the globe.[1] In the United States, specifically, whites enjoyed social, political and economic superiority over non-whites, including the imposition of a nearly 100 percent tax on black labor. Racially discriminatory poll taxes were an important part of preventing blacks from repealing the peonage tax, specifically, and the Jim Crow-apartheid system, generally.

But 1900 also marks the beginning of the demise of white supremacy, across the globe and in the United States. Intra-group competition and numerous outright wars between whites ensured that global white supremacy would not be absolute, even at its height. When they weren't openly rebelling and resisting, non-white nations in the twentieth century carefully negotiated between competing European forces. The concept of whiteness itself began to fray, fracture and fall apart. Early twentieth-century eugenists tried to restrict "whiteness" to the northwestern portions of Europe. The concept of Aryanism was growing and further distinguished between peoples understood up until that time to be "white." The 1924 Anti-Immigration Act sought to restrict social, political and economic control only to those of the purer white stock, by excluding those from many Southern and Eastern European countries, as well as Middle Easterners and other Asians. It was expressly designed to "preserve the ideal of American homogeneity" (i.e., white supremacy).

Eventually, World Wars I and II along with the Cold War loosened the grip Europeans had on the rest of the world. It would take considerable time for the demise of white supremacy to be felt or observed, however. But twentieth-century national independence movements across the globe and the civil rights and black power movements here in the United States exemplified the decline of white supremacy.

In 1900, however, whites in the south (however constructed) were in full control of private and public institutions and sought to maintain their socio-economic-political position by implementing an apartheid system in the United States, called "Jim Crow." More than 250 blacks were lynched during the year 1892, dispelling any doubt about the failed state of Reconstruction and the intent of whites to reenslave blacks in the South. After *Plessy v. Ferguson* in 1896, whites understood that government resources could be enlisted toward maintaining white supremacy so long as it was done without stating its intended purpose. Thereafter, whites devised ways to maintain racial subordination without expressing that purpose in those laws supporting the convict leasing-sharecropping system.

During Jim Crow apartheid, the nearly 100 percent tax on black labor was supported by four political tactics: 1) convict slavery, 2) the denial of public education and market exclusion, 3) voter disenfranchisement via poll taxes, and 4) the discriminatory disbursement of tax revenue. Each of these tactics was stated in neutral terms and justified on neutral grounds, while the clear, unstated purpose was to maintain white socio-political-economic supremacy.

First, the convict slavery system intimidated blacks into accepting the nearly 100 percent tax that came along with sharecropping. The brutality of convict slavery not only dealt with blacks who did not comply with the system, it also kept peonage sharecroppers from complaining about their conditions, because they knew to complain would likely mean being charged with and convicted of an illusory crime. This meant that landowners did not have to pay their black sharecroppers.[2] Second, denying public education to blacks and excluding them from markets outside of farming prevented blacks from escaping neo-slavery. Per pupil spending on black children plummeted, as states granted counties the authority to distribute funding for schools as they chose. By 1910, black children in the South attended school for about half the time required of white children, and almost 70 percent of white children attended school, while only 37 percent of black children were afforded the opportunity.[3]

Third, blacks were disenfranchised from voting so that they could not repeal laws that excluded them from lucrative markets, that denied them public education, nor could they repeal the laws designed to criminalize almost every aspect of their private lives. During Reconstruction, blacks in the South exercised their voting privileges and enjoyed some of the respect that accompanies political power. But by 1900, the southern judicial system had been reconscripted toward white supremacy. And by 1901, blacks had been almost entirely disenfranchised in every southern state. Nor could blacks serve on juries, hold state or local office, and predictably there were hardly any black sheriffs or police officers.[4]

Lastly, *Plessy v. Ferguson* gave whites the space to spend tax revenue on anti-poverty programs designed strictly for poor whites[5]:

> By World War II, millions of white southerners had been raised from profound poverty, illiteracy, and ignorance to at least modest middle-class status. Free public schools, consistent medical care, passable roads, clean tap water, electricity, even the concept of regular hourly wage work . . . were promulgated upon millions of the most dispossessed of Americans with a speed and efficacy that in hindsight made the Great Society initiatives of the 1960s appear timid and indolent.[6]

REPEALING THE 100 PERCENT TAX ON BLACK LABOR

The 100 percent tax on black labor via the convict-leasing/sharecropping system could not have been maintained without complicity from the federal government. For decades, the Justice Department had received numerous complaints and petitions to investigate, from both private individuals and a concerned public official or two. In 1941, President Franklin Delano Roosevelt acknowledged there had been a policy of ignoring such complaints: "Five days after [the attack on Pearl Harbor, Roosevelt's administration] issued a directive . . . to all federal prosecutors acknowledging the log history of the unwritten federal enforcement policy to ignore most reports of involuntary servitude."[7] Even then, not everyone in the federal government was enthusiastic, perhaps least of all, FBI director J. Edgar Hoover, who did not see a need to change policy. The 100 percent tax on black labor finally ended after World War II, thanks to Justice Department prosecutions and new, more stringent laws against peonage.

As far back as 1899, there had been sporadic yet unsuccessful attempts by individual federal prosecutors to stop the 100 percent tax on black labor. Until the 1940s, they all encountered similar problems: identifying what if any law actually outlawed slavery via convict leasing and slave labor sharecropping contracts, getting witnesses to come forward and protecting them, and combating white public scrutiny and complicity in the system. "A few southerners stepped forward to genuinely condemn the new slavery system—but very few."[8]

Even when prosecutions occurred and were carried out to conviction, the end result was always a slap on the wrist. In Georgia, John Pace was tried for holding scores of black workers on his farms as slaves. At first, Pace was convicted and sentenced to five years in the federal penitentiary, but remained free on bond during his appeal, which he won. Pace ultimately pled guilty to a lesser charge and paid a $1,000 fine. In 1906, President Theodore Roosevelt pardoned John Pace for his crimes. "In 1909, an internal review of all peonage prosecutions in Alabama in the first decade of the century found that of forty-three indictments issued—including those of Pace and his co-conspirators, all ended in acquittals, dismissals, suspended sentences, or presidential pardons. A total of $300 in fines had been collected from the defendants; four of those convicted served short periods in jail."[9]

Emboldened by the fact that there would be no consequences even if convicted, the neo-slave system reached new heights (depths?). Unsuccessful federal interventions amounted to a license to continue. Others like Pace, who were prosecuted and pled guilty, were ordered to pay fines, which they ignored. In fact, the only person to serve jail time for neo-slavery "was a black man named George Hart. For his role in selling a teenage girl to Frank McRee for $25, Hart spent thirty days in jail." As for John Pace, he won a new contract from Tallapoosa County to lease all of that county's convicts.[10]

When a federal district court judge attempted to dismantle the convict slave system, which supported the private slave market, the Supreme Court continued to charade their concern for "equality" and equal protection of the laws by upholding the validity of federal anti-peonage statutes in 1904, while at the same time holding that federal courts had no jurisdiction to dismantle Georgia's convict slavery system which sold prisoners into peonage in 1905. Moreover, the attorney general of the United States refused to seek habeas corpus for the prisoners. "The Supreme Court's renunciation of Speer's attempt to outlaw the misdemeanor convict leasing system was so complete that the opinion was not even written, but issued summarily and orally. . . . The old southern window dressing of legal rights for African Americans won the day again."[11]

Only the most egregious cases of peonage were ever prosecuted. For example, in 1920, "A total of eleven African Americans were murdered to conceal slavery on the Williams farm."[12] As it turns out, Williams was THE only white man found guilty of murdering a black man in the state of Georgia from 1877 to 1966.

There was little incentive to stop it, because whites on the tertiary of the system got paid . . . well. Sheriffs willing to "capture" poor blacks and sell them to local employers could make $20,000 to $30,000 a year, in the 1920s! Even as late as 1941, "Charles E. Bledsoe pleaded guilty in the federal court in Mobile, Alabama, to a charge of peonage for holding a black man named Martin Thompson against his will. Using the same technique as John Pace in 1903, Bledsoe didn't resist the charge and trusted that federal officials and the US District court judge would not deal harshly with a white man holding slaves. He was correct. Bledsoe's punishment was a fine of $100 and six months' probation."[13]

Finally, the Department of Justice prosecuted the US Sugar Company for enslaving black men in the sugarcane fields of Florida, as well as some of the county sheriffs who sold them. The defendants were found guilty of the pre-Civil War Slavery Kidnapping Act and sentenced to federal prison. The 100 percent tax on black labor was finally and officially repealed in 1948, when the U.S. Code was amended, and in 1951 Congress passed a federal statute criminalizing slavery in almost any form (except in respect of the "duly convicted").

The fact that the blacks were leaving the South in droves may have influenced the federal government's willingness to finally end the 100 percent tax on black labor. In the 1940s and 1950s, blacks from the Mississippi Valley migrated in huge numbers to Chicago and the north-midwest, as well as to California on other points west. Many black men in the South found the army a much better alternative than slavery and abject subjugation in the South, and when World War II ended, some blacks soldiers stayed in Europe rather than return to apartheid. Thus, Derrick Bell's interest convergence theory helps explain why the 100 percent tax on black labor effectively ended during World War II—to prevent enemies of the United States from using slavery as a tool of propaganda.[14]

Neo-slavery, Jim Crow, and American apartheid demonstrated to the rest of the world that the United States was not the meritocracy it claimed to be. "President Franklin D. Roosevelt instinctively knew the second class citizenship and violence imposed upon African Americans would be exploited by the enemies of the United States."[15] Like Lord Dunmore before, communist countries and other foes of the United States used racism as a wedge between Americans. The civil rights movement, culminating in the Civil Rights Act and the Voting Rights Act, reflect a successful national response to this threat.

THE CIVIL RIGHTS MOVEMENT AND POLL TAXES

The 100 percent tax on black labor and Jim Crow apartheid probably could not have existed without another tax, the poll tax. Since blacks in the South represented an overwhelming majority in some cases, maintaining the 100 percent tax on black labor or neo-slavery (as well as any other form of institutionalized group subjugation) could only continue if blacks were disenfranchised. And if poor whites noticed that black slave labor had the effect of depressing their own wages, well, poll taxes were originally designed to disenfranchise them too.[16]

Many southern blacks at the turn of the century were very proud they had gone from slavery to something looking like full citizenship. They had earned the right to vote and tried to participate in public life. In 1885, an incredible 98 percent of African Americans voted. But after Southern legislatures introduced all types of newly conceived poll taxes and other prerequisites to voting, the percentage of blacks who voted in 1905 fell to a paltry 10 percent. With this electorate, it cannot be surprising that slavery and the 100 percent tax on black labor continued into the 1940s.

In Alabama, black voting fell to less than 2 percent. After Virginia imposed its poll tax in 1903, black voter participation fell to 15 percent, while it remained almost 80 percent for whites. Other restrictions included requirements that one own real property, or hold more than, say, $300 of personal property, or read and write to the satisfaction of the board of elections, or be regularly employed.

Actually, poll taxes were not invented to disenfranchise blacks in the South. They have a longer history. Earlier, in the eighteenth and nineteenth century, poll taxes disenfranchising poor whites were the norm. It was generally asserted that only wealthy whites had sufficient interest in community affairs to be trusted with the franchise. Of course, this was not true even then—Robin Einhorn demonstrates that poor whites and wealthy slaveholders very well knew when their interests diverged, like with the taxation of slavery, and fought each other vigorously in state and county legislatures. The original, eighteenth-century reason for poll taxes as well as state tax uniformity clauses was to prevent poor whites from taxing slavery out of business.

But in the twentieth century, post-Reconstruction whites in the South, poor and wealthy, propertied and nonpropertied, banded together politically in order to maintain social and economic supremacy.[17] "Grandfather clauses" prevented these new Jim Crow poll taxes from disenfranchising millions of illiterate poor whites in the South. Poor whites were allowed to vote simply if their grandfather was able to vote. Veterans were also exempted, although black veterans were typically not acknowledged as such.

Jim Crow poll taxes disenfranchised even those blacks who had some savings and who would have spent a portion of it on the right to vote but for confusing or compounding regulations. Atiba Ellis exposes the more subtle, discouraging features of southern poll taxes.[18] The poll tax, for one, was not a mandatory tax and there was no one in government who had an interest in informing blacks when, where and how to pay it. In addition, the process for paying the tax was exceedingly burdensome for most, since the majority of blacks at the time could neither read nor write, and since literate blacks were routinely discouraged and often openly prevented from participating in public life. The tax was also cumulative. You also had to pay taxes for one to three years in order to vote in the election for which they were trying to register. The tax had to be paid by a deadline. And last, a black person had to hope that after paying the tax, getting a receipt, and delivering it to the proper official, that that official or some group of white citizens wouldn't refuse them the right to vote anyway.

The Supreme Court first upheld poll taxes in *Williams v. Mississippi* (1898),[19] two years after *Plessy v. Ferguson*. In *Williams*, the court held that the Mississippi poll tax statutes "do not on their face discriminate between the races, and it has not been shown that their actual administration was evil, only that evil was possible under them." The same court that totally ignored the inequality of separate provisions for blacks in *Plessy* similarly ignored in *Williams v. Mississippi* any proof that actual evil was intended and in fact being done pursuant to the Mississippi statute. Plessy was overturned in 1955, by *Brown v. Board of Education*. But it took another decade for the court to reverse *Williams* in *Harper v. Virginia*, 383 US 663 (1966).[20]

Forty years after Williams, the court in *Breedlove v. Suttles* (1937)[21] rejected a challenge to Georgia's poll tax filed by a white man who argued that poll taxes on the poor violated his right to equal protection and an unconstitutionally abridged his privileges and immunities. And in 1951, the court in *Butler v. Thompson* (1951) rejected a challenge to Virginia poll's tax even though the black complainant demonstrated that members of the Virginia Constitutional Convention who sponsored and enacted the statute intended specifically to disenfranchise blacks. The Butler court stated, "It is well settled that a law that is fair on its face and is also fairly administered is not rendered invalid by the evil motives of its draftsmen."[22] "Fair" in this sense could only mean skin complexion.

As mentioned before, World War II and the burgeoning Cold War dramatically changed world politics. Blatant racism and racists, nationally and globally, were vulnerable. Anti-colonization and anti-apartheid movements gained momentum across the world. In America, the United States could not maintain Jim Crow and present itself to the world as the bastion of meritocracy, all at the same time. Consequently, the civil rights movement took hold, most notably evidenced by *Brown v. Board of Education* (1955), which rejected *Plessy's* separate but equal doctrine, the crux of Jim Crow apartheid. While the promise of desegregated schools has not been achieved, *Brown* at least marks the point when express advocacy for white supremacy became not just legally, but socially taboo or "politically incorrect." Martin Luther King Jr., Rosa Parks and the Montgomery Bus Boycott, Malcolm X, the black Panthers, and the March on Washington all became iconic symbols of the American progress. The attack on racist taxation was but a small yet important part of the story.

In 1964, the people of the United States enacted the Twenty-fourth Amendment to the United States Constitution abolishing the poll tax in all federal elections. Indeed, the Twenty-fourth Amendment against poll taxes is the only constitutional amendment obtained by the civil rights movement. Yet poll taxes in federal elections had not been the means for disenfranchising blacks in the South. State and county poll taxes were. Thus, the poll tax was not really abolished until 1966, by the case of *Harper v. Virginia*, in which Justice Douglass wrote for a unanimous court that "wealth, like race, creed, or color is not germane to one's ability to participate intelligently in the electoral process. Lines drawn on the basis of wealth or property, like those of race are traditionally disfavored."[23]

The state of Virginia argued that the poll tax was a minor, legitimate requirement because "groups least able to pay are also the ones least interested in voting." The court finally rejected this specious argument that somehow held sway for years, holding that "Wealth or fee paying has, in our view, no relation to voting qualifications."[24] Thus ended poll taxes in the United States—unless of course the cost of obtaining photo identification is a poll tax.

The Twenty-fourth Amendment along with *Harper v. Virginia*, represents the height of the civil rights movement. Whatever date one could choose for the beginning of the civil rights movement—Jackie Robinson's integration of Major League Baseball in 1947, or perhaps as far back as the less remembered Houston jitney cab boycotts of the 1930s—it was in full swing by 1964 when the Twenty-fourth Amendment was enacted. The Civil Rights Act of 1964 and the Voting Rights Act of 1965 follow. And in 1966, *Harper v. Virginia* was decided. The country pushed forward, as the 1970s represented a decade of changing order. But by 1980, there emerged new, less overt strategies to maintain white male supremacy. Legal and social prohibitions against out and out racists and overt discrimination gained momentum, but the nation had not addressed the massive inequality in wealth that engendered from over two centuries of redistribution and market exclusion through slavery and apartheid, and attempts to specifically address racial economic disparities would be attacked under the banner of "color-blindedness" and "post-racialism." Ironically, neo-liberals use the remaining out and out racists to excuse the bulk of white folks, who because they pretend to ignore race are allowed also to ignore the fact that many of their economic privileges emanate from slavery and apartheid . . . you know, the good ol' days.

RETRENCHMENT AND THE SEEDS OF POST-RACIALISM

Together, two tax cases in the early 1980s, *Bob Jones University v. U.S.*, and *Allen v. Wright*, demonstrate the Supreme Court's 'modern' attitude on race, disapproval of outward expressions of white supremacy combined with ambivalence toward the institutional maintenance of black subordination. *Bob Jones* stands for the proposition that the executive branch may not interpret federal tax laws in a manner that promotes or maintains racial subordination, but counter-productively, *Allen v. Wright* stands for the proposition that aggrieved citizens have no standing to compel a presidential administration or executive agency to actually enforce the *Bob Jones* standard. Furthermore, a nontax case, *Heckler v. Chaney* (1985), adds that even if black folks had standing, the judiciary is presumptively prohibited from compelling the executive to enforce the *Bob Jones* standard.

In *Bob Jones University v. United States* (1983), the court upheld the Internal Revenue Service's determination that a "charitable" organization pursuant to section 501(c)(3) of the Internal Revenue Code does not include a private institution that discriminates amongst its students on the basis of race. Bob Jones University and literally thousands of private southern schools were thusly ineligible for tax exemption and donations to it became nondeductible. The court could have been mild and relied on its longstanding practice of deferring to the Treasury's formal interpretations of law in the realm of taxation and held that it was permissible for the Treasury to assume that Congress did not intend for its tax subsidies to support white supremacist institutions. They did not. Instead, the court held that all three branches of government had a compelling interest in combating racism. While the court acknowledged the presence of a vocal and committed minority in Congress who were outwardly supportive of racial subordination, it nevertheless attributed to Congress as a whole an intention that its legislation not be enforced or implemented in ways that maintain, promote or exacerbate racial subordination.[25]

Bob Jones is a phenomenally underappreciated case. Hailed by civil rights activists as an important victory when it was decided, its rhetorical disavowal of institutionalized white supremacy goes well beyond even *Brown v. Board of Education.*[26] But since then, critical race theorists have barely cited to *Bob Jones University v. United States* in support of the notion that the judiciary must consider the racial impacts of federal legislation.

However, the conservative backlash against so-called "judicial activism" took flight after *Bob Jones*. One year after *Bob Jones*, the Supreme Court admonished and stripped itself of its theretofore longstanding role as primary interpreter of federal statutes, in *Chevron v. NRDC* (1984).[27] President Ronald Reagan elevated the lone dissenter in *Bob Jones* to rank of chief judge. And the court has since been packed with conservative justices who openly tout their disdain for so-called judicial activism, who have led the court's post-Reconstruction-style abdication of affirmative action, and who inanely claim that neutrally worded laws are the antidote to racial discrimination, as if hundreds of years of history has not already proven that such demonstrably false claims are typically deployed in service of white socio-political-economic supremacy.

By the mid-1960s, the civil rights movement was turning the tide against white supremacy. Despite the abolition of racist poll taxes, concerns over taxation remained an integral part of the civil rights movement because whites seeking to avoid the integration of public schools mandated by *Brown v. Board of Education* began enrolling their children in racially segregated private schools. In response to Title VI of the Civil Rights Act, which forbids racial discrimination and segregation in schools that received federal funds waves of racially segregated private schools were created to serve the purpose of "white flight":

> In some communities, the white student body moved en masse to a new private school, taking the indicia of the old schools, such as the school colors, symbols, and mascots. Pledging massive resistance, many Southern state governments encouraged establishment of private schools, enacting legislation mandating or allowing the closing of pub-

> lic schools to resist desegregation or providing state tax credits and tuition grants to students attending private schools.[28]

Hundreds of segregated private schools opened after the passage of Title VI, including more than 150 by the various southern "white citizen's councils." Some schools attached themselves to religious organizations and believed their racial views were protected by First Amendment protections on the freedom of association and freedom of religion. In 1967, the IRS general counsel's office under President Lyndon Johnson provided informal guidance to revenue agents *not* to revoke the tax exemption of racially discriminatory private schools unless they received state aid. In order for the IRS to revoke a school's tax exemption, the general counsel's office believed they must first find some "state action." Under this ruling, the proliferation of segregated private schools expanded.[29]

In 1969, black parents in Mississippi represented by the Lawyers Committee for Civil Rights challenged 1) that state's tuition grants which allowed white children to attend racially segregated private schools and 2) the IRS's policy of granting federal tax exemptions to those schools. First, the district court in *Green v. Kennedy* held that the Mississippi state tuition grant program was unconstitutional, but that the IRS tax exemption policy was permissible because there had been no state action. A three judge panel reversed the initial decision with respect to the IRS policy, holding that tax exemptions for racially discriminatory schools were unlawful. The court granted a preliminary injunction preventing the IRS from granting tax exemptions for racially discriminatory private schools in Mississippi. But this ruling did not apply nationally.[30]

Then, in 1970, the IRS under the Nixon administration changed course, issuing a press release declaring that it would deny tax exempt status for these new waves of private schools if they were racially discriminatory in their admissions. Furthermore, the IRS held that in order to get federal tax exemption private schools had to publish a nondiscrimination policy. In 1971, the court in *Green v. Connally*[31] permanently enjoined the IRS from granting tax exempt status to racially discriminatory schools in Mississippi, holding that it was against public policy to interpret the statutory term "charitable" to include segregated schools. The Supreme Court affirmed the injunction relating to Mississippi without opinion in *Coit v. Green* (1971).[32]

In successive years, the IRS steadily raised the standard for what was considered discriminatory. They adopted the language and rationale of Judge Leventhal's opinion in Green, declaring that charitable organizations could not operate contrary to public policy. Then, in 1972, they issued guidance for schools seeking to adequately publicize their nondiscrimination policy.

The IRS understood that schools would announce nondiscriminatory policies at the same time they were still segregating in admissions or otherwise. So, in 1975, under the Ford administration, the IRS ruled that for a private school, including religious ones, to be considered a racially nondiscriminatory school, a school must "include a nondiscriminatory policy in its charter, brochures, and catalogues; publicize its policy by public notice broadly to the community; maintain racially nondiscriminatory policies with respect to employing staff; operate all scholarship and loans on a racially nondiscriminatory basis; and keep data on the racial composition of its student body, faculty, administrative staff, and the scholarships and loans awarded."[33] Thereafter, President Carter's IRS proposed a regulation requiring schools with a minority population less than 20 percent to rebut the presumption that they were racially discriminatory.

A strong backlash emerged from segregationists like Strom Thurmond. Southern congressmen, under the leadership of Trent Lott and others, raised the issue of religious schools and the First Amendment. They argued that southern denominations had few black members and, therefore, would be unfairly considered presumptively discriminatory. Senator Robert Byrd, chairman of the Subcommittee on Taxation and Debt Management, and former member of the Klu Klux Klan, accused the IRS of implementing a quota system. The House voted in favor of preventing the IRS from using funds to enforce these proposed regulations, but the Senate rejected that plan.[34]

On the other hand, the NAACP Legal Defense Fund argued for an even more stringent standard.

Segregationists in Congress continued attempts to thwart the IRS policy, but failed. Some of those bills would have required the IRS to seek a judicial finding that a school was racially discriminatory before revoking a schools tax exemption. The number of these failed bills waned each year after 1971, and most did not even challenge the court holding that racial discrimination in the private sphere was against public policy. Instead, they criticized the IRS ability to "easily" determine that a school was racist.[35]

But segregationists were fighting against a strong tide in the 1970s. Congress enacted a law in 1976 that prohibited the IRS from granting tax exemptions to private, social clubs. They reversed a district court ruling a year earlier that racially discriminatory private clubs indeed qualified for federal tax exemption—essentially the opposite of *Green*. And in the ten years between 1967 when the Johnson administration believed it had no basis for revoking tax exemptions from racist private schools and 1976 when Congress reversed a district court holding the same, clearly a national policy had emerged that overt racial discrimination in any public setting was strictly verboten.[36]

Grasping for straws, Bob Jones University and the Goldsboro Baptist Church wanted to carve out an exception to the IRS policy for private, religious schools. Goldsboro maintained that "God separated mankind into various nations and races." Its admissions policies, however, only discriminated against blacks. At first, Bob Jones University discriminated against blacks in admissions. But later, they limited their racial segregation to a prohibition against interracial dating. The IRS revoked Bob Jones University's tax exempt status in 1975, but made it retroactive back to 1970. If the IRS was successful, Bob Jones would have to pay close to half a million dollars in income taxes, as well as interest and penalties and delinquent employment taxes.[37]

District courts split on the issue. The district court in the Goldsboro case held that the denial of tax exemption to a racially discriminatory school was neither an improper reading of the statute nor did it offend the Constitution's guarantee of religious freedom. Conversely, the district court in *Bob Jones* held that the IRS violated the First Amendment when it denied tax exemption to Bob Jones. But, on appeal, the Fourth Circuit reversed the district court and upheld the IRS' revocation of Bob Jones' tax exemption. They held that "the government interest in eradicating discrimination was sufficiently compelling to justify any burden" on the religious freedoms of Bob Jones University.[38] After all, tax exemption is a governmental subsidy without which a religious order is still perfectly free to operate.

By the time the case of *Bob Jones* reached the Supreme Court, the civil rights era fervor against racial discrimination had ebbed. Economic crises in the late 1970s brought forth a new (or old) conservative attitude. According to Olati Johnson and others, "The country had moved to the right."[39] Even though most white citizens agreed that racial discrimination was wrong and against public policy, many began to chafe at losing the privileges that had inured to them under American apartheid. Racial integration was a laudable ideal to most, but many whites rejected the personal cost of having either their children "bussed" to minority schools, or minority schools being "bussed" to schools in predominately white neighborhoods. Equal opportunity in employment became a national norm, except that many whites rejected the government taking affirmative action toward leveling the playing field. It was one thing to forbid discrimination in public settings, but it was quite another for the government to make it more costly for whites to privately disassociate from black people.

Ronald Reagan was elected president in 1980 in a landslide, and support for Bob Jones University was part of his campaign platform. Early in his first term, while the case of Bob Jones was before the Supreme Court, Reagan reversed the IRS's nondiscrimination policy with respect to all private schools. In 1982, the IRS released a statement declaring that they would not use "public policy" to revoke the tax exempt status of otherwise charitable organizations. Also, conservative members of Congress attached a rider to an appropriations bill preventing the IRS from using specific funds for investigations of private church related schools unless they were initiated prior to the 1978 rule changes. Reagan, Trent Lott, and others reframed busing, tax exemption denials, affirmative action and other strategies for combating racial oppression from an attack on racial subordination to impermissible and unconstitutional judicial activism and executive overreaching. They questioned whether the judiciary or the executive had the constitutional capacity to determine the existence and content of "public policy."[40]

In a move that was either abjectly strange or wisely politically calculated, Reagan declared that separation of powers was the damning issue and revoked the IRS nondiscrimination policy, but then he sponsored legislation prohibiting tax exemption for racially segregated private schools to prove his commitment to civil rights. Many conservatives thought Reagan had capitulated, while civil rights activists believed he designed his proposed legislation to weaken the IRS' standards. What he did was implement a new rhetorical strategy, to invoke grand principles like democracy or equal opportunity to reject civil rights remedies. At the same time Reagan claimed to endorse civil rights, he could scuttle any executive remedies that were not specifically mandated by Congress in the name of democracy. This rhetorical two-step is the hallmark of post-racialism today.

Civil rights groups cried foul at the Reagan administrations turnabout. "[E]mployees of the Justice Department's Civil Rights Division, including half of its attorneys, sent . . . a letter protesting the change in policy." Veteran Deputy Solicitor General Lawrence Wallace was taken off the case, and the administration began to argue that the case was moot since the IRS changed its policy and intended to restore the tax exemption for both Goldsboro and Bob Jones University.[41]

Even though Reagan revoked the nondiscrimination policy, the Supreme Court declined to moot the *Goldsboro* and *Bob Jones* cases because several church related schools had been refusing to cooperate with IRS' investigation into their racial practices, citing religious freedom. At the suggestion of Thurgood Marshall, the court appointed William Coleman, the first black member of the *Harvard Law Review*, first black Supreme Court clerk, and a chairman of the NAACP Legal Defense Fund, to represent the IRS. Numerous other amici briefs were filed, with an appreciable but not overwhelming majority on the side of the IRS.[42]

The court held 8–1 in favor of the IRS's nondiscriminatory policy. Chief Justice Burger wrote that the purpose of statute was to subsidize only those things that provide a "public benefit," and that modern standards of public policy trumped what was previously understood as charitable by either the 1894 Congress or 1917 Congress who enacted the tax exemption statutes. In particular, the court cited the 1976 federal law prohibiting tax exemption for racist social clubs, and other executive actions to demonstrate that there was now an overarching and compelling public policy against racial subordination. The court also noted that since the IRS changed policies in 1970 Congress never came close to overturning it. In addition, repeated attempts to weaken the rule or oppose certain features of the regulations typically failed to succeed past the committee process.[43]

Moreover, the court noted that when Congress prohibited tax exemptions for racially segregated social clubs in 1976, the legislative history supporting that enactment showed how Congress had accepted to the IRS's determination that racially segregated private schools do not provide a public benefit and thus do not qualify for federal tax exemption. In his concurring opinion, Justice Powell agreed that the amount of public and legislative attention relating to the IRS' policy provided "an unusually strong case of legislative acquiescence in and ratification by implication." According to Professor Olati Johnson, Burger's first draft was even more strident, stating, "over the past quarter of a century, 'every pronouncement of this court, myriad Acts of Congress and Executive Orders attest a firm national policy to prohibit racial segregation and discrimination in public education."[44]

Dissenting, Justice Rhenquist argued that the plain meaning of the word charitable included no exceptions for public policy. He noted that Congress had amended the statute several times since its enactment and could have added a public policy requirement if it chose. The court had to choose which "Congress" was most relevant to the "plain meaning" analysis—the 1894 Congress? 1917? 1954? 1976? 1983? The majority favored the current one, while Rhenquist relied on the one from America's apartheid era. From this point forward, legal scholars and theorists would debate originalism versus modern dynamics, with the neo-originalists winning a majority of the court's seats at present. In fact, Reagan appointed Rhenquist as chief judge soon thereafter, and it is no mere coincidence that after the Bob Jones decision, conservatives coalesced around a technique of statutory interpretation called the "plain meaning rule" that was intended to certify and cement the understanding of legislatures from "back in the day," rather than the understandings of a recent or current legislature. Justice Scalia, famous for his advocacy for the plain meaning rule, was appointed to the court. Justice Thomas, an even stricter textualist than Scalia, followed.

On one hand, *Bob Jones* is a remarkable decision that does not get nearly the attention it deserves from Supreme Court commentators, critical race theorists or otherwise. The court in *Bob Jones* held that Congress rejects white supremacy: "Government has a fundamental, overriding interest in eradicating racial discrimination in education—discrimiantion that prevailed, with official approval, for the first 1765 years of this Nation's constitutional history." This is only slightly more than 100 years after it declared in *Dred Scott* that white supremacy was the official, Constitutional, political, social, economic order of the United States. According to Yale law professor, Judith Resnick, *Bob Jones* "is a cram down of a national norm" against "an overtly racist educational environment."[45]

On the other hand, the court had previously ignored the racial impacts relating to the inequitable distribution of property tax revenue toward educational funding based on class in San *Antonio v. Rodriguez* (1971)[46] and the racial impact relating to tax deductions for private school tuition in *Mueller v. Allen* (1983),[47] respectfully. Through *Rodriguez* and *Mueller*, the savvy segregationist already had a blueprint for disassociating with blacks and perpetuating their economic and social subordination. Robert Cover criticized the *Mueller* court, arguing,

> It is a pious fraud to say that there is a commitment in America to combat racial discrimiantion in education while the courts open the way to such dramatic subsidization of white flight. The court that protects the sanctuaries of white flight and the administration that panders to it are more responsible for the patterns of segregation and inequality in education than are the misguided fundamentalist of Bob Jones.[48]

What has since become apparent is that the court intends to sanction only the unsophisticated and belligerent racist who materially impairs the perception of American meritocracy.

Even with the authority to revoke tax exemptions from racist private schools, Reagan's IRS was not actually enforcing these standards, just giving them political lip service. In 1976, the Lawyers Committee sought to reopen the *Green* case to force the IRS to actually revoke tax exemptions from Mississippi schools. That same year, black parents filed a national class action suit, alleging the same thing, that the IRS was not enforcing the law against the subsidization of racist private schools. This suit eventually became *Allen v. Wright*, it was decided one year after *Bob Jones*, and it stripped Bob Jones of much of its vitality.[49]

In *Allen v. Wright* (1984), the court held that black citizens have no standing to compel the Treasury to actually take action and revoke the tax exemption for racists. The court held that black parents could not demonstrate that white flight would cease if the tax exemptions were revoked. The court did not believe revocation of tax exemptions would stop white people from abandoning integrated public schools. Out of whole cloth, the court announced for the first time the "redressibility" doctrine, by which they could in the future foreclose the type of successes garnered by black parents in Mississippi and the Lawyers Committee on Civil Rights in *Green v. Connally* and *Coit v. Green*.

Buttressing *Allen v. Wright*, the court, a year later, in *Heckler v. Chaney* (1985), a nontax case, held that even if they had standing, black parents cannot force the President or his agents to enforce the *Bob Jones* standard.[50] The court held that "prosecutorial discretion" is a core executive function which the courts are generally not able to review. This means that the IRS decision whether or not to revoke the subsidy for any particular racist institution is outside the purview of the Supreme Court. Now, prosecutorial discretion does not shield the executive from discriminating on the basis of race, *Webster v. Doe*.[51] But unless the executive openly states, discloses, reveals or admits to discrimination, the administration is well protected against claims of recism, especially since it is unclear what level of disparate impact, if any, would support judicial oversight of enforcement decisions and consequent rebuke.

Bob Jones University v. United States, *Allen v. Wright*, along with *Heckler v. Chaney*, perfectly reflect the court's version of twenty-first-century post-racialism, which allows the pretext of racial equality to be undermined by actual practice. Ultimately, the court allows the Executive almost complete discretion to subsidize racist institutions through the tax code, because blacks and other concerned citizens cannot force the courts to intervene if and when an administration drops the ball. So long as the President and his officials are not daft enough to announce racial subordination as their intended goal, the court will allow it to cause that effect.

Granting even more authority to the President, the court in *Chevron v. NRDC* (1984) restricted the judiciary's power to resolve legal questions, like whether "charity" includes racist private schools. The *Chevron* doctrine allows each presidential administration to determine for itself whether "charitable organization" includes racist schools. And since the *Bob Jones* court did not expressly state that their holding flowed from the plain meaning of the term "charity," the case of *National Cable & Telecommunications Association et al., v. Brand X* (2005) allows the IRS to reverse the *Bob Jones* holding anyway.[52]

CONCLUSION

A tax history of racism shows that because whites have deployed both openly discriminatory and neutrally worded taxes toward institutionalizing economic, political and social supremacy, and because the country once before committed to racial egalitarianism in Reconstruction before quickly and violently retrenching, and because the court similarly retrenched from the promise of *Bob Jones University v. United States*. and other civil rights cases, critical race theorists and critical race tax theorists, like Beverly Moran, Dorothy Brown, Karen Brown and others, rightly carry the responsibility of examining this nation's tax laws to determine when, how, and the extent which they are intentionally or unintentionally producing consequences that support or re-establish white social, political or economic supremacy in the United States.

Ultimately, tax laws, by themselves and in combination with others, served three functions toward the installation and maintenance of institutionalized racism in America: establishing a racial order, redistributing black wealth to whites generally, and excluding blacks from lucrative marketplaces. Open racially discriminatory taxation in the eighteenth and early ninenteenth century helped to define the racial order of the United States as one dedicated toward white economic and social supremacy. Poll taxes and capitation taxes reflected and promoted the social order in that they were levied highest on free blacks to discourage their presence, then slightly less on slaves, lesser still on free white men and no tax on white women. Such taxes were sometimes abolished for white men, when they were needed in greater numbers to protect against slave or Indian uprisings.

Taxes on slavery redistributed wealth which ought to have vested in black laborers from them to slaveowners and then to whites generally. First, this contends that slavery itself was a 100 percent tax on black labor, which unjustly redistributed the fruits of labor from the black slave to the white slaveowner. Then, the wealth of slaveowners and other merchants and traders along the several points of the slave industry was redistributed to those who did not hold slaves through flat fees, poll and capitation taxes, ad valorem property taxes, estate taxes, and all manner of excise taxes. And while the federal government seldom taxed slavery directly, the federal tariff indirectly redistributed substantial amounts, perhaps even a majority of the wealth from slavery, away from the south to northern merchants. Moreover, the Thirteenth Amendment repeal of the 100 percent tax on black labor was ineffective. "Real" slavery, according to Douglas blackmon and others did not end until at least 1945, as the Jim Crow South convict leasing/sharecropping system perpetuated the 100 percent tax on black labor, informally but hardly less effectively.

A tax history of racism in the United States is also the story of marketplace exclusion, as slavery as a tax and racially discriminatory taxation on free blacks, foreclosed the opportunity for blacks to compete in burgeoning American markets worth billions. To protect the market for white labor, southern polities levied occupational and other excise taxes on free blacks engaged in specific trades, vendors and merchants who dealt with free blacks or who hired slave labor, and on slaveowners who deployed their slaves in non-agricultural operations. Taxes provided a regulatory mechanism by which whites turned what should have been a "free market" into one where the imperfections, costs and externalities of the market were distributed disproportionately to blacks while the benefits of the market were distributed disproportionately to whites. Ultimately, the tax history of racism in the United States shows how redistributions and asymmetrical market imperfections have brought us today to the brink of a loose, racial socio-economic-political caste system.

However, the tax history of race in the United States also reflects the demise of white supremacy. This country's earliest tax laws demonstrate that the American colonies began without a commitment to a strict racial order, that white supremacy as the "official" racial order was not established until the early ninenteenth century, and that it reached its apogee at the turn of the twentieth century. The absence of facially discriminatory tax laws reflects the fact that white socio-political supremacy has been in certain decline since the end of World War II, Jackie Robinson, *Brown v. Board of Education*, and the civil rights movement. This trend away from apartheid and toward real meritocracy is exhibited in our tax laws through the abolition of federal and state poll taxes, by the Twenty-sixth Amendment and *Harper v. Virginia*, in 1964 and 1966 respectively. Then, in 1983, the Supreme Court decided *Bob Jones University v. United States*, upholding the IRS's interpretation of a federal income tax statute that "charitable" organizations could not include those who discriminate on the basis of race because Congress does not intend for its laws to exacerbate racial inequalities. *Bob Jones University v. United States* is remarkably underappreciated as an express, official disavowal of institutionalized white supremacy in the United States. It is a repudiation of *Dred Scott v. Sanford*.

But perhaps *Bob Jones University v. United States* is somewhat ignored by the larger legal community because the court quickly diminished its impact one year later in another tax case, *Allen v. Wright*. There, the court heightened its standing requirements which prevented exceptionally affected black citizens from forcing the IRS to revoke the tax exemption and federal subsidization of racially discriminatory schools. Buttressing *Allen v. Wright*, the court in *Heckler v. Chaney*, held similarly that agencies have almost absolute prosecutorial discretion to bring or not bring enforcement actions, in the case of the IRS, to revoke anyone's tax exempt status who is advocating for white supremacy or racial discrimination. Limiting the reach of *Bob Jones* even more, the court also held in *Chevron v. NRDC* that unless Congress has precisely spoken to the issue of racial subordination agencies like the IRS have the discretion to change their interpretation to one where racially discriminatory organizations are deemed "charitable" and subsidized by the federal government. These cases, all from the 1980s, are predicates for twenty-first-century claims of post-racialism, where express advocacy for white supremacy is socially and sometimes legally unacceptable while at the same time there is almost universal suspicion regarding programs and projects and activities toward affirmatively addressing racial subordination and inequalities (i.e., anything that actually diminishes white economic supremacy).

NOTES

1. Tomas Piketty, Capital in the 21st Century (2014)
2. Douglas blackmon, Slavery by Another Name (2008).
3. Ibid.
4. Ibid.
5. Juan F. Perea, "*Doctrines of Delusion: Bakke, Fisher and the Case for a New Affirmative Action*", http://papers.ssrn.com/sol3/papers.cfm?abstract_id=2312630; Daria Roith-

mayr, "*Locked In Segregation*," 12 Virginia Journal of Social Policy and the Law 197 (2004); "*Locked In Inequality: The Persistence of Discrimination*," 9 Michigan Journal of Race and Law 31 (2003).

6. Ibid.
7. Ibid.
8. Ibid.
9. Ibid.
10. Ibid.
11. Ibid.
12. Ibid.
13. Ibid.
14. Bell, Derrick A., "*Brown v. Board of Education and the Interest-Convergence Dilemma*", Harvard Law Review 518 (1979-80).
15. Douglas blackmon, Slavery by Another Name (2008).
16. Robin L. Einhorn, American Taxation, American Slavery (2006).
17. See Ira Katznelson, When Affirmative Action was white (2005).
18. Atiba Ellis, *The Cost of the Vote: Poll Taxes, Voter Identification Laws, and the Price of Democracy*, 86 Denver L. Rev. 1023 (2009).
19. *Williams v. Mississippi*, 170 US 213 (1898).
20. *Harper v. Virginia Bd. of Elections*, 383 US 663 (1966).
21. *Breedlove v. Suttles*, 302 US 277 (1937).
22. *Butler v. Thompson*, 341 U.S. 937 (1951).
23. *Harper v. Virginia Bd. of Elections*, 383 US 663 (1966).
24. Ibid.
25. *Bob Jones University v. United States*, 461 US 574 (1983).
26. 347 U.S. 483 (1954).
27. *Chevron U.S.A., Inc. v. Natural Resources Defense Council, Inc.*, 467 U.S. 837 (1984).
28. Olati Johnson, *The Story Of Bob Jones University V. United States: Race, Religion, And Congress' Extraordinary Acquiescence*, in Statutory Interpretation Stories (2011).
29. Ibid.
30. Ibid.
31. *Green v. Connally*, 330 F. Supp. 1150 (1971).
32. *Coit v Green*, 404 US 997 (1971).
33. Olati Johnson, *The Story Of Bob Jones University V. United States: Race, Religion, And Congress' Extraordinary Acquiescence*, in Statutory Interpretation Stories (2011).
34. Ibid.
35. Ibid.
36. Ibid.
37. Ibid.
38. Ibid.
39. Ibid.
40. Ibid.
41. Ibid.
42. Ibid.
43. Ibid.
44. Ibid.
45. Judith Resnick, *Living Their Legal Commitments: Paideic Communities, courts and Robert Cover*, 17 Yale Journal of Law & the Humanities 17 (2005).
46. *San Antonio Independent School Dis trict v. Rodriguez*, 411 U.S. 1 (1973).
47. *Mueller v. Allen*, 463 US 388 (1983).
48. Robert M. Cover, *Foreword: Nomos and Narrative*, 97 Harvard Law Review (1983).
49. *Allen v. Wright*, 468 US 737 (1984).
50. *Heckler v. Chaney*, 470 US 821 (1985).
51. *Webster v. Doe*, 486 US 592 (1988).

52. *National Cable & Telecommunications Association et al. v. Brand X Internet Services et al.*, 545 U.S. 967 (2005).

SIX

Critical Race Tax Theory in Twenty-First-Century Legal Architecture

CRITICAL RACE TAX THEORY (CRIT)

Our post-racial Supreme Court penalizes actions that expressly advocate for white supremacy at the same time it allows for neutrally worded statutes that produce asymmetrical or disparate impacts on groups. It also allows for the nonenforcement of statutes intended to address racial inequalities.[1] Therefore, it is up to legal scholars to reveal circumstances when the effects of neutrally worded legislation have the intended or unintended consequence of maintaining white political, economic or social supremacy. Toward that endeavor a cadre of law professors in the 1980s came to be known as Critical Race Theorists, and in the 1990s a branch of these scholars became Critical Race Tax Theorists.[2]

In 1995, Karen Brown and Mary Louise Fellows edited a book entitled *Taxing America,* in which authors discussed tax statutes that had a subordinating effect on blacks, women, and other discrete groups.[3] With respect to race specifically, *Taxing America* included John A. Powell's "How Government Tax and Housing Policies Have Racially Segregated America." Professor Powell's concern was, "Government subsidies for home mortgages and tax deductions connected to home ownership have played a large role in creating and maintaining racially segregated neighborhoods," as well as the larger critical race project, "and perpetuating the racially discriminatory distribution of resources."[4]

Dorothy Brown's piece in *Taxing America* commented on how the so-called tax marriage penalty also has a disparate impact on blacks. The next year, Beverly Moran and Bill Whitford published "A Black Critique of the Internal Revenue Code" in the *Wisconsin Law Review.* Whereas feminist critiques of the tax law and policy were featured prominently in

Taxing America, Moran and Whitford focused strictly on "a black critique" and asked whether the Internal Revenue code was racist.[5]

Without necessarily rejecting the notion that facially neutral taxation can produce disparate impacts on race and gender, Lawrence Zelenak in "Taking Critical Tax Theory Seriously" responded to these works by questioning the quality of critical tax scholarship.[6] His reflected a growing hostility toward critical race theory generally, although his criticisms were a tad gentler than others. Others have argued that critical race tax theory is wholly irrelevant because disparate racial impacts related to taxation are subsumed by discussions of class, or because they believe that traditional notions of tax equity already account for race since blacks are represented in lower income strata and thus pay less tax than whites.[7] Of course, previous chapters regarding a tax history of racism in the United States was designed to demonstrate how racial subordination can be accomplished through taxation in various ways, without references to the amount of tax actually paid. Moreover, the critical race tax project is justified simply by the fact that "traditional" tax equity scholars have ignored the racial implications of poll taxes, discriminatory occupational taxes, asymmetrical subsidies, etc.[8]

It is an uphill battle getting "mainstream" legal commentators to accept critical theory and critical tax theory as a "legitimate" scholarly discipline. And even if legal scholars analyze the impact of tax laws on race does not mean the Supreme Court has to. When, in *Banks v. Commissioner* (2005), the Supreme Court ignored the obvious racial implications of a facially neutral tax doctrine, the assignment of income doctrine, it aligned itself with those scholars who choose to avoid discussions of racial subordination if at all possible.[9] The story of *Banks* was basically this:

In 2000, Laura Sager and Stephen Cohen published "How the Income Tax Undermines Civil Rights Laws."[10] They demonstrated how the federal taxation of civil rights attorneys' fee awards penalized or at least discouraged civil rights plaintiffs from enforcing the civil rights law. The legal question was whether a civil rights plaintiff is in receipt of "income" when, pursuant to the civil rights statute they are suing under, the defendant is required to pay the plaintiff's attorneys' fees, even if the plaintiff did not request such fees and never had actual physical possession of the funds. The IRS determined that the legal fees were received first by the plaintiff as income and then assigned or transferred to the attorney. The IRS further determined, correctly and unremarkably, that when the plaintiff's adjusted gross income is high enough to trigger the alternative minimum tax (as it was in the *Banks* case, and as it would be in the typical civil rights fee shifting case), the plaintiff will not be allowed a deduction for the payment of attorney's fees. Therefore, the civil rights plaintiff is not appreciated as a "private attorney general," but saddled with a huge financial burden instead.

Sager and Cohen argued that taxing the attorney's fee portion of a civil rights recovery was inconsistent with the intent of Congress when they shifted the legal fees to the defendant in the first place. Congress, according to Sager and Cohen, recognized that the civil rights plaintiff acted as a private attorney general and wanted to relieve them of the cost of ridding racial discrimination from the national economy. If correct, then taxing their recovery, especially the attorneys fee portion, countermands the legislature and undermines the effectiveness of the civil rights law.

Cohen and Sager asked us to imagine a civil rights plaintiff who wins only an injunction for the defendant to stop discriminating along with attorney's fees. This plaintiff has recovered nothing for herself, yet must pay the government for the opportunity to rid the national economy of a racial discriminator. Further consider how absurd it would be if the discriminator were the federal government itself![11]

In *Banks* , the Supreme Court granted certiorari over this issue after the federal circuit courts of appeal split in three ways.[12] Some circuits held that a plaintiff is taxed on the attorneys' fee portion of a judgment if the taxpayer is in a state that only gives attorneys a creditors claim over unpaid debts, while the taxpayer is not to be taxed on the attorney's portion if state law grants the attorney an equity claim over their rightful part of a judgment. These courts looked to state law to determine whether the attorney "owned" a portion of the award. One of the problems with this approach was not only did it cause a federal inter-circuit split, where taxpayers in one circuit are taxed differently than another, these holdings created an intra-circuit split, where taxpayers within the same circuit are taxed differently depending on which state they lived in.

Alternatively, the Sixth Circuit determined that if income requires an "accession to wealth, realized, over which the taxpayer has dominion and control," then the civil rights plaintiff never has "dominion and control" since in almost every instance they rely necessarily on their attorney to win the case and will never physically handle the fee payment. On the other hand, the Seventh Circuit opinion, written by Richard Posner, who some consider no friend of civil rights, held that the civil rights plaintiff and all other litigants always have dominion and control over the cases they instigate, for they alone can decide whether to continue pursuing the cases or not.[13]

An interesting thing happened on the way to the court, though. Congress passed the American Job Creation Act and provided in it that attorney's fees relating to civil rights cases would be considered what is called an "above the line deduction"—which means that, regardless of the alternative minimum tax, plaintiffs would recognize attorney's fee awards as income first and then to deduct attorneys' fees from gross income in all civil rights cases. This approach would result in no gain or loss, and thus, would not discourage the enforcement of civil rights laws. Since Congress provided the answer during the pendency of the case, it was unclear if the court would even decide the case, and if so, how? Would they dismiss the case as moot? Would they decide the case by simply pointing to Congress' intent as manifested in the AJCA? Or keep the opportunity to more clearly define the assignment of income doctrine?

Instead of deciding the case strictly based on the legislature's clearly expressed intent on the matter, as represented by the AJCA, the court analyzed the contours of its assignment of income doctrine and expanded its reach to situations where taxpayers have no tax avoidance motive with respect to the assignment, like civil rights cases. The court cited Judge Posner's 7th Circuit opinion which found an attorney to be an agent of the litigant no different than a retail sales clerk to a shopkeeper. The shopkeeper, like the litigant, is to be taxed on all receipts regardless how important the agent was to the sale. The court's opinion has logical appeal. But why did the court go there when the answer was a simple matter of legislative intent, which the AJCA showed quite clearly? Was it rejecting the *Bob Jones* court's technique of considering the intent of a more current Congress over the intent of an older one?

I believe the *Banks* court eschewed any discussion of race and civil rights because it "fits" its post-racial attitude—that it is permissible, nay, preferable for institutions to publicly disparage racial discrimination while ignoring meaningful racial inequalities. Surely, the court was aware of the racial implications. Not only did Sager and Cohen identify the tension between the civil rights laws and the assignment of income doctrine, but other commentators weighed in with other approaches, and several amici briefs were filed with the court regarding the case's impact on race and civil rights.

Ultimately, the court mentioned the AJCA in a footnote, contending that it mooted the impact on civil rights. The court saw that Congress addressed the impact on civil rights by passing the AJCA, but it somehow failed to see that the AJCA resolved the main question as well. Or they did in fact see it, and ignored it so that they did not have to talk about race except in a footnote. This is marginalization, quite literally. According to Robin Einhorn in "American Taxation, American Slavery," this is an American tax tradition.

One might defend the court by arguing that its decision-making process, being text based, does not allow for it to consider the implications tax statutes have on subordinated groups. But, first, not all members of the Supreme Court are strict textualists or strict formalists, and, therefore, several members of the court should be openly receptive to hearing how tax statutes might subordinate or subjugate.[14] Second, even those justices who typically eschew realist or dynamic forms of interpretation—in other words those who consider group subordination to be an illegitimate concern of the judiciary (i.e., judicial activism)—slip up and consider group subordination when it suits them. For instance, in *Craft v. United*

States (2002), Justice Scalia, author of multiple books espousing textualism, dissented because the majority's decision as it related to tax collection procedures would harm "divorced women."[15] After Scalia's dissent in *Craft v. United States*, it seems that everyone's a CRIT!

Jurisprudential theorists, particularly formalists, tend to reject the notion that a judge should consider racial subordination in any context much less in federal taxation.[16] Moreover, tax scholars in search of theories of optimal taxation also tend to ignore racial subordination in the tax context because they claim it does not fit neatly into their "standard" conceptions of horizontal or vertical equity.[17]

To help them come out of the closet, so to speak, Anthony Infanti demonstrates in "Tax Equity" how traditional views of the optimal tax system can and ought to examine the asymmetrical effect tax laws have on groups generally as well as groups that have experienced intense subordination or subjugation already.[18] Here we attempt to take a step further and explore traditional concepts of tax fairness, as well as jurisprudential techniques such as textualism, intentionalism, purposivism, dynamism, and others, to determine if there is a place in any of them for the consideration of racial subordination through the federal tax code. The short answer is yes . . . in all of them.

CRITICAL RACE TAX THEORY AND TAX EQUITY?

Is critical race theory and critical race tax theory a creditable part of the legal academy? Is the scholarship of critical race tax theorists of any importance or quality? If the essence of critical race tax theory is a concern for group subordination, how is the law supposed to "think" about these issues, if at all?

Those of us who research and write about the relationship between taxation and racial subordination think we are doing something useful and important. Others do not think so highly of us, however. In fact, some argue that even if there is some relationship between tax and race, the law is not allowed to consider, or is better off ignoring, those dynamics. There are two strands of this irrelevance argument, each with subtle permutations. The first strand relates strictly to tax and typically revolves around the notion that conventional tax policy's consideration of income and class (vertical equity) subsumes race. The other argument against scholarship on tax and race relates to statutory construction and the formalist prohibition against judges considering social policy. The following chapter debunks these arguments and then demonstrates precisely how racial subordination relates to traditional concepts of tax equity, as well as the most popular techniques for constructing tax statutes—textualism, intentionalism, purposivism, and dynamism.

Tax equity, traditionally conceived, stands for the proposition that a good tax system should be efficient, simple, and fair.[19] It should "minimize interference with economic decision making," be "easy to administer and comply with," and respect "vertical and horizontal equity." Horizontal equity means that similarly situated taxpayers should bear the same responsibility. Vertical equity suggests that those with the ability to pay more should bear a greater responsibility.

Fairness in terms of vertical and horizontal equity has recently come under philosophical scrutiny. In fact, each component of tax equity has been challenged as to whether they independently represent goodness, whether they have significance without reference to some other norm outside of tax.[20] Nevertheless, tax equity or tax fairness is a prominent feature of tax law conversations, scholarship, and, to some extent, judicial opinions.[21] Critical race tax scholarship has typically been analyzed under the lens of vertical and horizontal equity, and the evaluation from the mainstream has not been kind.

According to those who have difficulty "taking critical tax theory seriously," concerns regarding the disparate impact of tax law on race and other types of group subordination are either entirely irrelevant, irrelevant because those concerns are already accounted for within the concepts of vertical and horizontal equity, or critical tax concerns unduly diminish simplicity or efficiency even if they are relevant. Others who are less dismissive would nevertheless require critical tax theorists to satisfy a set of confining conditions in order for our scholarship to count.[22]

In "Tax Equity," Anthony Infanti does much of the heavy lifting in terms of defending critical race tax theory against detractors in the legal academy. He contends that the traditional concept of tax equity does not subsume discussions of race and other types of group subordination and that discussing the racial dynamics of tax statutes adds something important to the standard conversation which is usually limited to horizontal and vertical equity and economic efficiency. According to Infanti, traditional tax equity discussions of race miss the mark because 1) traditional tax equity concerns itself strictly with income while ignoring billions of dollars in tax subsidies, 2) tax equity theorists wrongly believe that income disparities are the exclusive evidence of racism or group subordination, and 3) the unruly and complicated nature of real tax law demonstrates that legal actors are not very much beholden to traditional tax equity concerns anyway.[23]

This chapter adds that 1) traditional concepts of tax equity deal more properly with an ideal society that has not already violated requirements of justice toward all of its citizens, and, 2) even an ideal society should care whether its tax system creates disparate impacts for identifiable groups.[24] Moreover, we should understand that American law operates in a public choice environment where groups or factions compete over the content of law, and that Professor Steve Johnson's criteria for good critical tax scholarship is best understood as a negotiation stance toward multi-racial anti-subordination coalition building—albeit perhaps an unreasonable one.

Tax Equity?

To be fair, some of the commentators who have been accused of disparaging critical tax theory were instead being critical of a particular statement: that the Internal Revenue code is racist.[25] Asking whether the code as a whole is racist is different from asking whether particular provisions in the code cause disparate impacts relating to a subordinate member of an identifiable group. The critics correctly point out that identifying one provision of the code that benefits whites more than blacks does not necessarily mean that the entire code is racist, because it could be the case that other provisions disproportionately benefit blacks.[26] But, what's interesting is none of those critics themselves pointed to any provision other than the rate structure to countermand the disparate impacts identified by Karen Brown, Beverly Moran, Dorothy Brown, et al.

The degree to which the entire code discriminates against blacks, if at all, must change year to year as new provisions are added, old ones are taken out, and the tax relevant activities of black people change from year to year. And even if the code were deemed "nonracist" as a whole, this would not negate the critical tax project, for critical tax theorists also demonstrate how neutral tax provisions, like poll taxes, have a subordinating effect outside of the tax world:[27]

Simplicity

The first tax equity critique of critical race tax theory relates to simplicity. One commentator argues, "that any attempt to tailor the system to meet the criticisms of feminists or racial groups rapidly becomes a nightmare of dilemmas that are just not resolvable. One needs only to observe lifestyles of friends, colleagues, neighbors, and relatives and one becomes keenly aware that to design a tax regime to meet the gender and race consideration of each case would create a statutory maze of confusion many times worse confounded than the current system."[28] Infanti paraphrases the simplicity argument as such, "taking the reality of invidious discrimination into account makes tax policy analysis far too complicated and messy. Tax policy analysis is much simpler and tidier when the possibility of discrimination is flatly ignored."[29] Professor Infanti makes an even more salient point with respect to simplicity, that it has long been sacrificed in favor of other societal goals: "Commentators often speak of the need to simplify the tax system; however, when faced with a choice between simple rules, on the one hand, and efficient or equitable rules, on the other, the efficient or equitable rules usually win out." He is suspicious that simplicity is a "forgotten stepchild" that is brought ought only when confronting "questions of race, ethnicity, gender, sexual orientation, disability, and or/other characteristics that form the basis for invidious discrimination."[30]

But, moreover, the claim that considering race and gender would create more confusion is simply not true, or at least not necessarily true. It could be that a race or gender analysis leads to the conclusion that tax subsidies and complexities within the code, generally, inure disproportionately to whites or males, and thus a race or gender solution could be to simplify the code by taking out all the deductions and credits and other provisions unrelated to determining true income. To the extent those provisions that already make the code maddeningly complex are designed to benefit whites, simplicity would make the code fairer to blacks.

Fairness – Vertical Equity

That blacks are overrepresented in lower income strata leads to another strand of critiques against critical race tax scholarship: since race issues are nothing more than class issues, and since class is represented in terms of vertical equity, then race is irrelevant because it is already accounted for in tax law. Under this conception, one commentator contends that it is actually whites who are discriminated against, since they are overrepresented in higher income strata and thus pay more taxes.[31] But this argument about whites being discriminated against is particularly strange, since the reason why whites pay more is because vertical equity demonstrates its "fairness." If the demands of vertical equity are discriminatory toward whites, then vertical equity is itself a faulty lens with which to adjudicate the goodness of a tax system.

Besides, focusing exclusively on income strata is an incomplete proxy for racial or group subordination. Mylinh Uy fears that, because Asians are fairly well represented in higher income strata, exclusively focusing on income perpetuates the Asian as model minority myth and serves to deny their racial experiences in the United States.[32] Not only does focusing exclusively on income ignore other forms and techniques of group subordination, the myth of the model minority is improperly summoned against claims of subordination.

Fairness – Horizontal Equity

Focusing strictly on the income side leaves a blind spot for the flip side, horizontal equity, or racial subordination in terms of tax subsidies. The income model of horizontal equity holds that similarly situated taxpayer should bear the same responsibility, and that income determines who is similarly situated.[33] But first off, income is an inadequate determinant for the similarly situated because it does not refer to accumulated wealth. Under an income tax that takes no account of accumulated wealth, an extremely wealthy person who puts none of that wealth to productive economic use can certainly afford and has a duty to help pay for the government that protects and makes such wealth possible, yet pays no income tax. Moreover, tax subsidies in the form of deductions inure disproportionately to whites because the progressive rate structure makes deductions more valuable with respect to higher income brackets.

Secondly, tax subsidies—the bevy of deductions and credits and other tax planning opportunities available to reduce one's tax liability—may inure disproportionately to whites, because of the nature of the activity being subsidized.[34] In 1999, Beverly Moran demonstrated how the marriage penalty relates to black women in a way different from white women.[35] In 2012, Dorothy Brown demonstrated how tax incentives for homeownership disproportionately favor whites because "white flight" makes black homeownership less lucrative than white homeownership.[36] Also consider how taxes on dogs in the nineteenth century were designed to disarm and further emasculate free blacks in the south.[37] These are examples why focusing exclusively on the income side, horizontally and vertically, ignores the effect tax subsidies have on the asymmetric distribution of society's burdens and benefits.[38]

Redistribution

Traditional tax equity theorists also ignore racial subordination that can occur through the inequitable redistribution of tax revenues. Neither vertical nor horizontal equity based on the income model concerns itself with whether each person or group of people derives equal benefit from the expenditure of tax revenues.[39] If it is true that wealthier people derive more of a benefit from the existence and practices of government, then tax equity's sole concern with ability to pay is too myopic a lens with which to judge the goodness of a tax system. The inequitable distribution of tax revenues, if proven, would throw current tax equity discussions entirely out of whack.[40]

Basing taxes strictly on income causes a redistribution from blacks to whites if government services are provided in greater proportion to whites than blacks with respect to every income strata, or if blacks are denied government services regardless of their income strata, or such services are provided on a separate and unequal basis. The tax essence of Jim Crow apartheid was that blacks paid for government services but did not receive them, while whites who paid for government services got that which blacks paid for.

Economic Efficiency

Despite the criticisms of neoclassic economics, critical tax theory scholarship can promote the concept of economic efficiency. On one hand, efficiency with respect to a tax code could be limited to "minimizing interference with economic transactions."[41] This concept of efficiency tends to focus on individual taxpayers engaged in discrete, identifiable transactions. But as we have seen with the rise of law and economics as an academic subdiscipline over the last several decades, the concept of economic efficiency has taken different shapes and forms for differing contexts. It is high time critical legal scholars add internal criticisms of law and economics to the myriad external ones.

A critical tax perspective can very well discuss whether any aspect of the income tax system detracts from an efficient economic system.[42] If a perfectly free market system requires that everyone is a profit maximizer, then it is useful to determine whether a given tax law or set of tax laws detract from that motivation, and then it is also useful to determine whether any one provision or set of provisions discourages one group more than others. For example, the 100 percent tax on black labor not only redistributed wealth from blacks to whites, it is partly responsible for discouraging blacks as a group from committing to profit maximization and the American free market system. After three hundred years of slavery and peonage where hardwork was just as often punished as it was rewarded, it should not surprise that a troublesome number of blacks in the United States have yet to commit to the same entrepreneurial spirit as others who were not similarly oppressed. In this way, taxation has contributed to an "asymmetrically imperfect commitment to profit maximization relating to race."[43]

The same goes for the ideal market concept of perfect competition. If a perfectly free market system requires that everyone is able to enter or exit any market they choose, then taxes that foreclose lucrative markets or lock people into declining markets are inefficient. Slavery and discriminatory occupational taxes, for example, created asymmetrically imperfect market competition relating to race. Perfectly free markets require perfect information, and the same analysis applies. Taxes that restrict the flow of information are bad for the economy. Taxes that restrict the flow of information to one group more than another are even worse. Therefore, poll taxes, tax subsidies for racist private schools, and the mal-distribution of property tax revenue to predominately white schools are inefficient in the long run because they promote asymmetrically imperfect information relating to race.[44]

A perfectly free market assumes no transaction costs, including taxes. But since there are plenty of transaction costs and externalities, efficiency should demand that those costs be properly distributed. Fortunately, concepts of tax equity try to ensure that the burden is evenly distributed.

Unfortunately, racial concerns outside of the traditional tax equity construct have not. For example, poll taxes were an example of unevenly distributed transaction costs, and, worse than that, the disenfranchising effect of poll tax left blacks without political power that would prevent legislatures from heaping even more transaction costs upon them, like say environmental waste. Therefore, race CRITs should analyze tax laws that produce asymmetrical market imperfections relating to race. Others concerned about group subordination ought to do likewise to the extent the law produces or maintains asymmetrical market imperfections relating to any identifiable group.

Idyllic Systems

Part of the problem with deploying traditional concepts of tax equity to critical tax scholarship is that tax equity deals with the creation of a brand new tax system from scratch, one that is not already flawed. Once the flaws of the current tax system—complexity, nonvertical equity, nonhorizontal equity, nonefficiency—are acknowledged, tax equity concepts are not designed to judge specific items of reformation. An analogy can be made to John Rawls' theory of "justice as fairness" and affirmative action. According to Thomas Nagel, a student of Rawls, Rawls supported affirmative action even though there are very good arguments that it violates his meta rule that political justice requires a fair opportunity for each individual.[45] That rule, justice as fairness, is appropriate, according to Nagel's interpretation of Rawls, in an ideal situation, when one is constructing government institutions on a blank slate. But if an existing government has already violated the rule of justice as fairness, it should be restricted from invoking justice as fairness for the purpose of thwarting reforms and retaining the benefits of past injustices. It is similarly inappropriate to invoke idyllic tax fairness concepts against tax reforms proposed by critical tax theorists that respond or at least relate to past injustices.[46]

And yet, as Professor Infanti points out, current discussion of tax equity are inadequate even if we were talking about a fresh start. What would be gained by a new nation to ignore proof (or at least a strong hypothesis) that its tax laws have disparate impacts on identifiable groups in society.[47] If that society were exclusively based on individualism and there were no groups, perhaps then there would be no need for studies and examination relating to group subordination and the current tax equity concepts will be successfully applied. But where there are groups, and where there is evidence that the mere existence of groups produces factional solidarity,[48] and where such group solidarity includes the receipt of intra-group esteem from intergroup conflict,[49] then scholars must take note when they believe one group is conscripting government institutions toward the subordination of other competing groups. Simply put, a nation does not vigorously guarding its domestic tranquility to the extent it ignores unjust group subordination.

In chapter 2 of *Faces at the Bottom of the Well,* Derrick Bell imagines a volcano erupting in the Atlantic Ocean and forming a new island halfway between the Americas and Africa.[50] For whatever reason, only black people can breathe on this island. Derrick Bell uses this scenario to discuss how whites with different interests have reacted to black emigration in the past. For our purposes here, I imagine that black people emigrate to this island and have the opportunity to construct laws and institutions from scratch. In that context, I think it is clear that government, legal and academic institutions of Afrolantica are right to want to know when, whether, how and to what degree provisions of any of its laws, including taxes, create asymmetrical market imperfections relating to specified groups. If the smoke cleared and other races were able to breathe on the island and in fact emigrated there, good governance would include noticing if, when and how tax laws were disadvantaging a particular group. This is a matter of domestic tranquility without regard to past injustice. It is also simply a mark of affluence and intelligence for a nation's educational institutions to confront societal issues, like unjust group subordination, by, first, seeking to know all that can be known, then, determining whether "something should be done about it."

Quality of Critical Tax Scholarship

For some, critical tax scholarship is irrelevant if it cannot show that blacks or some other group pays more than whites pay in income taxes. If the critics were serious then I think the appropriate question they would pose in terms of fairness is whether blacks or some other group pay more than their *fair* share, which requires not only consideration of vertical equity as some critics correctly point out, but which also requires scholars to consider the tax expenditure side, and which requires scholars to also consider the distribution of government goods and services, and which requires some formula to weigh them altogether. A true analysis of fairness would be exceedingly complex, which is probably why the reductionist world of tax equity is so attractive to some.[51] But, it is one thing to argue that critical tax scholarship does not fit the tax equity mold, and quite another to say that the scholarship is inadequate or poor if it does not comport with such an artificial construct that holds little sway in actual practice.

In *Taking Critical Tax Seriously,* Professor Steve Johnson attempted to establish a reasonable standard for assessing the quality of critical tax scholarship.[52] He contended that for critical tax scholarship to be "fully persuasive" it must demonstrate that: 1) There is some particular code feature that operates to the substantial disadvantage of some group. This would involve showing that, as a result of the code feature, group members pay proportionately more tax than nonmembers. 2) The offending code feature is not compensated for by other aspects of the code that disproportionately benefit the group in question. That is, there must be an on-balance or on-net evaluation, a showing that the unfavorable code aspects hurt group members more than the favorable code aspects help them. 3) The appropriate way to redress the problem would be changing the code, rather than changing non-tax rules or practices. 4) A reasonable solution exits. That is, a way exists to reform the offending code section, and that way is technically feasible, efficacious, and unlikely to create other serious problems.

Professor Infanti correctly critiques the first two prongs because it is unjustifiably myopic toward the question of who pays more taxes, rather than dealing with whether taxation causes group subordination.[53] Of course, demonstrating that blacks pay more total tax than whites would be a serious accomplishment and a serious condemnation of American meritocracy, but that is not the aim of critical tax theorists. Critical race tax theorists are more likely argue that blacks or other groups pay more than their fair share, which requires an analysis of not only income, but also, type of income, tax expenditures, and the government's distribution of good and services post-assessment.[54]

Infanti also dismisses the want of simplicity, since it is not required in other contexts. Identifying simple, efficacious solutions makes scholarship better, more persuasive; but it doesn't discount much from a thorough identification of a major problem relating to racism or group subordination. The third prong, that the solution must be a tax solution is also tangentially related to good scholarship. While it might be difficult for a tenured tax professor to evaluate junior tax scholarship that offers a nontax solution to a "tax problem," the academic enterprise does not or ought not demean the scholar who has advanced knowledge by precisely identifying a problem yet has not also found a solution that is otherwise "technically feasible, efficacious, and unlikely to create other serious problems."[55]

Consider again Sager and Cohen's article, "How the Income Tax Undermines Civil Rights Law," a wonderful piece of critical tax scholarship that violates each of Steve Johnson's prescriptions.[56] In it, they describe how a civil rights plaintiff who accepts an injunction against the defendant's discriminatory behavior along with attorney's fees will be assessed a large tax on the attorney's fees as income. Because of tax laws, private attorney generals who were outing racial discrimination sometimes had to pay for the "privilege," rather than being compensated for doing an important national service. This discourages some from seeking to make America more meritocratic. This issue that Sager and Cohen identified produced a three-way circuit split and was eventually resolved in 2006, when the Supreme Court decided *Banks v. Commissioner*. Not only that, while the case was pending before the court, Congress attempted to fix the problem in the American Jobs Creation Act. But Johnson's formula discounts Sager and Cohen's work as fairly useless scholarship.

Sager and Cohen violated prong number one because although they identified features that operate to the substantial disadvantage of minority groups, they did not show nor could they show that it causes minorities to pay more tax than nonminorities. Nor could they feasibly satisfy prong number two, which requires them to analyze every single provision of the code to determine whether the harm to civil rights laws is "offset" by tax provisions that disproportionately benefit minorities. Now Sager and Cohen come closer to satisfying prongs three and four, which required a simple and effective tax solution, as they, and others, proposed legislative and jurisprudential solutions. But their scholarship would have been just as good if it determined that there was no simple and effective tax solution and that minority groups should instead focus on private protest tactics rather than legal changes.

For another example, the first chapter, "Does it Matter What Slaves Thought Direct Tax Meant in the U.S. Constitution?" poses an interesting question of tax and statutory interpretation from a critical perspective, without identifying any code provisions that are detrimental to blacks and proposing no solutions.[57] It simply uses a critical tax perspective to show that "Scalian" textualism is not as efficient as some of its proponents suggest. Moreover, this project here, "Black Tax," only satisfies half of prong one, and offers nothing to satisfy prongs two through four.

While other critics seem intent on dismissing the entire critical tax project, I find Professor Johnson's critique, along with some others, to be a genuine attempt at academically (nonpolitically) separating the wheat from the chaff—though it is still wanting. First of all, critical theorists by their nature believe politics cannot be removed from any part of law or any field of study, no matter how formalized the process. Secondly, Professor Johnson's standards for good scholarship really seem to be conditions upon which white male law professors will tend to agree that racism or group subordination is afoot. This is not surprising if we take Derrick Bell's Interest Convergence Theory seriously.[58] Professor Bell contends that whites will join with blacks to fight racism only when it is in their interest to do so, and, historically, preventing damage to the perception of American meritocracy has been the interest that typically compels elite whites in America to address systemic racism. From this view, we can recast Professor Johnson's "academic standards" into conditions for coalition.

But the standards are set unreasonably high, if white tax scholars will never believe that taxation contributes to unsavory race relations in the United States unless it is shown that the entirety of the tax code disproportionately burdens blacks. Furthermore, showing that the entirety of the code is racist can't be done in the language those scholars understand because tax equity (vertical and horizontal equity) does not consider tax expenditures and the distribution of goods and services. Perhaps critical race tax theorists could establish such a method, a worthy project indeed. But individual critical race theorists and their scholarship ought not be discounted because of its absence.

It is simply a valid and interesting use of brain power and research tools to notice and describe how "some particular code feature . . . operates to the substantial disadvantage of some group."[59] And, because of the nascent nature of critical tax theory, it is not unreasonable to think that critical race tax theory may someday develop such a framework that integrates tax incidence, subsidies and redistribution. Furthermore, focusing solely on how the Internal Revenue code is affected instead of how citizens of the United Sates are being treated is unwarranted. It is destructive to civil rights because it is designed to take efficacious solutions off the table, simply because they don't fit a form or because they disturb some falsely imagined analytical tidiness. Johnson's standards privilege even the most marginal savings in simplicity, efficiency and convention over huge gains to civil rights and national tranquility.

Actually, Johnson's third and fourth prong are reminiscent of *Allen v. Wright*, where the court refused to force the IRS to fully respect and implement anti-subordination laws because to do so might only whittle at the problem rather than redress the harms entirely. In other words, if the race problem can't be resolved by a silver bullet, then elite whites want no part of it, and blacks will simply have to respond without the help of a coalition. But to say that identifying a problem is not useful unless whites or some representation thereof are satisfied by the proposed solution is an unreasonable academic standard, and one that is not applied to all tax scholarship.

CRITICAL RACE TAX THEORY AND STATUTORY INTERPRETATION

After defending critical race tax theory on the grounds that closed conventions like tax equity should be expanded and integrated with the rest of law as well as important social norms, this part describes how the consideration of group subordination with respect to tax law (and critical race theory for that matter) fits within the larger legal framework of the United States. Like with respect to tax equity, some try to ignore and subvert discussions of race by claiming that even if race is real out in the world, and even if legal actors wanted to address it when it is relevant to a particular legal decision, some claim the law itself does not and cannot recognize and think through issues of race.

Of course, critical race theorists reject the idea that the law doesn't and can't consider race from a variety of perspectives. Some reject the entire ideal of law as an independent construct with its own way of thinking. Crits believe that law is subservient to politics and power.[60] This discussion, on the other hand, is intended to be entirely internal.[61] I contend that even if we accept that the law thinks in a bounded way, its deliberative processes are capable of recognizing and digesting racial phenomena, even with respect to federal tax statutes.

Roy Brooks also takes an internally critical view and believes the consideration of racial phenomena fits within existing, prominent structures of legal decision making.[62] He agrees with the ideal that democracy requires judges to subvert their personal, normative utility functions. On the other hand, Brooks disagrees with the traditional model by placing the nomos of the community on par with the intent of the legislature, like theorists such as Richard Posner[63] and William Eskridge.[64] Brooks demonstrates how judges who consider race are not simply deciding cases any which way they choose, nor are they simply implementing their personal policy preferences. Considering the institutionalized and hierarchical structure of the judiciary, the personal policy preferences of any one judge cannot stand to the extent they are out of touch with the communities preferences as understood by the judiciary as a whole. Moreover, the judiciary, even after taking life tenure into account, is certainly conscious of the fact that the legislature, the President and the People can reverse their decisions. Under this view, judges are well within the democratic tradition when they consider policy to the extent and in the manner they believe the community would want them to.

Here, I attempt to go a half-step farther and claim that so long as judges consider race in the manner they believe the community would expect, judges are not only well within the rubric of democratic legitimacy, but that the consideration of race fits within each currently prominent method of statutory interpretation, and thusly fits well within the concept of law as an independent, self-referential social construct. From this perspective, critical race theorists who develop constructs that recognize and digest racial phenomena in a manner the community would expect, or at least in a manner they would accept, are strengthening law rather than annihilating it, as the most rigid of formalists have accused.[65] After demonstrating how race legitimate consideration whatever jurisprudential technique a judge or any other legal actor may deploy, I offer the concept of asymmetrical market imperfections relating to race as a method for a judge to analyze and explain the degree with which a law or legal provision or interpretation may impact racial inequality. With respect to critical race tax theory, then, legal advocates and decision makers should, when appropriate, consider whether taxation produces transactions costs that asymmetrically burden a particular group, whether tax laws otherwise produce asymmetries relating to information available to or about black people, and whether taxation produces asymmetrical opportunities to enter or exploit lucrative markets.

How the Law Thinks

Even if we acknowledge that a judge or jury has a lot of discretion, and even if we admit we can never really know if they actually followed instructions, we still find it useful to play the game and we expect decision makers to think through the case as the law would have them do it.

We expect that a juror, who is told that a statement he has in fact heard is nevertheless stricken from the record, will at least try to obey the command and render a decision as if he had not heard the statement. The appellate review process follows a similar "dream of interpretation."[66] Each judge writes their decision fully aware that superior courts, commentators, particular academics, expect consistency with previous examples of legal thinking in similar contexts (e.g., legal precedent). We will overturn the decision of juries we believe did not follow instructions and the decisions of judges who have similarly failed the law's dictates.

Even if there are some judges who simply do whatever they want to do, as we saw in the last chapter with respect to convict leasing in the Jim Crow era, I think the reason judges willingly earn less than they could on the open legal market, less than most of their similarly ranked law school classmates, is because they value being "right," and part of that rightness is gaining the agreement of other judges, particularly superior ones. In other words, I think the vast majority of judges find it both a professional and personal affront to be overturned by an appeals court. I do not mean at all that a judge will not risk being overturned if she believes her personal sense of justice requires something that precedent prohibits. I mean only that discretion is, in fact, limited. This does not mean that law is pure or immune to politics. But if I may blaspheme against my critical legal colleagues, I do believe that law is politics, just not "all the way down."

Consider law in Afrolantica, the mythical land imagined by Derrick Bell to be halfway between America and Africa, and upon which only black people can breathe. I highly doubt that the Afrolantican juridical system would capitulate entirely to the notion that law is bullshit and eschew formal legal opinions, therefore. It is important to the survival of law as a regulatory system for those who have lost a legal battle to believe that the decision against them was not based on individual whim. We want them to believe that the law represents the community and that the adjudicator represents the law. When law receives instructions from the community and when adjudicators receive instructions from the law, we expect those instructions to be followed, especially when we personally have skin in the game, but also if we care about the effectiveness of the system. Clients challenge lawyers and law clerks to figure out what the "law says" about this or that. Great pains are made sometimes to convince the disappointed that no person is responsible or even happy about an adverse decision. "The law requires it," they are told.

So exactly how ought the law think through legal problems? Using the American legal system as the reference point, judges justify their choice between competing interpretations by emphasizing, first, the degree with which their choice is consistent with specific legal principles and, second, that the choices they refused are inconsistent with the same or other legal principles. The winner is that interpretation which *most* coheres with *most* of our *most* important legal principles. Ultimately, a survey of the United States Supreme Court's federal income tax cases in the twenty-first century confirms what twentieth-century debates over legal theory revealed: The principles most important to legal deliberation are text, intent, purpose, and modern dynamics.[67]

Legal theorists have debated which of these principles are relevant or legitimate, as well as how to rank them.[68] Those debates have waned as a hierarchy seems to have emerged, within the *Roberts* court at least, where text is the most important, intents and purposes next, while modern dynamics are to be considered only as a tie breaker if at all. Nevertheless, each of these techniques allows for the consideration of race or group subordination, regardless how much weight is ultimately given to it. Even though we can't know or explain how the law thinks with mathematical precision, the contours are fairly discernible, enough that we can show that the consideration of race fits within each currently acceptable deliberative function. Therefore, critical race tax theorists need not be bashful about advocating for judicial recognition of racial phenomena.

Text, or textualism, is the consideration of what people think a word or term means when they come upon it.[69] Intent, or intentionalism, is the consideration of what the author might have meant when they wrote it.[70] These two deliberative functions comprise formalism. They focus on meaning. They are interrelated in that some argue, not unpersuasively, that the best evidence of what an author meant is how the people understand it: "I meant what I said, and I said what I meant." On the other hand, when the words of a statute do not precisely capture the legislature's intent, some blame words for being inherently vague and ambiguous, while others blame intent for being ethereal or fictitious. Justice Scalia argues that the President approves of and signs the text of the law without reference to any mythical intent of the legislature—that the search for intent of an organization or a corporate body is a wild goose chase.[71] Notwithstanding Justice Scalia's admonitions, the Supreme Court invokes both text and intent as part of its deliberative process.[72]

Purpose and modern dynamics represent the flip side of the coin—legal realism.[73] Instead of focusing on whether the meaning of a word must be faithful to the author (legislature) or the intended readers (citizens), as formalism does, realism in statutory interpretation is represented by the consideration of consequences interpretations would likely produce. A judge might consider the real-life consequences an interpretation might produce after that judge has first determined that there is something of a tie between what it seems the legislature meant (intent) and what the citizens likely understood a statutory term to mean (text). For a more radical example, a judge might choose the meaning of a word that is less faithful than others to the intent of the legislature or the text of the statute or both simply because of the bad consequences produced by the other, more faithful interpretations. The term "radical purposivism" is meant to denigrate the practice of emphasizing purposes more than text or intent.

Purposivism is considered the more democratically legitimate version of realism, because purposivism is the consideration of consequences the legislature intended to produce or avoid.[74] More offensive to formalists is dynamism, the consideration of consequences untethered to legislative expectations.[75] Dynamism, the formalists tend to say, is anti-democratic because it places the policy preferences of life tenured judges over the popularly elected legislature.[76] Dynamism is derided as "policy analysis" or "judicial activism." The saving grace for dynamism, however, lies in the fact that there is no principled way to differentiate those consequences a legislature implicitly or objectively intended for judges to consider, versus, those they implicitly or objectively intended for the judiciary to ignore.

Professors William Eskridge, Roy Brooks, Richard Posner, and others defend the democratic legitimacy of considering modern dynamics.[77] Professor Brooks claims, more or less, that the institutional framework of the judiciary as a whole supports the authority of judges to vindicate clearly held public policies (i.e., policy vindication). According to Brooks, renegade policy creations, the injection of norms that do not appropriately represent the majority of citizens, (elite citizens?), are routinely excised from the law (or otherwise squelched) by the appeals process, the legislative and constitutional amendment process, sometimes and to a limited extent by actions of the executive and executive agencies, and perhaps to an even more limited extent by the press and public opinion.

The following is intended to demonstrate that critical race theory, critical race tax theory, the consideration of race and racism, the consideration of group subordination—can all be incorporated and considered under each of these deliberative aesthetics. Dynamism is where the consideration of group subordination is usually placed—derisively labeled as a policy consideration. There, racism and group subordination can be acknowledged as a real-life problem and, yet, categorically ignored as an affront to law or democracy or institutional competence, etc. But here I intend to show that, among other things, a central tenet of textualism requires judges to avoid absurd consequences, including the exacerbation of group subordination, and that there is also evidence to suggest that the Congress never intends for its statutes to be interpreted in a manner that either produces racial subordination or exacerbates it.

Textualism (Plain Meaning)

Despite the fact that most people associate textualism with Justice Scalia's "plain meaning rule," textualism is actually a two-step process, perhaps even three.[78] First, the plain meaning rule requires a judge to choose the meaning that is consistent with what ordinary people understand the word to mean. For example, in *US v. Galletti* (2004), the court held that the IRS need not "assess" an employment tax liability against each individual partner after it had already assessed the employment tax liability with respect to the partnership.[79] The court relied on *Black's Law Dictionary* to ascertain the plain meaning of *assessment*, which according to the court relates only to the determination of a tax liability and not toward who owes it. Somewhat similarly, the court in *Knight v. Commissioner* (2008) relied on *Webster's Third New International Dictionary* and the *American Heritage Dictionary* to determine the meaning of "would."[80]

While Knight and Galletti are both resolved on the grounds of plain meaning, they demonstrate some of the difficulties regarding the plain meaning technique: To whom is the meaning plain? Which interpretive community is most relevant or relevant at all? Galletti cited *Black's Law Dictionary*, suggesting that lawyers constituted the relevant community. Whereas Knight cited *Webster's* and *American Heritage*, suggesting that the entire body politic is the relevant interpretive community. What if there are disagreements within a particular community? The important question for the critical race scholar and the critical race tax scholar is what to do if the meaning of a term within the black community differs from the meaning assigned to it by mainstream authorities (be they lawyers, the general public, white males, etc.). If mainstream authorities conflict on this point, might the views of women, minorities, gays provide the tiebreaker?

I address these questions in chapter 1, Does it Matter What Slaves Thought Direct Tax Meant in the United States Constitution.[81] The Constitution prohibits direct taxation unless it is uniform throughout and apportioned amongst the several States. Yet, no one knows exactly what "direct" means.[82] The Supreme Court is unclear, and scholars are in fierce debate. Apparently, even the Framers of the Constitution knew that "direct" taxation had no plain meaning. But under the plain meaning rule, the intent or thoughts of the Framers is irrelevant: The only thing that matters is what the people of 1787 thought the term meant. Some complain that this type of originalism requires judges to become historians, and I add that argument that to be a good one, the judge-historian must consider, to the extent they differ from the prevailing views of the time, what women, blacks, Native Americans thought direct tax meant. This is not meant to say that using a dictionary is not a reasonable proxy for what the people thought a particular statutory term meant, nor do I contend that the benefits of becoming a great judge-historian necessarily exceed the costs.[83] Still, critical race theorists and critical race tax theorists should very well identify where there are meaningful differences between interpretive communities.

Textualism (Statutory Context)

The second step in a textual analysis is to consider whether a particular meaning offered for one statute is either consistent or causes a conflict with the meaning, intents or purposes of another related statute. For example, in *Gitlitz v. Commissioner* (2001), the issue revolved around whether a discharge of indebtedness to an insolvent taxpayer qualified as an "item of income."[84] Some scholars argue that discharges of indebtedness, which are typically considered income, are not income at all in the case for an insolvent taxpayer. The tax definition of income requires an "accession to wealth, clearly realized," and one cannot accede to wealth while still insolvent, so some say.

The court rejected this view, but it did not hold that the plain meaning of "income" to the ordinary person includes discharges of indebtedness in every case. Instead, the court noticed that Congress accounted for the discharge of indebtedness for an insolvent taxpayer in a section entitled "exclusions from income," situated amongst other statutes that referred to "exclusions of income." The court reasoned that it would be inconsistent with section 108 not to treat all discharges of indebtedness for an insolvent taxpayer as income. Similarly in *Boulware v. Commissioner* (2008), the court rejected a lower court's interpretation of the term "deficiency" in a civil tax fraud statute because the lower court included an element of intent that would be inconsistent with the way in which other sections, sections 301 and 316, determine a tax liability.[85]

For another example, in *Knight v. US*(2008), the court found the Second Circuit's construction inconsistent not only with plain meaning, but with statutory context as well. Section 67(e) also requires that the costs be "paid or incurred in connection with the administration of the . . . trust." This portion of the statute is rendered redundant by a construction of 67(e) that covers only costs that an individual is incapable of incurring. As the court noted, "We can think of no expense that could be incurred exclusively by a trust but would nevertheless not be "paid or incurred in connection with its administration." Under the taxpayer's construction, all costs fitting the first provision automatically satisfied the second provision, which rendered the second provision superfluous.[86]

Consequently, critical tax theorists should identify when the interpretation of a tax statute or the application of some tax law doctrine conflicts with civil rights statutes or causes some other unintended consequence relating to group subordination. Sager and Cohen's "How the Income Tax Undermines Civil Rights Laws" is a fine example.[87] In it, they demonstrate how certain interpretations of the assignment of income doctrine were inconsistent with the effective enforcement of civil rights statutes. Eventually, Congress passed the American Jobs Creation Act as a statutory fix to the problem Sager and Cohen identified.

Critical theorists should take particular note of statutory context, because in tax cases it has been used to trump plain meaning! In *EC Term of Years Trust v. United States* (2007), the court invoked statutory context to reject the plain meaning of the statutory term "any civil action."[88] *EC Term of Years* sought to challenge an IRS levy under sections 7426 and 1346, respectively. The lower courts held that their petition under section 7426 was untimely, and that section 1346 was unavailable even though the petition was timely and the plain language of this statute granted jurisdiction over "any" case. Relying on several precedents in a variety of contexts, the court held that where general jurisdiction statutes avail courts to "any civil action" Congress intends for them to hear any civil action except those that are the subject of a "more precisely, drawn detailed statute," and especially where "resort to a general remedy would effectively extend the limitations period for the specific one." The court held that despite the unambiguous term "any" section 1346 is unavailable to third-party challenges to an IRS levy, because otherwise section 7426's more stringent limit on administrative and judicial remedy would be meaningless.

In addition to *EC Term of Years Trust* (2007), the court followed roughly the same decisional procedure in *Hinck v. US* (2007),[89] and *United States v. Clintwood Elkwood Mining* (2008).[90] This trilogy of cases stands for the proposition that where Congress provides for a specific administrative and judicial remedy litigants may not avoid the strictures of such a scheme by attempting to proceed under a more general (and presumably more favorable) jurisdiction statute, even if the plain meaning of the more favorable statute seems to allow it. *EC Term of Years* involved a challenge to an IRS levy of property from a person other than the owing taxpayer, *Hinck* concerned a taxpayer challenge to an IRS refusal to abate interest, and *Clintwood Elkhorn* extends the principle to constitutional challenges. In *Clintwood Elkhorn,* the taxpayer paid taxes erroneously assessed but did not file an administrative claim "within three years of the filing of a return or two years of payment of the tax" because the tax collected in 1978 was not found unconstitutional until 1998. Although their claim for refund fit under the literal terms of the "more forgiving" Tucker Act, the court held that when Congress enacts precise, detailed administrative and judicial remedies, like section 7422, it intends to foreclose resort to more general procedures. Similarly, critical race theorists should argue that consistency with civil rights statutes trumps plain meaning.

Textualism (Absurd Consequences)

The third step in the textualist process is to guard against absurd consequences. The court in *EC Term of Years Trust* also noted that 7426's more stringent time limitation is "no accident . . . since after seizure of property for nonpayment of taxes [an IRS] district director is likely to suspend further collection activities against the taxpayer" and allowing taxpayers to resort to section 1346 would entirely frustrate Congress' intent to ease the IRS' administrative burden. Surely, the court would not hold that interpretations that cause extra burdens on the IRS are "absurd" per se, but they can be sometimes.

Moreover, *United Dominion Industries v. US* (2001) shows that something less than "absurdity" is required in order for the court to then examine deliberative functions other than text (i.e., intent, purpose, modern dynamics).[91] The court in *United Dominion Industries* would not rest, even though the court believed the taxpayer's argument was more consistent with the statutory text than the IRS'. The court's "textual disposition quotient" was left unsatisfied, however, and the court resorted to consideration of intent and purposes. Therefore, the soft textualist style of the Supreme Court forces/encourages critical tax scholars to engage in debates about how plain is plain, plain to whom, and which related statutes and consequences might cause the judiciary to reject the plain meaning—if and when adherence to the plain meaning would maintain or exacerbate racial subordination. Of course, Justice Thomas, as the strictest textualist on the court, would have relied on a canon of statutory construction in *United Dominion*, rather than consider intent and purposes.

Ultimately, even hardcore textualism allows/requies critical tax theorists to identify when and where interpretations of tax statutes produce consequences relating to group subordination and argue that those consequences are legally "absurd." For example, in *Bob Jones v. US* (1983), Justice Burger could have reasoned that despite the fact the plain meaning of charitable as understood by the people of 1890 and 1917 clearly allows for racially discriminatory private schools, adopting that definition would produce the absurd consequence of promoting and exacerbating racial subordination and subverting domestic tranquility.[92] There is an obvious congruence between "public policy" in tax jurisprudence and "absurd consequences" in textualist literature, and critical race tax theorists must take hold of it.

Intentionalism and Purposivism

Critical race tax theorists should also identify evidence that proves legislatures *intend* for their statutes to be interpreted in ways that do not maintain or exacerbate group subordination. Purpose and intent are closely related. They are often linked and sometimes hard to distinguish, because each is dependent on an imaginatively constructed legislative intent, as to both form and consequence. Intent relates to the meaning the author of a text had in mind, while purpose relates to the consequences the author sought to produce or avoid. Imagine that when a legislature prohibits vehicles in the park, they may have intended to prohibit carbon-powered things with two or more wheels that can travel over 30 mph (intent), because such things produce accidents, as well as noise and air pollution (purposes).

Law, American-style, is based on the idea that the legislature is supreme, while the judiciary is subordinate and enforces legislative commands. Adherence to the concept of "interpretation" supports this conception of legislative supremacy, even though it permits wide discretion. Evidence of legislative intent and purpose can be found in the text of the statute at issue and related statutes, as well as legislative work papers, subsequent legislative actions or inaction, administrative pronouncements, as well as judicial opinions. Judges and commentators in search of legislative intent differ wildly about which of these categories of evidence is best. For one example, courts used to rely on so-called legislative history to glean legislative intent, but not much anymore.[93] For another, Justice Scalia suggests that the best evidence of legislative intent is the plain meaning of the words they used.[94]

The quest for intent is fraught with many interpretive questions. How much weight should courts give to legislative inaction after a judicial or executive pronouncement? Should courts assume that a legislative re-enactment incorporates all of the undisturbed prior judicial decisions under that statute as the putative intent of the Congress? Is this not also the true import of stare decisis with respect to statutory interpretation? Should administrative interpretations be similarly credited as the putative intent of the legislature? If so, what constitutes an "official" or "authoritative" executive interpretation? These questions amount to one: Which Congress are we speaking of, the enacting, the subsequent, the present? What about imagining an "objective legislature"?

Inaction of the legislature means something, even if we are not 100 percent sure what.[95] See the case of *Bob Jones University*, for example. Therefore, considering legislative inaction for a second demonstrates how unruly the search for intent can be. In *Boeing v. US* (2003), the court states, "the fact that Congress did not legislatively override [the regulation] in enacting the FSC provisions in 1984 serves as persuasive evidence that Congress regarded that regulation as a correct implementation of its intent."[96] Consider also that in *Craft v. US* (2002) the court credited a particular interpretation as the likely putative intent of the legislature because it believed Congress failed to codify the interpretation only because it was thought to be unnecessary.[97]

Consider, on the other hand, that in *Commissioner v. Banks* (2005), the court ignored the fact that Congress passed the American Jobs Creation

Act while the case was still before the court. The AJCA provided an above the line deduction for litigation expenses in a discriminations suit, thereby clearly expressing the legislature's intention that the litigant owns the case and receives all of the income and "needs" an unlimited deduction for the expense.[98] The court suggests in *Banks* that the views of the current legislature are irrelevant; which, by the way, is inconsistent with the court's approach to intent in *Bob Jones* (1983). Legislative action/inaction is probably the least orderly feature of the Supreme Court's deliberative processes.

To some, these unresolved questions regarding legal interpretive practice, and others, reduce finding the "true" interpretation to "a dream" or a "wild goose chase."[99] But, despite the indeterminacy of intent, the court insists that that is the object of their inquiry in statutory cases. Therefore, critical tax theorists must deal with it. Crits must gather and present evidence suggesting that Congress does not mean for its statutes to increase racial inequalities. The case of *Bob Jones* supports such an intention, as does Geoffrey Parsons Miller's research on the meaning of "necessary and proper," which we will discuss later.

This task is not only important with regard to appellate advocacy. Because of the Chevron doctrine, the administrative process is now more than ever where a great deal of law is made, and its lodestar is also legislative intent. Critical theorists, then, must also engage with the administrative process and demonstrate there that Congress does not want federal programs implemented in ways that exacerbate racial hierarchy.[100]

Intent and Purpose (Executive Pronouncements as Works for Hire)

Cleveland Indians Baseball (2001), *United Dominion Industries* (2001), *Fior D'Italia* (2002), and *Boeing* (2003) represent twenty-first-century tax cases in which the court determined whether and which Treasury regulations best represented the putative intent of Congress as to how important tax computations should be made. Consistent with the *Chevron* doctrine, those regulations formally promulgated via notice and comment rulemaking receive the highest emphasis, while those less formally promulgated interpretations typically but not always receive lesser emphasis.[101]

Even more helpful to the student of statutory interpretation, these cases distinguish between intent and purpose, and demonstrate that despite their close teleological relationship the two can often be in competition in practice. In each case (*Cleveland Indians*, *United Dominion*, *Fior D'Italia*, and *Boeing*), the IRS provided a method of calculation, which, under the Chevron/Mead Doctrine, presumably represented the intent of Congress; while the taxpayer argued that the intended method would produce consequences that Congress intended for the courts to avoid.

Consistent with the Chevron/Mead Doctrine, the court sided with the IRS when the interpretation was promulgated through notice and comment rulemaking, and was less deferential to the IRS when the interpretation had not. Because the Chevron Doctrine presumes that an official treasury interpretation, one that is duly promulgated through either notice and comment rulemaking or formal agency adjudication, has already taken notice of, considered and weighed all the relevant consequences tethered to legislative expectations, it is therefore incumbent upon critical tax scholars to influence the executive branch as much if not more than the judiciary.

In *Fior D'Italia* (2002), the court permitted the IRS to assess a restaurant's employment tax liability by estimating the amount of tips employees received using a sampling of credit card receipts, rather than using employee-made reports.[102] Even though Congress in another statute specifically relieved restaurants of the administrative burden of policing its staff over the issue of tip reporting, the court held that Congress did not intend to limit the range of duly promulgated methods the IRS might deploy in determining a deficiency. The taxpayer's argument seemed consistent with some clearly identified legislative purposes, yet the court would not disturb the IRS' use of long-standing methods for making assessments presumably because Congress is aware of them and did not anywhere explicitly limit the Treasury's ability to continue making assessments in the same manner. Inconsistency with statutory purposes could have rendered the IRS interpretation unreasonable, pursuant to step two of the Chevron Doctrine. But, it did not. The court rarely finds duly promulgated regulations to be "unreasonable" under step two of the *Chevron* analysis. *Fior D'Italia* demonstrates the strength of administrative pronouncements as the putative intent of Congress, and why critical theorists must engage in notice and comment rulemakings and other administrative procedures designed to produce regulations or interpretations carrying the force of law.

On the other hand, determining which of several regulations best evinces legislative intent can be a challenge in itself, and admits interpretive discretion. In *Boeing Co. v. United States* (2003), the court permitted the IRS to adjust the return of a parent and subsidiary domestic international sales corporation using an administrative rule that requires research and development costs to be allocated to all of the parent's product lines regardless whether those R&D costs were in fact dedicated to just one product line.[103] The court held that a proposed (but not yet duly promulgated) regulation, issued directly pursuant to the operating statute, which would allow dedicated costs to be distributed in respect of their product lines did not apply, because the Commissioner had already determined in another regulation, one that was duly promulgated but not under the statute in question, that the benefits from R&D costs are inherently speculative and may inure to all areas of production. A duly promulgated regulation promulgated under a related statute beat out a proposed regulation issued but not finally promulgated under the precise statute at issue. Why this is so, and whether it will be so in future cases is perhaps why Jack Beerman calls *Chevron* a failure.[104] I, on the other hand, believe uncertainty is not the failure of *Chevron*, but the inevitable consequence of depending legal outcomes on the concept of intent.

The dissent in *Boeing* would have emphasized the regulation under the operative statute even though it had not been duly promulgated. The majority, on the other hand, found that the regulations complemented each other, and that the taxpayer had to satisfy both. It remains a deliberative question whether and in what contexts a proposed regulation under the operative statute trumps a conflicting duly promulgated regulation under a related statute. Where such deliberative questions remain unresolved, critical tax theorists should consider whether a rule based approach to such deliberative questions is beneficial or detrimental to group subordination.

Intent and Purpose (Objective Purposes)

On the less "positive" side, Aharon Barak, justice of the Israeli Supreme Court, argues in "Purposive Interpretation in Law" that judges should consider those consequences a reasonable legislature would want a judge to consider.[105] Barak contends that there are goals an objective legislature would always seek to pursue, even without documentation confirming that belief. A formalist would probably reject the ethereal nature of these "objective purposes," because it makes purpose almost indistinguishable from modern dynamics (those consequences untethered to legislative expectations (i.e., public policy or judicial activism). However, the twenty-first century tax cases show that within tax law the Supreme Court considers some consequences like administrative efficiency or taxpayer notice that can reasonably be placed in the realm of objective purposes (i.e., consequences a reasonable legislature would expect a judge to consider without that judge finding evidence to do so in legislative history or some like positive representation). For another example, Deborah Geier suggests that the structure of the Internal Revenue code itself evinces certain purposes, like income and deduction matching, the progressive rate structure, etc.[106]

Twenty-first century Supreme Court tax cases decided on the basis of consistency with legislative purposes include *United Dominion Industries* (2001) (administrative efficiency and taxpayer convenience), *Banks v. Commissioner* (2005) (horizontal equity) and *Ballard v. Commissioner* (2005) (taxpayer convenience). Purposive concerns were also discussed in *all* the other cases, *Galletti, Gitlitz, Cleveland Indians, Craft, Hinck, Boulware, Boeing, EC Term of Years, Clintwood Elkhorn, Knight, Fior D'Italia* and *Ballard*.

The court most often considers the notion that a particular deliberative choice will facilitate or exacerbate tax avoidance. It also considers whether a deliberative choice is consistent with horizontal equity, judicial and administrative efficiency, and taxpayer convenience and notice. Because in these cases the court did not cite to legislative work papers to identify these concerns, these are best categorized as "objective" purposes, or perhaps even modern dynamics. If taxpayer notice and convenience and judicial and administrative efficiency are objective purposes that are eligible for the court's consideration, then the court should also consider whether a particular interpretation maintains or exacerbates racial subordination.

Intent and Purpose (Constitutional Purposes?)

Recent scholarship suggests that the Constitution requires federal courts to consider whether a proffered interpretation of a federal statute exacerbates racial or other group subordination. For example, Justice Stephen Breyer argues that the text of the Constitution as a whole evinces a purpose toward greater and fuller democratic participation.[107] The Constitution also references domestic tranquility. To the extent tax laws or the interpretation or enforcement thereof maintain or exacerbate racial subordination, they detract from these constitutionally derived goals.

More specifically, Geoffrey Parsons Miller, in "The Corporate Law Background of the Necessary and Proper Clause," suggests that the Necessary and Proper Clause "requires that federal law may not, without adequate justification, discriminate against or otherwise disproportionately affect the interests of particular citizens vis-a-vis others."[108] The Framers failed to define the terms "necessary" and "proper." Even Daniel Webster treated necessary and proper synonymously and equated them both with fit, best, and useful. Parsons' research shows, however, that corporate charters of that day routinely incorporated these terms, in conjunction as well as separately, and that those charters intended a particular meaning for "necessary" and "proper":

> Each of these contexts where "proper" plays a distinctive role is one affecting the interest of corporate stakeholders. The decision to declare a dividend affects the interest of shareholders; the decision as to when to call a meeting or levy a tax affects the interest of those who are supposed to attend the meeting or pay the tax. . . . Where the term "proper" is absent or rare . . . the relevant relationship are not between the corporation and its stakeholders but rather between the corporation and a third party acting at arms' length. . . . The term "proper" might therefore convey the idea that, in carrying out a given authority, the company to its managers should design the actions takes so as to consider the effects on stakeholders in the firm.[109]

Professor Miller's interpretation of the commerce clause supports critical race theorists in two ways: 1) That all federal statutes must be interpreted with respect toward whether they maintain or exacerbate racial subordination, and 2) that racial subordination includes express discrimination as well as disparate impacts. One could argue that the Necessary and Proper Clause is inapplicable to tax law since the IRC is not enacted under the Commerce Clause. However, in *Mayo Foundation* (2010), the court held that there is no reason to interpret federal tax statutes in any manner different from other federal legislation.[110]

The Supreme Court's holding in *Bob Jones v. United States* (1983) also supports the critical theorist's claim that all tax statutes should be evaluated toward whether they intentionally or unintentionally maintain or exacerbate racial subordination.[111] *Bob Jones University* stands for the proposition that all branches of government have a compelling government interest in eradicating racism, and Congress does not intend for its statutes to be interpreted in a manner that subsidizes racial subordination.

In 1970, the IRS instituted a new policy that disqualified private schools, including religious schools, from tax exemption if they were racially exclusionary. In subsequent years, the IRS ratcheted up the policy, including proposing a formula for testing whether schools were exclusionary. Despite vehement opposition from a vocal minority, Congress never repealed the IRS' position. Instead, Congress subsequently enacted a statute prohibiting racial discrimination in private social clubs. Chief Justice Burger noted that 1) Congress failed to repeal the IRS' policy even though the issue had been widely and publicly discussed in Congress and in the public, 2) bills calling for repeal did not get out of committee and garnered less support year after year, and 3) Congress enacted another statute prohibiting tax exemptions for private social clubs, agreeing in principle with the IRS' policy with respect to private schools. Burger held that Congress either acquiesced to or approved of the rule. Thus, *Bob Jones v. United States* can stand for the proposition that Congress never intends for its federal statutes to be interpreted so as to maintain or exacerbate racial subordination.[112]

On the other hand, *Chevron/BrandX* may limit *Bob Jones* to the proposition that the Treasury or any other executive *may* interpret statutes so as not to maintain or exacerbate racial subordination, then critical race theorists and critical race tax theorists must address the executive agencies as much as the courts in order to ensure that each federal agencies promulgate rules toward the recognition and eradication of racial subordination and/or that rules of general applicability do not have the effect of maintaining or exacerbating racial subordination.[113]

To some, *Bob Jones* provided the final and conclusive evidence that statutory interpretation is inextricably political, and was probably a key inspiration for the Chevron Doctrine. Not only was the judicial interpretation of "charitable" vexing as to whether it included those who discriminate on the basis of race, but the Reagan administration changed course in the middle of litigation and argued against the IRS regulation. In his *Bob Jones* concurrence, Justice Powell agreed only that the IRS construction was permissible, but not a necessary interpretation. Then, one year later, the court completely adopted Justice Powell's concurrence in *Bob Jones*. The court recognized in Chevron that a new presidential election brought in a new administration with a new evaluation of public policy that the court would be thereafter bound to respect. Thus, the court announced in *Chevron* that it was giving up the interpretation business to the executive, that the executive's official word will bind the public so long as it is not manifestly contrary to a specific and clearly ascertainable intent of Congress.

In a later case, the court held that Chevron Doctrine can even trump the doctrine of Stare Decisis.[114] So even though the court held in *Bob Jones* that charitable does not include those who racially discriminate or subordinate and that all statutes should not maintain or exacerbate racial subordination, the Chevron Doctrine permits the IRS to reverse a Supreme Court interpretation such as *Bob Jones* so long as the court did not base its decision on the "plain meaning." Again, critical race theorists and critical race tax theorists should understand that the Chevron Doctrine, which gives the executive power not only to interpret but also to reinterpret, requires them to lobby executive agencies for rules that eradicate racial subordination, or at least for rules that do not unintentionally or unwittingly maintain or exacerbate racial subordination.

Modern Dynamics

Dynamism represents the consideration of consequences untethered to legislative expectations. To some, *Bob Jones v. United States* was an example of political rather than principled decision making by the Supreme Court, because there was conflicting evidence as to whether Congress as a whole specifically intended to deny charitable exemptions to private schools who discriminate on the basis of race. The dissent complained that the plain meaning of charitable, especially at the time the charitable exemption statutes were enacted, included private schools even if they discriminated on the basis of race.[115] The court held that Congress rejected the original, plain, common law meaning of charitable, since they amended the statute several times over the years to contravene the common law and acquiesced to IRS interpretations that did the same. It held that even if Congress did not form a clear consensus over the specific question whether racist private schools should receive tax exemptions, the propenderance of the evidence suggested that a majority of Congress either approved or acquiesced to the IRS' interpretation. Moreover, the court noted that all three branches of government have expressed the view that eradicating racial discrimination was a compelling interest. Plain meaning was rejected as anachronistic, legislative intent seemed to favor the IRS, and combating racial discrimination as a reasonable and objective legislative purpose also clearly favored the IRS.

But was there really enough evidence to prove that the legislature intended for the IRS to strip racist schools of their federal tax exemption? Or, did the court simply inject their estimation of the public's feelings? Or, worse in terms of legislative supremacy, did the court inject their own policy preferences for racial conciliation? Judicial activism!

Judith Resnick for one believes the court was merely vindicating the policy preferences of the public. The court was lambasted by conservatives for unprincipled decision making, an unelected branch of government elevating its moral policies above the will of the people. This is theocracy, not democracy; or so the critics would contend. But *Bob Jones* and other dynamically decided cases, like *Brown v. Board*, can only be considered a highjacking of democracy if combating racial discrimination was merely the personal policy preferences of the court and not the policy of the people of the United States.[116] The *Bob Jones* court vindicated public policy rather than impose it: even if combating racial discrimination cannot be considered an objective legislative purpose, even if it is a dynamic or "policy" driven decision, Roy Brooks teaches us that such decisions can endure only when they vindicate public policy rather than impose it.[117] Looking back after thirty years, it is hard to believe that it was seriously argued that the will of the people was to subsidize racially discriminatory private schools, or that identifying the eradication of racism as a legislative purpose was somehow a usurpation of congressional authority. In this sense *Bob Jones* and the dynamic interpretation that produced it have been ratified and vindicated.

Justice Scalia, of all people, reveals to us in *Craft v. United States* that modern dynamics still matter, that courts should consider how interpretations of tax law affect discrete groups. *United States v. Craft* (2002) held that a federal tax lien can attach to property held as a tenancy of the entirety.[118] Although the court acknowledged that property held by the entirety is burdened by restrictions on alienation, it found that property held by a tenancy by the entirety is not unlike property held in the form of a partnership or a Texas homestead, each of which is subject to liens by the federal tax collector. Justice Scalia complained in dissent that the court's ruling is likely to have a detrimental impact on married women. Who knew that Scalia is not only a dynamist, but a critical theorist to boot!

Are we to ignore Scalia's concern because it was written in dissent? That seems odd, especially since judicial dissents tend to point at a legitimate concern the majority failed to consider or considered improperly. If the disparate impact on married women is a relevant and important consideration to the Supreme Court justice who has written books not only defending textualism but also teaching how to perform it, then group subordination must be an absurd consequence which provides cause for rejecting the statutes plain meaning. Or, textualism is merely a starting point in a deliberative process that includes the consideration of purposes and modern dynamics, like avoiding the maintenance or exacerbation of group subordination.

CRT AND LAW AS AN AUTOPOEITIC SYSTEM

American Law thinks in terms of text, intent, purpose and, to a lesser extent, modern dynamics.[119] Nicklas Luhmann, Gunther Tuebner, and Hugh Baxter conceive of law as an autopoietic system; a closed, self-referential system that can observe and process discourse from outside of itself. For them, law and justice are distinct systems whose language and way of thinking are symmetrical to some degree. By contrast, Dworkin believes justice and law are best seen as one and the same, rather than distinctly.[120] Regardless whether one is the hedgehog who knows one big thing or the wolf who knows lots of little things, if neo-pragmatism has indeed taken hold of the top theorists in the legal academy, as James Hackney suggests, then a focus on degrees and measurement should follow. Autopoiesis permits this.

Aesthetically speaking, law is alive in the sense that it is distinct from its environment (formalism), yet influenced by that environment (realism). Therefore, it is the duty of critical race theorists to inject forms and constructs into the law's decision-making processes which will allow it to recognize and digest institutionalized racism, or institutionalized group subordination in whatever context. The consideration of asymmetrical market imperfections relating to race, gender, sexuality, etc., is the framework I suggest will help law better recognize the extent and degree to which governmental practices perpetuate or exacerbate racial inequality or group subordination.[121] The consideration of asymmetrical market imperfections is compatible with text, intent, purpose and modern dynamics.

The once vibrant debate over legal theory has petered out for the most part.[122] Contrary to the chauvinistic debates over legal decision making in the twentieth century, law as an autopoietic system accepts both formalism and realism as indispensable parts of any good legal system.[123] The important questions for law commentators revolve not around which of these is correct, but the degree of accuracy and efficiency which a formal system can observe and digest the environment in which it finds itself.

James Hackney demonstrates in his latest work *Legal Intellectuals in Conversation* that many of the old great prize fighters have adopted a neo-pragmatist attitude, one where they accept that each jurisprudential theory has benefits and costs, and that it is impossible to determine which one is True.[124] Hackney calls this the death of theory. Pierre Schlagg describes it as "Formalism and Realism in Ruins."[125] The death of theory should be followed by aesthetic conceptions of law, including law as an autopoietic system. Aesthetic conceptions should focus on "degrees." Therefore, twenty-first-century statutory interpretation questions should not focus on "whether" to consider group subordination, but how much "emphasis" should be placed on it vis-à-vis other relevant concerns like simplicity, efficiency, etc.[126]

Of course, there are those who still believe that their approach is the correct, true, or best approach. But Schlagg, for one, demonstrates that formalism and realism cannot really do without each other, because neither answers hard legal questions by itself. Schlagg reduces legal theory debates from one where the players believe they are in search of truth to one where the contestants are simply trying to construct the most appropriate (the least assailable) aesthetic.[127] For example, the textualist mantra is that "the text is the law." This is a slogan, an effective one, but not a reason.

If formalism and realism are really of little use independent of each other, and if it is also true that legal theory is about providing the most appropriate aesthetic with which to describe law, its structures, apparatus and functions, then law should be conceived of as an autopoietic system because autopoiesis recognizes the indispensability of form and structure and all those things which make law distinct from its environment, yet also recognizes that law has always looked outside of itself when the rigidity of its internal processes produce decisions at odds with other social constructs, like justice or efficiency, for example. Without form or structure, without skin and bone and organs and tissue, the body of law is not distinct from its environment, it is annihilated as it melds into or yields to other constructs. Without respect for reality, on the other hand, the body of law is incompatible with constructs like justice and efficiency and, and for that reason falls into desuetude. If we conceive of law as an autopoietic system, however, we can then conceive of formalism as simply that which makes law distinct from all other systems, and realism as the system's capacity to respond to its environment. As Schlagg demonstrates, reality cannot be processed without forms and constructs. Therefore, even realists must inject into the law formal constructs appropriate for recognizing and processing the environment in which law operates.

From an autopoietic perspective, then, the careless critical race theorists simply demands that the law recognize racism, whereas the more effective critical race theorist develops or identifies a method by which the system can recognize racism. For example, Charles Lawrence does not simply demand that the Supreme Court recognize racism when deciding equal protection cases, he attempts to inject the construct of "cultural meaning" so that the body of law can recognize and process a wider variety of racial phenomenon.[128] Conceiving of racism as asymmetrical market imperfections is designed to accomplish the very same thing, except that it is intentionally congruent with neo-classical economics because such symmetry may make it easier for the body to accept the device.

Of course there is also the philosophically critical legal theorist who thinks it useless, even counter-revolutionary, to try and develop useful constructs and inject them into the system. To them, law is not distinct from its environment at all; it is subsumed by power and politics. And yet, the autopoietic project accounts for philosophical critical legal theory as well. Its critique is supplemental, in that it recognizes the fact that those with power have much greater ability to inject discursive constructs into the body of law.

The Supreme Court's federal tax opinions from 2001 to 2010 demonstrate the autopoietic nature of law, because they illustrate how the court relies on a self-referential process for making decisions while at the same time it keeps at least one eye open to reality. The court's decision-making process may resemble that of other constructs, and even uses the same terminology on occasion, but the court's process is justified by itself, not in relation to any other construct.

As we just attempted to demonstrate, in contrast with the open-ended decision-making process relating to abstract justice, for example, the law (according to the Supreme Court of the United States) thinks in terms of four guideposts, 1) text, 2) intent, 3) purpose, and 4) modern dynamics. Even if another social system restricts itself to these four considerations, the law assigns its own level of emphasis to each consideration, and it develops its own methods for entertaining these considerations. Moreover, its twenty-first-century tax opinions show that the court thinks algorithmically. It attempts first to resolve legal question by strictly considering text. But if a textual disposition quotient is not reached, the court resorts to considering the intent and purposes of the legislature (typically from the perspective of the Executive branch, see *Chevron*). Should the consideration of text, intent and purposes altogether continue to produce uncertainty in a given case, the court might then open its eyes to recognize modern dynamics, policy, consequences, or whatever one might call "reality."

Not only does the Supreme Court's twenty-first century tax opinions support the idea that the US law is relatively autopoietic, they also support the notion that to the extent the court can look outside of itself (*Craft*), it still chooses, as philosophical CRITs might predict, not to recognize race even when its relevant, as it did in *Banks v. Commissioner*. Toward greater recognition or racial phenomena, I offer next a critical race and economics concept of asymmetrical market imperfections as a discursive construct that critical race theorists can attempt to inject into the law's analytical processes.

ASYMMETRICAL MARKET IMPERFECTIONS RELATING TO RACE

Regardless whether one considers themselves a textualist, intentionalist, purposivist, or dynamist, each technique allows for judges to consider the effect a statute has on racial or group subordination. Each technique allows the law to see reality outside of itself, but then "the law" deliberates and justifies its decisions from within. The law prefers to stay within itself, but it also fears desuetude and will adjust to its environment, to preserve itself. Thus, in order to observe the environment yet remain independent of it, law uses internal structures that process discourse from the outside and transmogrify it into that with which it is more familiar. Ultimately, it is the role of legal "architects and engineers" to debate the extent which ought to observe its environment; and, it is incumbent on those who want it to see more than it does (realists and CRITs) to inject into the law constructs that help it do so.

The construct I offer for the judicial (as well as executive, legislative, and private) consideration of group subordination is a law and economics conception of racism as "asymmetrical market imperfections relating to race." In our conservatively constructed legal regime, appeals to justice (in all circumstances, not just race) are more persuasive to the extent they include obvious demonstrations of economic foul play.[129] Appeals for justice "fit" better within our legal architecture to the extent they deploy law and economics paradigms.[130] Of course, racial injustice like any other social phenomena cannot be reduced to economic theory and at the same time maintain perfect touch with reality. It would be far, far too much (flat out wrong even) to say that asymmetrical market failures define racism. The claim here is simply that expressing racial injustice in economic terms is a good, perhaps necessary complement to narratives, empiricism, and case analysis.

Asymmetrical Market Imperfections

We imagine that a free market distributes goods and services in a meritocratic manner goods and services are distributed to those who desire them most as evidenced by their willingness to pay for them. But the existence of a free market depends on a few things that are ignored in popular discourse. A truly free market requires that 1) everyone is a profit or utility maximizer, 2) everyone has a perfect ability to enter and exit all markets, 3) everyone has perfect information about goods, services and each other, and 4) all transactions costs are at least evenly distributed. Well, so much for a perfectly free and meritocratic market!

Everyone is not a profit maximizer, everyone cannot enter and exit any market they so desire, information is not perfectly had or even available to anyone, and transaction costs, like say environmental waste, are unevenly distributed.

Moreover, imperfections in the market relating to rationality, competition, information and transaction costs are asymmetrically imperfect with respect to race, gender, religion, etc. Thus, one can recognize and describe institutional racism as phenomena which maintain or exacerbate asymmetrical imperfections in the marketplace relating to race.[131] So long as asymmetries in market imperfections maintain racial subordination, the United States cannot claim the meritocratic economic environment it touts to the rest of the world. The degree with which we allow asymmetrical market imperfections to maintain racial subordination is also the degree with which our society can be considered a racial caste system. We are talking equality of opportunity, not necessarily results. Furthermore, the concept of racism as asymmetrical market imperfections is transportable to almost any and all forms of group subordination. It can also help describe racial marginalization in the marketplace of ideas or the market for legislation, etc.

Asymmetrically Distributed Transaction Costs

Most obviously, critical race theorists demonstrate how taxation produces or maintains asymmetrical market imperfections relating to race by showing how taxes cause an asymmetrical distribution of society's transaction costs. Asymmetrically distributed transactions costs are represented by the fact that blacks bear a greater burden of the nation's unwanted social and economic costs. For example, African Americans are disproportionately exposed to environmental waste.[132] Living near environmental waste causes blight, disease, and lower IQ scores, each of which negatively affects an individual's ability to think rationally, acquire information, and compete in today's marketplace. Because NIMBY's (Not In My Back Yard) are typically middle- to upper-class whites who can politically mobilize against environmental waste in their neighborhoods, the waste ends up near poor people, a disproportionate portion of which are black.

Taxation, regulation, and governmental decision making impose or shifts costs from one to another. Consider that even tort law can be conceptualized in terms of transaction costs—as a regulatory mechanism that puts a monetary cost on anti-social behavior so that the offending party can fully pay for their actions and not leave others holding the bag. Since the political process, from town, county, state to the federal government, is the mechanism for distributing transaction costs, lack of political access lies at the heart of asymmetrically distributed transactions costs.

Voting rights, then, lie at the heart of transaction costs and their (mal)distribution. Legal interventions into the electoral process that have expanded the electorate to include black voters, which allow for the election of black candidates, are designed to reduce the asymmetrical distribution of transaction costs. While those that have reduced the black electorate or the impact thereof, such as disenfranchisement through poll taxes, vote caging, voter fraud, and redistricting serve to disproportionately burden blacks with transaction costs and thusly further frustrate their attempts to compete in the general commercial market as well as the marketplace for legislation. Atiba Ellis examines the financial burdens of certain voting rules, and critical tax theorists might continue the discussion in terms of whether these costs amount to an unconstitutional poll tax.[133]

Consistent with racist taxation as asymmetrically distributed transactions costs, critical tax theorists have traditionally examined whether the incidence or burden of taxation falls disproportionately on blacks. Beverly Moran, for example, argues for a wealth tax that would make our system of taxation more progressive and, thus, fairer to black people who are disproportionately amongst the less propertied.[134] Critical tax theorists also question whether so-called tax expenditures or tax subsidies are asymmetrically distributed.[135] Dorothy Brown and others have examined tax subsidies for real estate and questioned whether such programs are of greater benefit to whites than blacks.[136] David Brennan's treatments of race in the tax exemption context might also be recharacterized in terms asymmetrically distributed tax subsidies.[137] Regina Jefferson's work on retirement taxation also fits this rubric, as does Daryll Jones', Reginald Mombrun's, Bobby Dexter's, Keeva Terry's, Phyllis Taite-Smith's. . . .

Asymmetrically Imperfect Competition

Critical theorists also demonstrate how taxation produces or maintains asymmetrical market imperfections relating to race by showing how taxes contribute to asymmetrical imperfect market competition relating to race. The first chapter of this book described different ways in which taxation was used to exclude blacks from many lucrative markets in the United States. Poll taxes, capitation taxes, discriminatory occupational taxes discouraged free blacks in the antebellum South from competing against free whites. Slavery itself was a nearly 100 percent tax on black labor that restricted blacks to a market that did not serve them, and prevented them from accumulating capital to deploy in more lucrative markets.

Since openly discriminatory market exclusions are prohibited at this point in time, asymmetrically imperfect competition relates principally to the fact that blacks have less capital (financial, human, and social) to enter or exit markets. Daria Roithmayr's "Locked In Segregation" examines the economic effect of the National Association of Realtors rule against interracial housing sales.[138] She shows how historical market exclusions can perpetuate income and wealth inequality well into future periods after the market exclusion has been removed. Toward the same end, Juan Perea examines the disproportionately distributed benefits of the GI Bill.[139]

Similarly, today's critical tax theorists might complain that because blacks are disproportionately concentrated in the labor market rather than the capital markets, a higher tax on labor than on capital is discriminatory in effect, because it contributes to or exacerbates the racially asymmetric nature of market competition. Also, Sager and Cohen show how taxation can relate to civil rights in surprising ways.[140] Civil rights laws, particularly those concerning fair employment, are designed for the principal purpose of increasing meritocracy and fair competition, and Sager and Cohen showed how tax law placed unreasonable burdens on the victims of racial discrimination who were expected to enforce those laws. Tax law in this context clearly had the effect of maintaining racially asymmetrical imperfections in market competition.

Asymmetrically Imperfect Information

Critical tax theorists can also demonstrate how taxation can produce or maintain asymmetrical market imperfections relating to race by showing how taxes contribute to asymmetrical imperfect information relating to race. Asymmetrically imperfect information has two important and interrelated components, the asymmetrical degree of information available to black people or the inequitable distribution of education, and the asymmetrical nature of information available about black people or the tendency for blacks to be depicted stereotypically as historically, intellectually, morally, and culturally inferior. Legal intervention has been hardly available as to the former and not at all as to the latter. Perhaps the difference in degree of legal intervention between asymmetric competition and asymmetric information relates again to interest convergence.[141] Excluding blacks from commercial transactions tends to also hurt whites who would otherwise profit in transactions with blacks, whereas excluding blacks from information tends to provide an incremental relative advantage to all whites. Still, Gary Becker argues that a nation's wealth is exactly that, the sum total of its citizens' human capital.[142] Thus, it is not wise national policy in the long run for blacks to be entirely devoid of the human capital that is information.

Where *Brown v. Board of Education* prohibits the state from providing separate educational facilities for blacks, but *San Antonio v. Rodriguez* permits the State to direct property tax revenue to wealthy neighborhoods that are disproportionately white and away from educational facilities that serve the poor who are disproportionately black and Latino.[143]

Of course, the current trend seems to be toward doing away with public schools in poor neighborhoods altogether and to subsidize education only for those who have sufficient income to pay for it. Since voucher programs do not pay the whole cost of private education, those with nothing to contribute are quickly transferred from the educational system to the prison system. Lest we stray too far from the immediate point, asymmetrically imperfect information stands for the proposition that blacks have less access than whites to accurate and useful information and endure more than whites false information about them. Whether our tax system helps or hurts the educational system as it relates to blacks is a worthy subject of both critical race theorists and critical race tax theorists.

Asymmetrically Imperfect Profit Maximization

Critical tax theory is less able to demonstrate how taxation can produce or maintain asymmetrical market imperfections relating to race by showing how taxes might contribute to asymmetrical imperfect information relating to race. Through media and other institutions, our society tends to encourage blacks more than whites toward destructive behaviors rather than productive ones. As Albert Einstein once stated, "those who meet such treatment [as an inferior class] themselves for the most art acquiesce in the prejudiced estimate because of the suggestive influence of the majority, and come to regard people like themselves as inferior."[144] Harvard philosopher Tommy Shelby ponders what can be done to address a lack of "vigor" amongst some African-Americans.[145] One excuse is that dealing with the constant micro-aggressions of institutionalized white supremacy drives black people crazy! Another reason, espoused by Malcolm X and which is very compatible with that expressed by Einstein, is that racism as an institution trains blacks to seek the back of the bus without being told.

Where does this backward culture come from, if not from slavery, if not from the effects of over two hundred years of a 100 percent tax on black labor? It is generally believed that high taxes squelch work ethic and innovation, so it should not be surprising at all that slavery and peonage as 100 percent tax on black labor poisoned the work ethic of black laborers for generations. The reward system under such a system is entirely perverted. Avoiding work becomes a revolutionary act, while working hard and producing strictly for the master's benefit is self-destructive and demeaning. Couple the 100 percent tax on black labor with other myriad informal taxes and costs imposed on "free" blacks, and it is not surprising that scores of poor black people simply believe the system is set up against them, to the point where there is not much point in trying. In the board game Monopoly, when a player does not believe he will earn enough going around the board to pay his expenses, he will roll the dice often hoping to land in jail.

CONCLUSION

Tax law demonstrates the degree with which the United States has been committed to racial group subordination or white supremacy. The absence of racial references in tax laws up until the end of the seventeenth century suggests that colonial America started without a commitment to racial hierarchy, even if it was clear that racial confrontation, admixture, and sometimes violent competition were set to increase. Near the end of the seventeenth century and extending into the Revolutionary period, some whites began to express notions of white superiority and black inferiority, notions which then found themselves expressed in law, including tax law. During the antebellum period of the nineteenth century, avocation for economic and cultural white supremacy was explicit and indiscreet, and law, including tax law, was expressly used to create and maintain racial order. Until the Civil War, this nation's state and local tax laws, particularly those of the southern states, clearly expressed the view that the United States as a nation was committed to white socio-economic-political supremacy.

From perhaps the Civil War to the present, white economic and political supremacy has been on the demise, in that outward indiscreet avocation for white supremacy has become disfavored to the point it is almost illegal. However, economic statistics today show that racial wealth inequality may be greater now than it has since the Civil War. Thus, the twentieth century may become most well-known for the long, slow march toward a bare de jure equality which allows whites to disingenuously disavow white supremacy while at the same time designing facially neutral laws like taxes in ways that maintain economic supremacy. In the twenty-first century, critical race tax theorists have accepted the responsibility of identifying facially neutral laws in taxation that distribute the burdens and benefits of taxation disproportionately, that maintain white economic supremacy. A complete demise of institutionalized white supremacy requires no less.

The general aim of the critical race theory project is to recognize that racism encompasses all manners, means and methods of group subordination, and not just abject discrimination. Despite its loose theoretical structure, CRT is practically unified in criticizing the Supreme Court's conception of racism, which focuses narrowly on "discrimination" to the exclusion of other racist phenomena.[146] In matters relating to the Equal Protection Clause, it tends to focus strictly on overt, legal discrimination based on race. Thus, whoever might look to law to help define social reality may come to believe that racism and overt discrimination is the same thing. It is not uncommon for law students and colleagues to express such a view. But the Supreme Court does not define racism. Its equal protection jurisprudence is designed only to determine what the government may do in terms of race relations. When it insists on findings of "discriminatory intent," it limits itself to seeing only overt expressions of white supremacy. Its reluctance to recognize statistical and other empirical evidence of discrimination allows for systemic and institutionalized group subordination in terms of race, gender, sexual orientation, ethnicity, etc.

Now, those who recognize race while ignoring racism tend to elicit the so-called free market in defense of economic disparities between blacks and whites.[147] The neo-liberal attitude does not ignore the huge economic disparities between whites in the aggregate and blacks in the aggregate. Instead, it usually places the blame on blacks themselves for not being able to take advantage of the free market and its promise of equal opportunity. Free market fundamentalists believe there exists a perfectly free market that produces equal opportunity of the type John Rawls would be proud.[148] According to this trope, the economic markets of the United States, or free market capitalism distributes wealth meritocratically. "DeMarquette" lords over our society and justly determines who succeeds and who fails. And if whites have more wealth than blacks, then it must be because of the licentiousness of black culture.

Yet, according to neo-classical economics, a free and meritocratic economic system cannot exist unless *everyone* is able to compete in any market they choose or refuse any market that serves them. We know not only that this perfect state of competition does not exist as a general proposition because of prior discrimination and oppression, the market is asymmetrically imperfect with respect to race (and gender, sexual orientation, etc.) blacks have less capital with which to compete, financial and otherwise. A free and meritocratic market requires perfect information—which is a fantasy of course. Yet government in the United States responds to the desires of its citizenry to increase the availability and accuracy of information, via public education, laws against fraud, libel and slander, etc.

Still, information available to and about black people is asymmetrically imperfect due to under-education, stereotypes, and other false notions of black inferiority. Moreover, asymmetrically distributed transaction costs, like taxes, drug and violence zoning, environmental waste, also perpetuate racial, economic inequality. By relying on the myth of the free market, postracialists, especially those who ignore that a truly free and meritocratic market requires certain preconditions, are also able to ignore racism and racial inequalities produced by social institutions that affect, even determine, the size, scope and operations of the marketplace.

Asymmetrical market imperfections as a concept demonstrate how the effect of past anti-competitive (racist) behavior is not limited to their specific time periods. Therefore, the foregoing tax history of racism focuses broadly on how taxes helped create and maintain racial economic inequality. It focuses on both tax as a mechanism for redistribution wealth according to the political desires of the citizenry, as well as tax as a mechanism for regulating competition in the marketplace.

And as far as a licentious black culture is concerned, consider that in the sharecropping/convict leasing system, employers routinely, fraudulently elongated the peonage contract of their most productive workers, until they worked many of them to death. Slavery and neo-slavery perverted the work ethic by penalizing effort and ingenuity and rewarding malaise, sloth and sabotage. If high taxation discourages productive behavior, then we should recognize how a 100 percent tax on black labor lasting over two hundred years could produce whatever lack of vigor is perceived by cultural critics.

NOTES

1. Darren Hutchison, *Preventing Balkanization or Facilitation Racial Domination: A Critique of the New Equal Protection*, 22 Virginia Journal of Social Policy and the Law (2014).
2. Critical Legal Studies, the legal branch of post-modernist philosophy, tends to concern itself with group subordination generally, while Critical Race Theory focuses on subordination relating to race specifically. Likewise, Critical Tax Theory analyzes whether and how tax law contributes to the subordination of any group regardless whether based on race, ethnicity, gender, sexual orientation, etc., while Critical Race Tax Theory projects like this tend to focus on how tax law relates to racial subordination strictly. Using this distinction, we might put scholars like David Brennen, Alice Gresham Bullock, Regina Jefferson, Phyllis Smith, Darryl Jones, Reginald Mombrun and Darryl Wilson's work in the Critical Race Tax Theory camp. Anthony Infanti, Nancy Knauer, Bridget Crawford, Marjorie Kornhauser, Neil Buchanan, Roberta Mann, Francine Lipman, Nancy Knauer and David Herzig, belong in the Critical Tax Theory camp. Of course, brilliant scholars such as Beverly Moran, Karen Brown, Mildred Robinson and Dorothy Brown can navigate seamlessly between the two.
3. Brown & Fellows, Taxing America (1995).
4. John Powell, *How Government Tax and Housing Policies Have Racially Segregated America*, in Taxing America 89 (1995).
5. Moran & Whitford, "*A black Critique of the Internal Revenue code*," 4 *Wisconsin Law Review* 751 (1996).
6. Lawrence A. Zelenak, *Taking Critical Tax Theory Seriously*, 76 North Carolina Law Review 1521–580 (1997).
7. Infanti & Crawford, Critical Tax Theory (2009); Lawrence A. Zelenak, *Taking Critical Tax Theory Seriously*, 76 North Carolina Law Review 1521–580 (1997).
8. Nagel & Murphy, The Myth of Ownership (2002).
9. *Banks v. Commissioner*, 543 U.S. 426 (2005).
10. Laura Sager and Stephen Cohen, "*How the Income Tax Undermines Civil Rights Law*," 73 Southern California Law Review 1075 (2000).
11. Ibid.
12. *Commissioner v. Banks*, 543 U.S. 426 (2005).
13. Another approach by Judge Beghe of the Tax Court compared the civil rights plaintiff to a sharecropper. Other scholarly approaches included considering the case a capital asset and characterizing the attorney's fee portion as basis.
14. Hon. Stephen F. Breyer, Active Liberty (2005).
15. *Craft v. United States*, 535 U.S. 274 (2002).
16. Roy Brooks, Structures of Judicial Decision Making (2005).

17. David Brennen, Karen Brown & Darryl Jones, Beyond Efficiency in United States Tax Law (2013); Nagel & Murphy, The Myth of Ownership (2002).
18. Infanti & Crawford, Critical Tax Theory (2009).
19. Richard Wood, *Supreme Court Jurisprudence of Tax Fairness,* 36 Seton Hall L. J. 421 (2006).
20. Nagel & Murphy, The Myth of Ownership (2002)
21. Richard Wood, *Supreme Court Jurisprudence of Tax Fairness,* 36 Seton Hall L. J. 421 (2006).
22. Compare North Carolina (1998), with Infanti & Crawford, Critical Tax Theory (2009).
23. Infanti & Crawford, Critical Tax Theory (2009).
24. Nagel & Murphy, The Myth of Ownership (2002)
25. Beverly I. Moran & William Whitford, *A black Critique of the Internal Revenue code,* 1996 Wis. L. Rev. 751.
26. Infanti & Crawford, Critical Tax Theory (2009).
27. Nagel & Murphy, The Myth of Ownership (2002)
28. 76 North Carolina Law Review (1998).
29. Infanti & Crawford, Critical Tax Theory (2009).
30. Ibid.
31. 76 North Carolina Law Review (1998).
32. Mylinh Uy, *Tax and Race: The Impact on Asian Americans,* 11 Asian Am. L.J. 117 (2004).
33. Richard Wood, *Supreme Court Jurisprudence of Tax Fairness,* 36 Seton Hall L. J. 421 (2006).
34. Moran & Whitford, "*A black Critique of the Internal Revenue code,*" 4 *Wisconsin Law Review* 751 (1996); Nagel & Murphy, The Myth of Ownership (2002).
35. Beverly Moran, '*Setting an Agenda for the Study of Tax and black Culture,*' University of Arkansas at Little Rock Law Review, 21 (1999). Also see D. Brown in Taxing America (1996).
36. Dorothy Brown, *How Home Ownership Keeps blacks Poorer Than whites,* Forbes Magazine (Dec. 10, 2012).
37. Infra
38. Nagel & Murphy, The Myth of Ownership (2002).
39. Ibid.
40. Nagel & Murphy choose not to go down this road, asserting that all people in society get roughly the same benefit from government expenditures, as compared to how all people would fare in a war of all against all. To disagree requires a critique of the "state of nature" as a concept, which might include the argument that poor people may do as well or better in a state of nature (as suggested by high rates of drug addiction and suicide in industrial countries). Nagel & Murphy, The Myth of Ownership (2002).
41. Neil Buchanan, "*The Role of Economics in Tax Scholarship,*" in Beyond Economic Efficiency in United States Tax Law. Ed. by David A. Brennen, Karen B. Brown and Darryll K. Jones) (2013).
42. Nagel & Murphy, The Myth of Ownership (2002).
43. Andre L. Smith, *Boycotts, Interest Convergence, and Asymmetrical Market Failures Relating to Race,* 56 Howard Law Journal 891 (2013) (Wiley A. Branton Symposium Issue); *Race, Law, and the Free Market: A Critical Law and Economics Conception of Racism as Asymmetrical Market Failures,* 4 Georgetown Journal of Law & Modern Critical Race Perspectives 39 (2012).
44. Consider the numerous works of Nobel Prize award winning economist Joseph Stiglitz on asymmetric information in the marketplace. Also see the works of co-Nobel Prize winners George Akerloff, Michael Spence, and others.
45. Thomas Nagel, *John Rawls and Affirmative Action,* Journal of blacks in Higher Education (2003).

46. Nagel & Murphy, The Myth of Ownership (2002). Sagit Leviner, *The Normative Underpinnings of Taxation*, in Beyond Economic Efficiency (2013).
47. Nagel & Murphy, The Myth of Ownership (2002).
48. Stephen M. Garcia, et al., "*Profit Maximization Versus Disadvantageous Inequality: The Impact of Self-Categorization*", J. Behav. Decision Making, 18 (2005).
49. Richard McAdams, *Cooperation and Conflict: The Economics of Group Status Production and Race Discrimination*, 108 Harv. L. Rev. 1003 (1995).
50. Derrick Bell, Faces at the Bottom of the Well (1992).
51. Nagel & Murphy, The Myth of Ownership (2002).
52. Calvin H. Johnson, Righteous Anger at the Wicked States: The Meaning of the Founders' Constitution (2009).
53. Infanti & Crawford, Critical Tax Theory (2009).
54. Nagel & Murphy, The Myth of Ownership (2002).
55. Infanti & Crawford, Critical Tax Theory (2009).
56. Laura Sager & Stephen Cohen, "*How the Income Tax Undermines Civil Rights Law*," 73 Southern California Law Review 1075 (2000).
57. Infra, chapter 1.
58. Derrick Bell, Faces at the Bottom of the Well (1992).
59. Nagel & Murphy, The Myth of Ownership (2002); Infanti, *Tax Equity*, 55 Buff. L. Rev. 1191 (2008).
60. Anthony Farley, *The Dream of Interpretation*, University of Miami Law Review (2002).
61. Roy Brooks, Structures of Judicial Decision Making (2005).
62. Ibid.
63. Richard Posner, Law, Pragmatism & Democracy (2003).
64. William N. Eskridge, Dynamic Statutory Interpretation 34 (1994).
65. Manning, John F. "*Textualism and the Equity of the Statute*," 101 Columbia Law Review 1 (2001); Antonin Scalia, A Matter of Interpretation: Federal Courts and the Law (1997); John H. Ely, Democracy and Distrust (1980).
66. Anthony Farley, *The Dream of Interpretation*, University of Miami Law Review (2002).
67. Andre Smith, *The Deliberative Stylings of Leading Tax Law Scholars*, The Tax Lawyer (2007).
68. James Hackney, Under Cover of Science (2007).
69. Antonin Scalia, A Matter of Interpretation: Federal Courts and the Law (1997). Manning, John F. "*Textualism and the Equity of the Statute*," 101 Columbia Law Review 1 (2001); Vermeule.
70. Stanley Fish, *There is No Textualist Position*, 42 San Diego Law Review 629, 649 (2005).
71. Antonin Scalia, A Matter of Interpretation: Federal Courts and the Law (1997).
72. Andre Smith, *Formulaically Describing 21st Century Supreme Court Tax Jurisprudence*, Houston Business and Tax Law Journal (2008).
73. Pierre Schlag, Formalism and Realism in Ruins (Mapping the Logics of. Collapse), 95 Iowa L. Rev. 195 (2009).
74. Aharon Barak, Purposive Interpretation in Law (2005).
75. William N. Eskridge, Dynamic Statutory Interpretation 34 (1994).
76. Antonin Scalia, A Matter of Interpretation: Federal Courts and the Law (1997); Manning, John F. "*Textualism and the Equity of the Statute*," 101 Columbia Law Review 1 (2001).
77. Roy Brooks, Structures of Judicial Decision Making (2005).
78. Antonin Scalia & Bryan Garner, Reading Law (2011).
79. *United States v. Galletti*, 541 U.S. 114 (2004).
80. *Knight v. Commissioner*, 552 U.S. 181 (2008). In *Knight*, the court was confronted with three tests among the circuit courts of appeal for determining whether a taxpayer has incurred "costs which are paid or incurred in connection with the administration of the estate or trust and which would not have been incurred if the property were not

held in such trust or estate." The court held that the statutory tem "would" plainly encompasses "custom, habit, natural disposition, or probability," that it naturally invokes a prediction "based on what would customarily or commonly occur." The issue was the deductibility of investment expenses, and since the statute "looks to the counterfactual question of whether individuals would have incurred such costs in the absence of a trust, . . . the question whether a trust related expense is fully deductible turns on a prediction about what would happen if . . . the property were held by an individual rather than by a trust."

81. Infra, chapter 1.

82. Calvin H. Johnson, Righteous Anger at the Wicked States: The Meaning of the Founders' Constitution (2009).

83. Hon. Richard Posner, *Judges are not Competent Historians*, ABA Journal, August 2012.

84. *Gitlitz v. Commissioner*, 531 US 206 (2001).

85. *Boulware v. US*, 128 S. Ct. 1168 (2008).

86. *Knight v. Commissioner*, 552 U.S. 181 (2008).

87. Laura Sager & Stephen Cohen, "*How the Income Tax Undermines Civil Rights Law*," 73 Southern California Law Review 1075 (2000).

88. *EC Term of Years Trust v. United States*, 550 U.S. 429 (2007).

89. *Hinck v. US*, 127 S. Ct. 2011 (2007).

90. *United States v. Clintwood Elkwood Mining*, 553 US 1 (2008).

91. *United Dominion Industries v. United States*, 532 U.S. 822 (2001).

92. *Bob Jones Univ. v. United States*, 461 U.S. 574 (1983).

93. Stephen Breyer, "*On the Uses of Legislative History in Interpreting Statutes*," 65 Southern California Law Review 845 (2000).

94. Hon. Antonin J. Scalia, Matter of Interpretation (1997).

95. Paul Caron, *Tax Myopia*, 13 Va. Tax Rev. 517 (1994).

96. *Boeing Co. v. United States*, 537 US 437 (2003).

97. *United States v. Craft*, 535 U.S. 274 (2002).

98. *Commissioner v. Banks*, 543 US 426 (2005).

99. Antonin Scalia, A Matter of Interpretation: Federal Courts and the Law (1997); Anthony Farley, *The Dream of Interpretation*, University of Miami Law Review (2002); Felix Cohen, *Transcendental Nonsense and the Functional Approach*, 35 Colum. L. Rev. 809, 814–17 (1935).

100. Richard Pierce, *What Factors Can an Agency Consider in Making a Decision?* Michigan State Law Review 67 (2009).

101. *Chevron U.S.A., Inc. v. Natural Resources Defense Council, Inc.*, 467 U.S. 837 (1984); *United States v. Mead Corp.*, 533 U.S. 218 (2001).

102. *United States v. Flor D'Italia*, 536 US 238 (2002).

103. *Boeing Co. v. United States* , 537 US 437 (2003).

104. Jack M. Beermann, *End the Failed. Chevron Experiment Now: How Chevron Has Failed and Why It Can and Should Be Overruled*, 42 Conn. L. Rev. 779 (2009).

105. Aharon Barak, Purposive Interpretation in Law (2005).

106. Deborah Geier, *Interpreting Tax Statutes: The Role of Purpose*, Florida Tax Review (1995).

107. Hon. Stephen F. Breyer, Active Liberty (2005).

108. Geoffrey Parsons Miller, *The Corporate Law Background of the Necessary and Proper Clause*, in the Origins of the Necessary and Proper Clause (2013).

109. Ibid.

110. *Mayo Foundation v. United States*, 562 US __ (2011).

111. *Bob Jones Univ. v. United States*, 461 U.S. 574 (1983).

112. Judith Resnick, *Living Their Legal Commitments: Paideic Communities, Courts and Robert Cover*, 17 Yale Journal of Law & the Humanities 17 (2005).

113. *National Cable & Telecommunications Association et al. v. Brand X Internet Services et al.*, 545 U.S. 967 (2005).

114. *National Cable & Telecommunications Association et al. v. Brand X Internet Services et al.*, 545 U.S. 967 (2005).
115. *Bob Jones Univ. v. United States*, 461 U.S. 574 (1983) (Burger, dissent).
116. William N. Eskridge, Dynamic Statutory Interpretation 34 (1994); Posner
117. Roy Brooks, Structures of Judicial Decision Making (2005).
118. *United States v. Craft*, 535 U.S. 274 (2002) (Scalia, dissent).
119. Gunther Tuebner, Law as an Autopoietic System (1993).
120. Ronald Dworkin, Justice for Hedgehogs (2013).
121. Andre L. Smith, *Boycotts, Interest Convergence, and Asymmetrical Market Failures Relating to Race*, 56 Howard Law Journal 891 (2013) (Wiley A. Branton Symposium Issue); *Race, Law, and the Free Market: A Critical Law and Economics Conception of Racism as Asymmetrical Market Failures*, 4 Georgetown Journal of Law & Modern Critical Race Perspectives 39 (2012).
122. James Hackney, Legal Intellectuals in Conversation (2012).
123. Pierre Schlag, Formalism and Realism in Ruins (Mapping the Logics of. Collapse), 95 Iowa L. Rev. 195 (2009).
124. James Hackney, Legal Intellectuals in Conversation (2012).
125. Pierre Schlag, Formalism and Realism in Ruins (Mapping the Logics of. Collapse), 95 Iowa L. Rev. 195 (2009).
126. David Brennen, Karen Brown & Darryl Jones, Beyond Efficiency in United States Tax Law (2013).
127. Pierre Schlag, Formalism and Realism in Ruins (Mapping the Logics of. Collapse), 95 Iowa L. Rev. 195 (2009).
128. Charles Lawrence, "*The Id, The Ego, and Equal Protection: Reckoning with Unconscious Racism*," 39 Stan. L. Rev. 317 (1987).
129. Bell, Derrick A., "Brown v. Board of Education and the Interest-Convergence Dilemma", Harvard Law Review 518 (1979-80).
130. Ronald Dworkin, Law's Empire (1986).
131. Andre L. Smith, *Boycotts, Interest Convergence, and Asymmetrical Market Failures Relating to Race*, 56 Howard Law Journal 891 (2013) (Wiley A. Branton Symposium Issue); *Race, Law, and the Free Market: A Critical Law and Economics Conception of Racism as Asymmetrical Market Failures*, 4 Georgetown Journal of Law & Modern Critical Race Perspectives 39 (2012).
132. Carlton Waterhouse, *Abandon All Hope Ye That Enter? Equal Protection, Title VI, and the Divine Comedy of Environmental Justice*, 20 Fordham Envtl. L. Rev. 51 (2009).
133. Atiba Ellis, *The Cost of the Vote: Poll Taxes, Voter Identification Laws, and the Price of Democracy*, 86 Denver L. Rev. 1023 (2009).
134. Beverly Moran,"*Wealth Redistribution and the Income Tax*," 35 Howard Law Journal 319 (2010).
135. Infanti & Crawford, Critical Tax Theory (2009).
136. See Dorothy Brown, Race and Class Matters in Tax Policy, 107 Columbia Law Review 790 (2007)
137. David A. Brennen, *Race and Equality Across the Law School Curriculum: The Law of Tax Exemption*, 54 J. Legal Educ. 336 (2004).
138. Daria Roithmayr, "*Locked In Segregation*," 12 Virginia Journal of Social Policy and the Law 197 (2004); "*Locked In Inequality: The Persistence of Discrimination*," 9 Michigan Journal of Race and Law 31 (2003).
139. Juan F. Perea, "Doctrines of Delusion: Bakke, Fisher and the Case for a New Affirmative Action," http://papers.ssrn.com/sol3/papers.cfm?abstract_id=2312630.
140. Laura Sager & Stephen Cohen, "*How the Income Tax Undermines Civil Rights Law*," 73 Southern California Law Review 1075 (2000).
141. Bell, Derrick A., "Brown v. Board of Education and the Interest-Convergence Dilemma", Harvard Law Review 518 (1979–1980).
142. Gary S. Becker, Human Capital (1994).
143. *San Antonio Independent School District v. Rodriguez*, 411 U.S. 1 (1973).
144. Rodgers & Taylor, Einstein on Race and Racism (2006).

145. Tommie Shelby, We Who are Dark (2007).
146. Richard Delgado & Jean Stefancic, Critical Race Theory: An Introduction (2012); Kimberle Crenshaw, Gary Peller & Neil Gotunda: Critical Race Thoery: The Key Writings That Started the Movement (1996).
147. Eduardo Bonilla-Silva, Racism Without Racists, Rowman & Littlefield (2008).
148. Joseph E. Stiglitz, Globalization and Its Discontents (2002).

Bibliography

Bruce Ackerman, *Taxation and the Constitution*, 99 Columbia Law Review 1 (1999); *The Living Constitution*, 120 Harvard Law Review 1727 (2007).

Terry Alford, Prince Among Slaves (2007).

Molefi Asante, Classical Africa (1994).

Kara Backus, *All Saints Church and the Argument for a Goal-Driven Application of Internal Revenue Service Rules for Tax- Exempt Organizations*, 17 S. Cal. Interdisc. L.J. 301, 302 (2008).

Aharon Barak, Purposive Interpretation in Law (2005).

Robert Bauval, Thomas Brophy, Black Genesis: The Prehistoric Origins of Ancient Egypt (2011).

Gary S. Becker, Human Capital (1994).

Derrick A. Bell, Derrick Bell, Faces at the Bottom of the Well (1992); *Brown v. Board of Education and the Interest-Convergence Dilemma*, Harvard Law Review 518 (1979–980).

Jack M. Beermann, *End the Failed. Chevron Experiment Now: How Chevron Has Failed and Why It Can and Should Be Overruled*, 42 Conn. L. Rev. 779 (2009).

Martin Bernal, Black Athena (1987).

Boris K. Bittker, The Case of Black Reparations (1973).

Blumrosen & Blumrosen, Slave Nation: How Slavery United the Colonies and Sparked the American Revolution (2006).

Eduardo Bonilla-Silva, Racism Without Racists, Rowman & Littlefield (2008).

David Brennen, Karen Brown & Darryl Jones, Beyond Efficiency in United States Tax Law (2013).

David A. Brennen, *Race and Equality Across the Law School Curriculum: The Law of Tax Exemption*, 54 J. Legal Educ. 336 (2004); *A Diversity Theory of Charitable Tax Exemption—Beyond Efficiency, ThroughCritical Race Theory, Toward Diversity*, 4 Pitt. Tax Rev. 1, 26 (2006).

Hon. Stephen F. Breyer, Active Liberty (2005).

Stephen Breyer, *On the Uses of Legislative History in Interpreting Statutes*, 65 Southern California Law Review 845 (2000).

Roy L. Brooks, Structures of Judicial Decision Making (2005); Atonement and Forgiveness: A New Model For Black Reparations (2004).

———., *Getting Reparations for Slavery Right—A Response to Posner and Vermeule*, 80 Notre Dame L. Rev. 251 (2004); *Rehabilitative Reparations for the Judicial Process*, 58 N.Y.U. Ann. Surv. Am. L. 475 (2003).

Alfred L. Brophy, Reparations Pro and Con.

———., *Losing the (Understanding of the Importance Of) Race: Evaluating the Significance of Race and the Utility of Reparations*, 80 Tex. L. Rev. 911 (2002); *Reconsidering Reparations*, 81 Ind. L.J. 811 (2006): *Some Conceptual and Legal Problems in Reparations for Slavery*, 58 N.Y.U. Ann. Surv. Am. L. 497 (2003);

Dorothy Brown, *How Home Ownership Keeps Blacks Poorer Than Whites*, Forbes Magazine (Dec. 10, 2012); *Race and Class Matters in Tax Policy*, 107 Colum. L. Rev. 790 (2007); *Race, Class, and Gender Essentialism in Tax Literature: The Joint Return*, 54 Wash. & Lee L. Rev. 1469 (1997).

Karen Brown & Mary Louise Fellows, Taxing America (1995).

Tamiko Brown-Nagin, *Elites, Social Movements, and the Law: The Case of Affirmative Action*, 15 Colum. L. Rev. 1436, 1472 (2004).

Neil Buchanan, *The Role of Economics in Tax Scholarship*, in Beyond Economic Efficiency in United States Tax Law. Ed. by David A. Brennen, Karen B. Brown and Darryll K. Jones) (2013).

Maxine Burkett, *Reconciliation and Nonrepetition: A New Paradigm for African-American Reparations*, 86 Or. L. Rev. 99 (2007).

Vincent Carretta, Equiano, The African (2007).

Maureen B. Cavanaugh, *On the Road to Incoherence: Congress, Economics and Taxes*, 49 UCLA L. Rev. 685 (2002).

Claessen & Skalnik, The Early State (1978); Claessen & Skalnik, The Study of the State (1981).

Kimberle Crenshaw, Gary Peller & Neil Gotunda: Critical Race Thoery: The Key Writings That Started the Movement (1996).

Robert M. Cover, *Foreword: Nomos and Narrative*, 97 Harvard Law Review (1983).

David Brian Davis, The Problem of Slavery in the Age of Emancipation (2006)

Martin R. Delaney, The Huts of America (1859).

Cheikh Anta Diop, African Origins of Civilization: Myth or Reality (1989); PreColonial Black Africa (1988); The Cultural Unity of Black Africa (1990).

Delgado & Jean Stefancic, Critical Race Theory: An Introduction (2012).

W.E.B. Dubois, Black Folk Then and Now (2007).

Ronald Dworkin, Law's Empire (1986); Justice for Hedgehogs (2013).

———., *The Arduous Virtue of Fidelity: Originalism, Scalia, Tribe, and Nerve*, 65 Fordham. L. Rev. 1249 (1997).

Atiba Ellis, *The Cost of the Vote: Poll Taxes, Voter Identification Laws, and the Price of Democracy*, 86 Denver L. Rev. 1023 (2009).

John H. Ely, Democracy and Distrust (1980).

Robin L. Einhorn, American Taxation, American Slavery (2006).

William N. Eskridge, Dynamic Statutory Interpretation 34 (1994).

Anthony Farley, *The Dream of Interpretation*, University of Miami Law Review (2002).

Paul Finkelman, Slavery and the Founders: Race and Liberty in the Age of Jefferson (2014).

Stanley Fish, Is there a Text in This Class?: The Authoritativeness of Interpretive Communities (1980).

Stanley Fish, *There is No Textualist Position*, 42 San Diego Law Review. 629, 649 (2005).

Toyin Folala, Africa, Volume 1 (2001).

John Hope Franklin & Laura Schweninger, Runaway Slaves: Rebels on the Plantation (2000).

E. Franklin Frazier, Black Bourgeoisie (1997).

Stephen M. Garcia, et al., *Profit Maximization Versus Disadvantageous Inequality: The Impact of Self-Categorization*, J. Behav. Decision Making, 18 (2005).

Deborah Geier, *Interpreting Tax Statutes: The Role of Purpose*, Florida Tax Review (1995)

James Hackney, Legal Intellectuals in Conversation (2012); Under Cover of Science (2007).

Nathan Hall, Hate Crimes (2005).

Cheryl Harris, *Whiteness as Property*, 106 Harvard Law Review 1709-91 (1993).

David Horowitz, Uncivil Wars: The Controversy Over Reparations For Slavery.

Darren Hutchison, *Preventing Balkanization or Facilitation Racial Domination: A Critique of the New Equal Protection*, 22 Virginia Journal of Social Policy and the Law (2014).

Infanti & Crawford, Critical Tax Theory (2009).

Erik M. Jensen, *Taxation and the Constitution: How to Read the Direct Tax Clauses*, 15 Journal of Law and Politics 687 (Fall 1999); *Interpreting the Sixteenth Amendment (By Way of the Direct-Tax Clauses)*, 21 Const. Comment. 355 (2004).

Calvin H. Johnson, Righteous Anger at the Wicked States: The Meaning of the Founders' Constitution (2009).

Calvin H. Johnson, *Fixing the Constitutional Absurdity of the Apportionment of Direct Tax*, 21 Const. Comment. 295 (2004).

Olati Johnson, *The Story Of Bob Jones University V. United States: Race, Religion, And Congress' Extraordinary Acquiescence*, in Statutory Interpretation Stories (2011).

Walter Johnson, River of Dark Dreams (2013).

Darryl K. Jones, et al., The Tax Law of Charities and Other Exempt Organizations: Cases, Materials, Questions and Activities (St. Paul, 2003).

Barbara Coleman Jordon & Angela HArris, Race and Economics, (2006)

See Ira Katznelson, When Affirmative Action was White (2005).

Charles Lawrence, *The Id, The Ego, and Equal Protection: Reckoning with Unconscious Racism*, 39 Stan. L. Rev. 317 (1987); *Unconscious Racism Revisited: Reflections on the Impact and Origins of The Id, the Ego, and Equal Protection* 40 Conn. L. Rev. 931, (2008).

Lawrence Lessig, *Fidelity in Translation*, 71 Texas L. Rev. 1165 (1993).

Ibn Battuta, Letzion & Hopkins, Corpus of Early Arabic Sources for West African History (2000).

Audre Lord, *The Master's Tools Will Never Dismantle the Master's House*, speech The Second Sex Conference, New York, New York (1979).

Manning, John F. *Textualism and the Equity of the Statute*, 101 Columbia Law Review 1 (2001).

Richard McAdams, *Cooperation and Conflict: The Economics of Group Status Production and Race Discrimination*, 108 Harv. L. Rev. 1003 (1995).

Geoffrey Parsons Miller, *The Corporate Law Background of the Necessary and Proper Clause*, in the Origins of the Necessary and Proper Clause (2013).

Charles Mills, Blackness Visible: Essays on Philosophy and Race (1998); The Racial Contract (1997).

P. G. Monateri, *Black Gaius: A Quest for the Multicultural Origins of the 'Western Legal Tradition'*, Hastings Law Journal (2000).

Beverly Moran,*Wealth Redistribution and the Income Tax*, 35 Howard Law Journal 319 (2010); *'Setting an Agenda for the Study of Tax and Black Culture'*, University of Arkansas at Little Rock Law Review, 21 (1999); *Capitalism and the Tax System: A Search for Social Justice*, 61 SMU L. Rev. 337 (2008).

Beverly Moran & Bill Whitford, *A Black Critique of the Internal Revenue Code*, 4 Wisconsin Law Review 751 (1996).

Thomas Nagel & Liam Murphy, The Myth of Ownership (2002).

Thomas Nagel, *John Rawls and Affirmative Action*, Journal of Blacks in Higher Education (2003).

D. T. Niani, *West Africa from the 12 th to the 16 th Century*, UNESCO General History of Africa (1990).

Robert Nozick, Anarchy, State and Utopia (1974).

Charles J. Ogletree, Jr., *Repairing the Past: New Efforts in the Reparations Debate in America*, 38 HARV. C.R.-C.L. L. REV. 279 (2003);

Akin Ogundiran & Toyin Folala, Archaeology of Atlantic Africa and African Diaspora (2007).

Philip Osafo-Kwaako & James A. Robinson, *Political Centralization in Pre-Colonial Africa*. Journal of Comparative Economics (2013).

Nell Irvin Painter, The History of White People (2009).

Juan F. Perea, *Doctrines of Delusion: Bakke, Fisher and the Case for a New Affirmative Action*, http://papers.ssrn.com/sol3/papers.cfm?abstract_id=2312630.

Harold Peckern, *Reparation Payments—An Exclusion Revisited*, 34 U.S.F. L. Rev. 705 (2000).

Tomas Piketty, Capital in the 21st Century (2014).

Richard Pierce, *What Factors Can an Agency Consider in Making a Decision?* Michigan State Law Review 67 (2009).

Eric A. Posner & Adrian Vermeule, *Reparations for Slavery and Other Historical Injustices*, 103 Colum. L. Rev. 689, 692 (2003).

Hon. Richard Posner, Law, Pragmatism and Democracy (2000); Overcoming Law (2005).

———., *Judges are not Competent Historians*, ABA Journal, August 2012.

Runoko Rashidi, *Iraq: The African Presence in Early Iraq*, in Encyclopedia of the African Diaspora (Ed. Carole Boyce Davies) (2008).

Judith Resnick, *Living Their Legal Commitments: Paideic Communities, Courts and Robert Cover*, 17 Yale Journal of Law & the Humanities 17 (2005).

Randall Robinson, The Debt: What America Owes to Blacks (2000).

Rodgers & Taylor, Einstein on Race and Racism (2006).

Daria Roithmayr, *Locked In Segregation*, 12 Virginia Journal of Social Policy and the Law 197 (2004); *Locked In Inequality: The Persistence of Discrimination*, 9 Michigan Journal of Race and Law 31 (2003).

Phillip F. Rubio, A History of Affirmative Action (2001).

Laura Sager & Stephen Cohen, *How the Income Tax Undermines Civil Rights Law*, 73 Southern California Law Review 1075 (2000).

Antonin Scalia, A Matter of Interpretation: Federal Courts and the Law (1997)

Antonin Scalia & Bryan Garner, Reading Law (2011).

Pierre Schlag, *Formalism and Realism in Ruins (Mapping the Logics of. Collapse)*, 95 Iowa L. Rev. 195 (2009).

Tommie Shelby, We Who are Dark (2007).

Andre L. Smith, *Boycotts, Interest Convergence, and Asymmetrical Market Failures Relating to Race*, 56 Howard Law Journal 891 (2013); *Race, Law, and the Free Market: A Critical Law and Economics Conception of Racism as Asymmetrical Market Failures*, 4 Georgetown Journal of Modern Critical Race Perspectives 39 (2012); *The IRS Don't Care About Poor Black People*, in Katrina: America's Unnatural Disaster (2008).

Joseph E. Stiglitz, Globalization and Its Discontents (2002).

Stanley S. Surrey & Paul R. McDaniel, Tax Expenditures (Cambridge, Mass., 1985).

Stanley S. Surrey, *Tax Incentives as a Device for Implementing Government Policy: A Comparison with Direct Government Expenditures*, 83 Harv. L. Rev. 705 (1970).

Aristide Theodorides, The Legacy of Egypt (1971).

Michal Tymowski, The Origins and Structures of Political Institutions in Pre-Colonial Black Africa (2009).

Gunther Tuebner, Law as an Autopoietic System (1993).

Mylinh Uy, *Tax and Race: The Impact on Asian Americans*, 11 Asian Am. L.J. 117 (2004).

Jan Vansina, How Societies are Born (2004).

———., The Kuba State, in The Early State (1978).

Ruth Vatvedt Fjeld, *The Lexical Semantics of Vague Adjectives*, in Vagueness in Normative Texts (2005).

Adrian Vermeule, Judging Under Uncertainty (2006). Cass R. Sunstein & Adrian Vermeule, *Interpretation and Institutions*, 101 Mich. L. Rev. 885 (2003);

Russ VerSteeg, Law in Ancient Egypt (2002).

Attiya Waris & Jeremy Leaman, Tax Justice and the Political Economy of Global Capitalism, 1945 to the Present (2013).

Carlton Waterhouse, *Abandon All Hope Ye That Enter? Equal Protection, Title VI, and the Divine Comedy of Environmental Justice*, 20 Fordham International Law Review 51 (2009); *Avoiding Another Step In A Series of Unfortunate Legal Events*, 26 B.C. Third-World L.J. 207, 262–65 (2006).

Robert Wesley, *Many Billions Gone: Is it Time to Reconsider the Case for Black Reparations?*, 40 B.C. L. Rev. 429 (1998).

Stephanie Willbanks, Federal Taxation of Wealth Transfers (2004).

John A. Wilson, Authority and Law in Ancient Egypt (1954).

George Ruble Woolfolk, *Slavery and Taxation in the AnteBellum South*, Journal of Southern History (1960).

Richard Wood, *Supreme Court Jurisprudence of Tax Fairness*, 36 Seton Hall L. J. 421 (2006).

Eric K. Yamamoto, Sandra Hye Yun Kim and Abigail M. Holden, *American Reparations Theory and Practice at the Crossroads*, 44 Cal. W.L. Rev. 1 (2007).

Naomi Zack, Philosophy of Science and Race (2002); Race and Mixed Race, (1993).

Lawrence A. Zelenak, *Taking Critical Tax Theory Seriously*, 76 North Carolina Law Review 1521-1580 (1997).
Howard Zinn, A Peoples History of the United States (2005).

Index

About the Author

Andre L. Smith is an associate professor at the Widener University School of Law, in Wilmington, Delaware, where he teaches tax law, sports law, and administrative law. Born in Philadelphia, Pennsylvania, Professor Smith graduated from the University of Maryland at College Park (B.S., Economics), the Howard University School of Law (J.D.), and the Georgetown University Law Center (LL.M, Taxation). He is an avid Philadelphia sportsaholic, an old school hiphop enthusiast, and the father of three, Lauren, Jasmyne, and Marley.

CPSIA information can be obtained at www.ICGtesting.com
Printed in the USA
BVOW07*0646270515

401622BV00002B/2/P

9 781498 503655